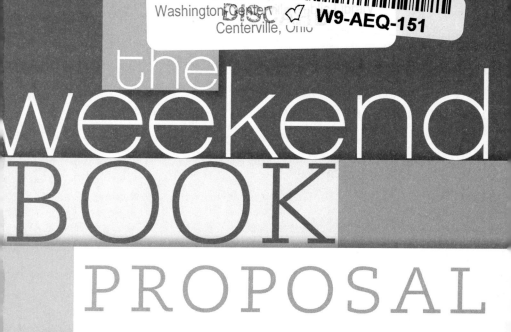

the weekend BOOK PROPOSAL

How to Write a **Winning Proposal** in **48 Hours** and **Sell Your Book**

RYAN G. **VAN CLEAVE**

WD

WRITER'S DIGEST BOOKS

WritersDigest.*com*
Cincinnati, Ohio

For more resources for writers, visit www.writersdigest.com.

18 17 16 15 14   5 4 3 2 1

Distributed in Canada by Fraser Direct
100 Armstrong Avenue
Georgetown, Ontario, Canada L7G 5S4
Tel: (905) 877-4411

Distributed in the U.K. and Europe by F&W Media International
Brunel House, Newton Abbot, Devon, TQ12 4PU, England
Tel: (+44) 1626-323200, Fax: (+44) 1626-323319
E-mail: postmaster@davidandcharles.co.uk

Distributed in Australia by Capricorn Link
P.O. Box 704, Windsor, NSW 2756 Australia
Tel: (02) 4577-3555

ISBN-13: 978-1-59963-757-0

Edited by James Duncan
Cover Designed by Wendy Dunning
Interior Designed by Michelle Thompson
Production coordinated by Debbie Thomas

media

About the Author

Ryan G. Van Cleave is the author of more than twenty books including *Memoir Writing for Dummies* and an award-winning young adult book, *Unlocked*. He is the Coordinator of Creative Writing at the Ringling College of Art + Design in Sarasota, Florida, where he lives with his wife, two daughters, and a feisty Shih Tzu named Ladybug. To find out more about Ryan, visit www.ryangvancleave.com and www.theweekendbookproposal.com.

Dedication

For all the students in my workshops and classes whose dreams of publishing their own books led me to write this one.

CONTENTS

INTRODUCTION

Like so many writers, my morning consists of sipping coffee, watching ESPN, scouring freelance writing job sites, creating new query letters, editing manuscripts, and firing off a dozen work-related e-mails. Later, I'll send out a slew of non-work-related e-mails, read the headlines off Yahoo's home page, stare into the backyard, and wonder if the neighbor's dog did its business there again.

I might knock out a page or two of my supernatural thriller or my presidential humor book while choking down a charred Lender's cinnamon raisin bagel that no coffee dunking can save. And that's all before 9:30 in the morning!

In short, I'm a busy guy. My life is one giant multitasking challenge. I have a wife. I have two daughters. I run private writing workshops. I teach at the Ringling College of Art + Design. I ghostwrite. I play pickup basketball (alright, I *used* to). I watch *American Idol*. I'm an NFL junkie. I jog (occasionally). And from time to time, I take my wife out for a nice dinner.

Simply put, I can no longer take my former dissertation director's advice:

"Time + Reflection + Patience = Writing Success."

Oh, and on his office wall was taped this Oscar Wilde quote: "I was working on the proof of one of my poems all the morning, and took out a comma. In the afternoon, I put it back again."

When I was a grad student, I could afford to take three days to consider the use of an epigraph in a short story. Now? I have to knock out rent and pay the orthodontist. Writing articles, fillers, short profiles, and book reviews are great for coming up with lunch money, but it's writing *books* that really pays the bills. It's writing books that lets you quit your high school janitor or prison guard job. And unless you're Stephen King, Stieg Larsson, or some other fiction überstud (and most of us are not), that means writing nonfiction books, which make up 85 percent of the new titles published every year.

Pretty good odds, right? But here's sobering news—99 percent of nonfiction book proposals are rejected (which explains Bowker's recent announcement that 211,269 titles were self-published in 2011), thanks to:

- higher publishing costs than ever before
- already-written books covering your topic

- editors and agents too overworked and underpaid to notice your brilliant literary potential
- a flailing US economy that has publishers scared to take on any book that might just break even, or worse, lose money

Let's be clear: Terrific ideas presented in a professional manner are regularly rejected every day. So why spend a couple of months on a proposal when a couple of days or even a handful of hours might be enough? Sure, it's a numbers game. But what's wrong with a numbers game when the numbers are *on your side*?

Why struggle for a year or two (or four) to finally land a publishing contract when you can write four, six, or eight proposals (or more) per year and have as many book contracts as you can handle?

Why struggle with writing humdrum proposals when you can create a laser-guided missile of a proposal that's sure to wow agents and editors alike? With an estimated forty thousand writing projects submitted to agents, editors, and publishing venues *every single day*, would-be authors need clear advice on how to push ahead of the ever-growing crowd.

And that 99 percent rejection statistic for nonfiction book proposals mentioned above: It only reflects the odds for *actual submissions*. What about the thousands upon thousands of writers living lives of quiet literary desperation and never getting to the point where they send something out?

I've polled the students in my writing workshops and spoken with award-winning professors and multitasking homemakers. I've chatted with teens living in hospice care and neighbors who've converted their cars to run on biodiesel. I've shared stories with stay-at-home web designers and grandmas who make the best blueberry custard ever (all of whom have enough material already to write a book). I've found that their excuses win out over their dreams of landing a book deal and being a published writer.

- "I wouldn't know where to begin."
- "I don't have enough time."
- "I wasn't born with the talent for it."
- "I don't have a Ph.D."
- "If only I could have a sit-down over coffee with the head of Random House …"
- "I just need to take one more writing workshop and then …"
- "The muse just hasn't arrived. Yet."

- "But I might get rejected!"
- "I'm just too stressed/tired/overcommitted."
- "Writing is too hard."
- "I'd feel guilty spending time writing when I have so many other things to do."

WORDS OF WISDOM

"No excuse is valid. You do not become a writer by wishing, or talking about it, or pitching ideas to writers." — Lawrence Watt-Evans

These people don't realize that 90 percent of all nonfiction books are sold by sending a literary agent or editor a proposal, not the entire manuscript! Anyone can write a book proposal when given the proper guidance. You don't need fancy degrees. You don't need to be able to type 1,000 words per minute. You don't need some magical, innate skill with wordplay. You don't even need oodles of time—forty-eight hours will suffice, as the title says.

Whether you're a true beginner or a seasoned writer looking to hone your skills, *The Weekend Book Proposal* reveals how to take your best ideas and create proposals that will ignite the interest of an agent or editor. This guide is jam-packed with expert advice, proven strategies, useful anecdotes, nuts-and-bolts sidebars, proposal samples, "Hit the Gas" tips (for those who want the proposal done *fast*), and clear explanations suitable for all learning styles. You'll learn how to succeed and prosper as a writer by using time-tested methods and attention-getting techniques to sell your book—before you've even written it.

And for those interested in the "other" topics most book proposal how-to guides ignore, this book offers specific chapters with marketing-savvy ideas, expert tips, and proposal examples for (a) memoirs, (b) textbooks, (c) literary anthologies, and (d) novels.

Now, you may be wondering, "Why should I listen to you?" I'm glad you asked. You should always learn about a potential source's authority before taking any advice. Here are my key writing and publishing experiences that inform all I'm sharing with you in this book:

- I've used proposals to sell many of my own books to such publishers as the University of Iowa Press, HCI Books, Oxford University Press, Pearson PLC, Wiley, Running Press, and (of course) Writer's Digest Books, to name just a few.

- I co-founded C&R Press (www.crpress.org), a nonprofit literary press, and served as executive director for nearly a decade. During this time, I read and reviewed countless book proposals, manuscripts, and pitches.
- I've served as a book doctor, manuscript consultant, and writing coach for years.
- I've worked as a freelance proposal reviewer for publishers like McGraw-Hill, Prentice Hall, Bedford, and Longman Publishing Group, as well as numerous indie and university presses.
- I earned a Ph.D. in creative writing and American literature from Florida State.
- I've taught creative writing and literature for nearly twenty years at Clemson University, Eckerd College, Florida State University, George Washington University, the Ringling College of Art + Design, the University of Wisconsin-Green Bay, and the University of Wisconsin-Madison. I've also taught writing at prisons, community centers, and urban at-risk facilities.

And if that's not enough, many of the ideas, tips, and techniques here are time-tested and approved by some of the best writers, agents, and editors in the business (many of whom you'll hear from directly within these pages). In short, what you'll find in *The Weekend Book Proposal* is the reason for much of their success. Let this book help launch you toward the literary success you deserve, too.

The world of publishing is always changing, and I'm always interested in learning new ways to navigate it better. Use the contact form at www.ryangvancleave.com to zip me a note about your own experiences. I welcome your ideas, insight, challenges, and questions. You can also reach me (and find many more samples and tips!) at www.theweekendbookproposal.com.

One of the greatest things I can experience as a writer is to have readers tell me they followed my advice and made their dream a reality. I hope that success story becomes *your* story, too. May your relationship with your readers be as wonderful as mine has been with my own.

Now let's get that book proposal written!

Part One

THE PROPOSAL

Chapter One

BOOK PROPOSALS:
SOME BASICS AND BACKGROUND

We're living in a fast-food, fast Internet, fast-paced world today. To deny that is to deny that the sun is hot. I mean, c'mon! Who doesn't have more work to do, places to shop, family members to hang out with (okay, friends then), or video games to play? We're multitasking machines with more tasks on our dockets than a team of clones could manage.

The Weekend Book Proposal is designed for busy people like you who are interested in writing a book but don't have months or years to devote to it. After all, without a publishing contract in hand (which a good book proposal can get you), your book-writing efforts are speculative, meaning there's a possibility that your writing efforts might amount to nothing. Sure, you could always go the self-publishing route, but the average self-published book:

- doesn't earn you an advance
- costs *you* $$$ to produce (and store and ship, if you make print copies versus e-books)
- is promoted and marketed by you (lots of time and $$$ can be spent here)
- sells fewer than 150 copies
- rarely generates movie or foreign rights deals

If that sounds appealing to you, go for it. Millions of people have self-published, and millions more will do so. A rare few—like Amanda Hocking and Robert Kiyosaki—will even do it successfully. But if you want to work with an established publishing company with money to offer you up-front as an advance, a PR department willing and able to promote your book, and a design/editorial team that can make your book both beautiful and grammatically sound, then read on because that's what a traditional publisher brings to the table.

Let me put it even more plainly. Here's what *The Weekend Book Proposal* offers:

- clear explanations on the elements of winning book proposals
- insider secrets on how to write book proposals *fast*

- ways to "think like an editor" to make your book proposals irresistible
- samples of successful book proposals (with annotations about their strengths and weaknesses)

The result of these features and benefits? If you want to maximize your writing efforts, generate book advances on books you haven't even written yet, and join the ranks of published writers (or add to your own already-existing catalog of published titles), then this book is for you.

YOUR INVITATION

This book is your invitation to join the ranks of published writers in the easiest, most efficient manner possible. How do I know? Because I'm lazy, and in the past twenty years I've still managed to have well more than twenty of my own books published, and many of those I didn't write until I had a book contract in hand.

GETTING THE IDEAS WRITTEN

I went to grad school at Florida State University in 1995 to study with Jerry Stern, a professor best known for his anthology of short-short stories, *Micro Fiction,* and a clever writing how-to book, *Making Shapely Fiction.* As a teacher, he was funny, popular, and accessible. With great regularity, students used to arrive during his office hours to announce some variation of "I've got this great idea for a story. It's about this dude whose head explodes but he doesn't die. He just walks around headless the whole time. Do you think that'd make a good story?"

Jerry always responded the same way. He gave each of these eager students a lengthy meditative stare, and then he folded his arms over his chest and said, "No text, no talk."

The translation? Ideas are cheap. A good idea handled poorly in writing isn't publishable. A boring idea handled wonderfully in writing might well be publishable. It might even be a bestseller. Until you develop your idea on the page, you'll never know if it'll work or not as a written text.

It's not what the students wanted to hear, but what they got was a useful albeit hard truth. That's what this book aims to deliver: useful albeit sometimes hard truths. And all of these hard truths are drawn from what I've learned through my experiences of teaching at a number of universities, interviewing other successful writers, and figuring things out myself through decades of trial and error via the School of Hard Knocks. It's also drawn from years of selling my own books via successful book proposals.

Jerry believed in the power of the book proposal, and so do I.

THE BOOK PROPOSAL ITSELF

Shakespeare didn't write book (or play) proposals. Neither did F. Scott Fitzgerald when he was banging out *The Great Gatsby* or *Tender Is the Night.* "Why the heck should I write one?" you might reasonably wonder. If you're a best-selling author or you've been lucky enough to have a publisher come to you and beg you to write a book on topic X, Y, or Z, you might not need to. The rest of us? We do.

HIT THE GAS

John Boswell, author of *The Insider's Guide to Getting Published,* says, "Fully 90 percent of all nonfiction books sold to trade publishers are acquired on the basis of a proposal." This is perhaps the best "Hit the Gas" tip of all. Write a book proposal first, *not* the book itself. Let's be clear: Creating a book proposal is an invaluable, time-saving, energy-focusing part of the process.

Being represented by a literary agent is the single best way to bypass the slush pile, which is the glut of manuscripts that arrive unsolicited—unasked for—at publishing houses. In the days before PDFs and DOCX files, this meant a mountain of envelopes stuffed with paper that often filled entire rooms. Publishing houses would take on interns whose sole job it was to read the first page or two of each and either pass it on to a junior editor (.5 percent chance) or send it back to the writer with a form rejection (99.5 percent chance). It was very much the idea of looking for a literary diamond in the rough.

One of the reasons to work with a literary agent is that they have direct connections to the decision makers at publishing houses. Here's just one example. A few years back, I was interested in doing a writing how-to book.

I sent a very, very short proposal to my agent, who sent it to the head of the Complete Idiots Guide series. Not a junior editor, mind you, but the man at the top of the entire series of those books. We received a very nice "no" response *within a day*, which primarily came about because they had a similar project in the pipeline already. No problem! That short proposal took me about two hours to write. Not a lot of wasted time there.

Here's the best part of this story. My agent had just made a connection with the folks at Wiley who run the For Dummies line of books, so I spent a couple more hours slanting the proposal to better fit the For Dummies line versus the Complete Idiots Guide line. I even wrote a single chapter as a manuscript sample (something I did not do with the previous proposal for the Idiots series, which was only a few pages long but gave a very clear overview of my plan). The result: a nice advance and a contract to write *Memoir Writing for Dummies*, which came out in early 2013.

Total time investment from start to contract, including the first "failed" proposal? Maybe fifteen hours over the course of a week.

That's why you write book proposals versus complete book manuscripts. Doing so saves everyone time and also makes it easier to change gears or tweak something if you (or your agent or an editor) decide you missed the mark. Plus, for a writer, you don't have to spend much effort on a speculative project. It took me three full months of my writing time to actually write that For Dummies book. What if I wrote the entire thing and then sent it in only to find that someone else who sent in a book proposal was now under contract for that topic? What an incredible waste of time that'd be! What if the publisher said, "Oh, we like this, but we really wish you'd gone a different way from chapter three on ..." ?

Nearly every literary agent prefers to read proposals before they see a full manuscript. Why? It's a simple math problem. Many of the best literary agencies receive hundreds of submissions a week. If each was book length, they'd need a forklift to merely handle the weight of them. Just think about how much time they'd need to read through it all! Worse, they're going to reject 99 percent of it, so reading through that much to find the 1 percent is a fool's errand.

Like I said, it's simple math. Agents need ways to reduce the volume of text they have to read, so they do it incrementally.

Here's a common path a new writer should take in order to get a book manuscript sold to a commercial publisher.

- **What you do first:** Send in a well-written, polished, professional query letter (more on this one- or two-page item in chapter ten).

- **What the agent or editor does first:** Invites you to send more because you've tantalized them with good writing, good ideas, and a strong sense of the marketplace.
- **What you do next:** Send in a book proposal, which includes a manuscript sample. (For fiction, this usually includes the entire finished manuscript rather than a sample or proposal, but as I shall note later, sometimes a full book proposal can be beneficial.)
- **What they do next:** Either offer you a contract (a literary agent will offer a contract for representation/an editor will offer a publishing contract) or ask to see the full manuscript, because by now, they're interested and invested in the book.
- **What you do last:** Write the entire book.

Just to reinforce what you've learned here: Where does "Write the entire book" fall in this process? At the end. The very, very end.

INSIDER TIP

If you're a fiction writer, here's a hard truth: You should write the actual manuscript before sending out queries, samples, or proposals. An agent or publisher will wait a few months for delivery of a requested nonfiction book manuscript. They won't for fiction. Why? There's often a very strong correlation between a strong nonfiction book proposal and a strong nonfiction book. With fiction? That correlation is far less pronounced. So why write a book proposal for fiction? Three reasons.

1. It helps you get your ideas in order about story, audience, and marketing.

2. It's likely that someone along the publishing food chain might request one (or at least many of the parts you've included in one).

3. It's possible to sell a book or series off a proposal alone. See chapter thirteen for examples.

BUT I WROTE THE WHOLE DARN BOOK ALREADY!

You did? Well, first let me congratulate you on having an idea and following through with the dedication to write the entire thing. That's a huge accomplishment. The good news is that *The Weekend Book Proposal* will still help you. Since editors and agents want proposals, you can use the strategies in this book to reverse engineer a proposal for the already-written book. A proposal is all about promise, and it gives editors the sense that they can help shape the forthcoming book (although they rarely do much shaping these days). Don't tell them the book's written. Give them the proposal and sample chapters, and then easily deliver the whole thing on time once the contract is in hand.

THE ANATOMY OF A BOOK PROPOSAL

Despite what experts might tell you, there's no one perfect blueprint for a book proposal, no one-size-fits-all fill-in-the-blank template. That's exactly why I've included a range of different book proposals in this book and at www.theweekendbookproposal.com. There's a very big difference between nonfiction (the most common) and fiction proposals, so I devoted chapter thirteen to fiction proposals. I've also included chapters on anthologies (chapter fourteen) and memoir (chapter fifteen) since both of those are often sold through proposals as well.

All book proposals, however, have certain common elements. Any of these might be enough to excite a literary agent or editor to take on your book, which is your goal. However you manage to achieve that end sounds like a good book proposal to me.

The most common and important elements of a book proposal are:

- attention-grabbing title
- book description
- marketplace analysis
- list of competing books
- promotions/marketing ideas
- author background
- table of contents
- chapter summaries/outline
- manuscript sample
- endorsements

Book proposals might also include the following:

- back matter
- concept statement/elevator pitch
- production details

HOW TO GET THE MAXIMUM BENEFIT FROM THIS BOOK

The how-to books that impress me the most always offer multiple ways to make them work for the reader. While the title of this book says it only takes a weekend to write a complete draft of a book proposal, there are plenty of different ways to accomplish that task. Follow one of the methods listed below, or simply create your own.

Hour-by-Hour Plan

This plan is simple. Spread a weekend's worth of work over a week or even longer if you need to. If you need ten days, take it. Need a month? Fine. Take on the task of writing a book proposal in bite-size pieces. The challenge with doing it this way is to keep up your momentum. A great way to do that? Work on it every day, even if it's just for a fifteen-minute stretch. This way, the idea of your book is always fairly fresh in your mind and you'll be working on it nonstop, even if you don't consciously realize it.

I like the hour-by-hour plan because it's flexible. You make it work around your own schedule. If you have a full load of classes or if work requires a lot of time, sandwich the hour-by-hour plan around it. A completed book proposal could be anywhere between 3,000 and 15,000 words, depending on the length of your sample chapter, with most full proposals averaging about 9,000 words. Knock out a few hundred words per hour and you're on your way!

The Weekend Plan

"That hour-by-hour stuff is too slow," you might be thinking. Fine. Give the weekend plan a try. Select a weekend where you have a big chunk of free time and binge write. Put in five, eight, or even ten hours at once for a couple of days. Seriously, just shut the door and get to work. Hang up a "Rabid Guard Dogs at Work" sign on the door. Put on headphones or earplugs so you won't be distracted.

Plenty of writers do this kind of thing at writing retreats—they get away from the distractions of real life so they can focus on the writing without the constant interruptions that life brings. Borrow a friend's cabin and do your own weekend writing retreat, where you can put in enough hours to walk away with the proposal done. Rent an inexpensive hotel room. Take a couple of days in the middle of the week, find a quiet coffee shop, and don't tell anyone you know that you'll be there. (Be sure to shut off your phone, too—no Angry Birds or texting while writing!).

A few inherent dangers come with the blitzkrieg/marathon method. The first is that Murphy's Law will make sure the cat starts throwing up, the kids will suddenly need a ride from practice, and the fridge will go on the blink, threatening to rot the house supply of food. Ignore it all as best you can. Why? There will *always* be things that clamor for your attention.

HIT THE GAS

The Internet is a huge time suck. Get around it by investing in an Internet blocker like Freedom or Self-Control. Both can be set for a certain amount of time during which your computer will not talk to the Internet no matter what. Internet excuse gone!

Patch a Leaky Pipe Plan

This one's a popular choice because nothing is more frustrating than a writer who's done 75 percent of the work but can't seem to hit that finish line. Maybe you finished pieces of the manuscript. Maybe you've sold magazine articles that feature some of the ideas for your book. Maybe you have a great outline, a stack of notes (or note cards), or a clear idea of what you want to do since you've been mulling it over for months, years, or decades. Maybe you have part or all of a book proposal completed, though you recognize that it's not yet good enough to send out.

This plan asks you to identify where you're stuck and to focus on those areas first. Take a look at this book's table of contents and skip ahead if you need to. Sure, the other chapters provide benefits, but you can always go back to them and strengthen what you've accomplished. For the Patch a Leaky Pipe plan, start by putting the medicine where it's needed most.

The Do It Yourself (DIY) Plan

I confess that the DIY plan is the one I use most often. I've bought lots of writing how-to books in the past, and I don't think I've ever read one front to back. I'm unsure if I'm ADD, dyslexic, or just a little convoluted in how I choose to proceed, but I like to grab a new book and plunge right into whatever interests me. If I like a particular title for a chapter, BAM, I start there. On the other hand, there are a few writing how-to books in which I've read 90 percent of the book but not chapter one or the introduction. And then there are those that I've read only one or two chapters from. I've also been known to read the entire glossary and index before starting on the main part of a book.

If you're a DIY-er, don't let me get in your way. Find your own path to success, and let this book be of whatever help you can make of it. I simply put it together in a logical order for those who like to work from start to finish on a book proposal.

DON'T FORGET TO REVISE!

This topic gets a brief mention because it's the key to any successful writer's career. Stephen King does at least three drafts of every manuscript before sending it to his publisher. Even Kurt Vonnegut revised. I revise, too, even if it's just a quick e-mail I'm sending to my literary agent or to my department head at my college. Be a professional no matter what the writing opportunity. Get it right even though it's hard to do so. Mark Twain supposedly said, "I didn't have time to write a short letter, so I wrote a long one instead."

Please remember, too, that there's a huge difference between editing and revision. Editing is where you target grammar issues. You fix the commas. Get the spelling right. Change *affect* when you really meant *effect*. It's where you work with what you already have in order to make it read better. Revision is where you "redo" the "vision." It's where you might hack and slash entire paragraphs and change big things as you re-envision the writing. Both are needed, but remember that there's a difference. Too many people think light editing is enough. As a teacher and writing coach, I can assure you—rarely is that the case.

If it were my proposal going out, I'd want it to be bulletproof, razor sharp, and tight as a drum (maybe without the clichés, but you get the point).

A FINAL THOUGHT

One final thought that I really want to impress upon you about the entire process is that it's all about audience. Of course, you should always start with a book idea that you yearn to write (see chapter two for more regarding this), but you're not the one buying your own book. Others will be. So keep them and their needs in mind throughout every part of the process. Be a giver. Share, share, and share some more. Do that, and good things will follow.

TOP TIPS TO REMEMBER

- Book proposals save you time and energy. Write the proposal first and the book only once the contract arrives.
- Agents and editors expect certain common elements in book proposals. Make sure you incude all possible elements that they might wish to see.
- Editors and agents are your partners, not the enemy.
- Submit only your *very best* work.
- Edit and revise like your life depends on it.
- When you think about the audience for your book, ask yourself, "Is this book really just for me (not the most commercial/viable idea) or is it for a specific group of people (a better option)?"

Chapter Two

CONSIDER THE AUDIENCE:
CREATING ELEVATOR PITCHES, TIMELY TOPICS, AND WELL-STRUCTURED BOOKS

This is a chapter that's all about ideas, purpose, and structure. But before we get into any of those topics, let's start with your book proposal's audience: agents and editors. These poor souls are overworked, underpaid, underappreciated, and (often) one bad book acquisition away from being reprimanded or canned by the bean counters at the top. Let's put ourselves in their shoes for a moment to understand where they're coming from. Once we see that, we might better understand how to approach them and what we, as writers, need to deliver.

Too many writers ignore the editorial and business aspects of publishing to the detriment of their artistic careers. You'll recognize these folks by their grumblings about being published ... someday. The more you know about the business side of the equation—the elements that agents and editors deal with daily—the better (and faster) you'll be able to achieve the success that you desire.

THE EDITOR'S WORLD
As we discussed in the last chapter, agents must contend with an onslaught of queries and book proposals. So, too, must editors, but editors don't just sit around acquiring books all day long. As a matter of fact, they rarely make those acquisition decisions alone anymore; they have editorial meetings where they meet with fellow editors to share the projects they're most interested in. After receiving input from their colleagues, they each decide which projects they'll prepare to present (sometimes as infrequently as once a month) at a meeting called a publication board (often called a "pub board" or "ed board"). Here, all the top people of a publishing house are included in the final decision to say "yes" or "no" to a proposed book.

I'm not just talking about a bunch of editors at these meetings but also the head of sales, the head of marketing, the publisher, and sometimes even the president, vice president, and other administrative-level people. In short, every publishing house bigwig is the monthly audience for each editor's pitch for the proposed book projects they're serious about acquiring.

It's possible that all of this can happen behind the scenes while authors have no idea that their proposals are moving along toward a contract. Often, though, they're made aware because the editor who intends to present the project needs revisions or more material to make the presentation stronger, so they ask the author for assistance.

A lot of people need to be convinced that the book has a viable audience, whose consumer sales will offset the costs associated with publishing the book, and nowhere in that description did I mention anybody worrying too much about it being a *good* book. The decision of whether or not to acquire the book is primarily made according to how strong the market is for the book. The assumption is that the editor can help make the book good (or good enough). Plus, any book that an editor has bothered to take to a pub board is assumed to be competent: What editor would prepare a presentation for a book that wasn't up to snuff?

INSIDER TIP

Carol Traver, senior acquisitions editor for Tyndale House, says, "There is a huge creative and mission-minded component of publishing. It's just gotten so freakishly competitive these past few years that the financial piece is every bit as important. First-time authors so rarely take the business/marketing side of things into consideration, and it really shows in their proposals."

At a big publishing house, each editor will pitch maybe a half dozen books, and on a good day, half of those will go through. One or two of the other half will be tweaked and later pitched again, with the hopes of answering some of the questions and concerns that came up in the previous pub board. The rest will fall away. At smaller publishing houses (those that put out fewer books per year), editors might be happy with a single green light.

Why am I telling you all of this? Because your job is to give an editor what she needs to satisfy and create a consensus from all of those other people at the publishing house.

And it all starts here, with a strong idea for a book.

WHAT'S YOUR BOOK IDEA?

Now that we see what an editor and a book proposal are up against, let's look at your idea. Already have one? Fantastic. If you don't, then here are some tips on how to come up with an idea that might work as a successful book.

- **Start with a successful nonfiction book and "fix" it:** Take an existing book whose subject matter you like, and then add your own twist. For example, I'm going to do Dr. John Gray's *Men Are from Mars, Women Are from Venus ...* for dogs.

- **Start with what you know:** Consider your jobs, your education, and the places you've lived. I grew up near Chicago and loved it, so small wonder that I pitched *City of the Big Shoulders: An Anthology of Chicago Poetry.* I also saw a lot of kids fail out of college at Northern Illinois University (where I was an undergraduate) and at the other seven colleges and universities where I've since taught. The reason? Playing video games at the expense of homework and overall health. What book idea might come from this fact of life? *Gaming Their Way Out of School: A Parent's Guide to Stop the Self-Destructive Habits of Pathological Video Gamers.*

- **Think about your own interests:** I'm interested in fantasy role-playing games, for instance. And I like reading *Psychology Today.* Why not a book entitled *The Anatomy of a Geek Mind: An Insider's Look at the World of Dungeons & Dragons*?

- **Think about your audience's interests and needs:** What book does your grandmother wish she had? Maybe go with *The Art of Aging: How Teaching Painting to Retirees Increases One's Health, Raises the Level of Happiness, and Prolongs Life.*

- **Ask a question you've had:** Write a book called *Why Don't Our Stomachs Digest Themselves? & Other Strange Facts We Ought to Know.*

- **Trust Google:** Use Google AdWords' keyword tool to find search terms/phrases that get over 500,000 queries per month, and then put a little spin on it for a great book idea. An example? Over 675,000 global searches are done each month for some version of the phrase "writing prompts." So how about this book idea? *101 New Writing Prompts to Bring out the Novelist Within You.*

- **Examine newspaper headlines:** A recent *New York Times* article explains how a new 100 percent online master's degree from the Georgia Institute of Technology might be the new frontier of online education. One could readily turn that idea into a book like *The Professional Cheater: How Online*

Test Cheaters Are Making Millions by Scamming Online MBA Programs. Or, if you prefer to write a novel, have the hero be an online educator who receives a request to meet face-to-face with a failing student in a local strip club. He declines. Soon after, cyberstalking and danger ensues.

- **Get on professional listservs and newsletters:** Every profession has its own online vehicle to receive the latest news and updates particular to its world. Learning about the latest updates in technology from Shelly Palmer's blog and newsletter might lead you to this book idea: *Never Alone: How the Digital World Is Watching Us ... Even When We're Not Online.*

Once you have your idea, it's time to test its sizzle factor. We do that by creating a short book description called an elevator pitch.

HIT THE GAS

A regular writer will wait around until she gets excited by an idea. Then she'll start writing it. A professional writer will brainstorm twenty ideas and pick the best one in light of the realities of the publishing world. Then she'll start writing that one.

Who'll succeed faster and more often? No contest here.

THE NOW FACTOR

If your idea has a timeliness to it, you're in even better shape because an editor can say, "Well, Y2K is in twenty months, and we don't have a Y2K book in the pipeline." An older example, yes, but you get the point. There's *actionable immediacy* to that statement. Don't try to pretend your book idea has timeliness if it doesn't. But if it truly does, arm the editor with that information in the elevator pitch of the book overview (I'll go over that in a bit). Timeliness will jump out to him and will be a key factor in his own pitch to the pub board.

Some good examples of topics with timeliness? The 2012 Mayan Doomsday date. The Black Hawk crash in the 1993 Battle of Mogadishu. Michael Jackson's death. The fiftieth anniversary of the Apollo 11 moon landing. Occupy Wall Street. Facebook's one billionth user. Do you notice how all of these events are already in the past? Make sure you're looking ahead when you plot and plan your book idea.

ELEVATOR PITCH/LOG LINE

Both of these terms mean roughly the same thing: In fifty words or less, what exactly is your project about? Two pieces of information need to be included here: (a) what my book is and (b) what my book does. At its most fundamental level, that's really what a book is about.

An elevator pitch for a nonfiction book needs to communicate the genre of the book, what's new/different about this book, and what promise(s) it's designed to fulfill. An elevator pitch for a novel includes the who (main character), what (conflict), when (time period), where (setting), and why (motivation/stakes). Other types of books will use a combination of elements to describe the book. Here are a few examples of possible log lines for various types of projects.

- **From a movie (*Raiders of the Lost Ark*):** Just before the outbreak of World War II, an adventuring archaeologist named Indiana Jones races around the globe to single-handedly prevent the Nazis from turning the greatest archaeological relic of all time into a weapon of world conquest.

- **From a nonfiction book (Nicholas Carr's *The Shallows: What the Internet Is Doing to Our Brains*):** The Internet has made the information universe much larger, and at the same time, it has altered the way we think, read, and pay attention. We're now shallower creatures living in an increasingly more fragmented world, asking for more interruptions even though we know on some level that these interruptions work against concentration, contemplation, and creative thought.

- **From a memoir (Jonna Ivin's *Will Love for Crumbs: A Memoir*):** Raised by a single alcoholic mother, Jonna learned to put her own needs on the back burner. After her mother dies of cancer, she goes on a journey for enlightenment, eventually winding up as a volunteer in the relief effort following Hurricane Ike, where she meets a twenty-year veteran of the Army Special Forces who will forever change her life.

- **From my book *Memoir Writing for Dummies*:** In the highly readable For Dummies style, Dr. Ryan G. Van Cleave reveals how to successfully start *and finish* the most important story you know—your own! Now you can discover how to avoid the most common pitfalls, know which details to put in (and leave out), and create a clear vision for your life story.

Why do editors love log lines? Because they can usually tell from investing the thirty seconds in reading one whether it's worth reading the rest. A great log line is sometimes enough to push a proposal all the way to the contract stage. It's an efficient, handy, useful tool for authors *and* editors.

SCOPE OF THE BOOK

To move beyond an elevator pitch, you need a strong vision of the finished book. How in-depth will it be? How many topics and subtopics will you cover? What's the estimated word count—will it be a pamphlet or a doorstop? Will it contain extra elements that will hike up the cost of the book's production, such as photographs or tear-out sheets? Take notes on these elements. Jot them down as if you were creating a baseball card for your book with all of its stats included—with the understanding that they might change as you write the proposal—and keep this info for later. You don't need to decide all of these things now, but the clearer your idea of what the book might look like in its final incarnation, the clearer a path you'll have before you.

CONCEPT STATEMENT/VISION STATEMENT

Whichever term you use, this one- or two-paragraph sales statement is a fuller extension of your elevator pitch. The elevator pitch is the massive tease. This statement is where you deliver. It's the type of exciting, clear, purposeful writing that generates reader interest. It's the sort of paragraph that book reps use to sell to stores, publishers use in their catalogs, and Amazon puts on their book description pages.

Here's what appears in Amazon's book description for Stephen King's *On Writing: 10th Anniversary Edition: A Memoir of the Craft.*

> "Long live the King" hailed *Entertainment Weekly* upon publication of Stephen King's *On Writing*. Part memoir, part master class by one of the bestselling authors of all time, this superb volume is a revealing and practical view of the writer's craft, comprising the basic tools of the trade every writer must have. King's advice is grounded in his vivid memories from childhood through his emergence as a writer, from his struggling early career to his widely reported, near-fatal accident in 1999—and how the inextricable link between writing and living spurred his recovery. Brilliantly structured, friendly and inspiring, *On Writing* will empower and entertain everyone who reads it— fans, writers, and anyone who loves a great story well told.

It's not much more than an extended log line, no? But a number of things are made clear in this one dynamic paragraph, such as:

- the author's credentials ("one of the bestselling authors of all time")
- the book's intended audience ("fans, writers, and anyone who loves a great story well told")
- the book's subject ("part memoir, part [writing] master class")
- the book's features ("master class") ("revealing and practical view of the writer's craft")
- the book's benefits ("empower and entertain") ("friendly and inspiring")
- the book's uniqueness (grounded in his vivid memories)

When a publisher is handed a great concept statement like this, she's going to use it. Check out the Amazon book description on other books you admire. Look at book descriptions in publishers' catalogs on their websites. See how others are juggling as many tasks as King (or his publisher's first-rate PR writers) did above.

So why take the time to create a rock-solid concept statement? Because an editor with this pithy paragraph has a much better chance of selling your book to the pub board.

CREATING AN OVERVIEW (A.K.A. ABOUT THE BOOK SECTION)

Okay, you've hooked an editor with an elevator pitch and then wowed her with the concept statement. She's excited and eager for more. The next step is to deliver a sizable sample of your own writing that's called the "overview" or the "about the book" section. This might be as many as four or five pages long, and it takes the concept statement and shows how that idea can be expanded to fill an entire book. This is the time to present evidence that you can write well for an extended period of time and that there's firm footing beneath your ideas.

As with any extended piece of writing, you have to make it reader-friendly. Remember those nasty five-paragraph essays you had to write in high school? Some of those structural ideas are useful in writing your overview, too. A reasonable format for your overview might be:

1. Begin with a strong lead.
2. Show the context/timeliness for your book.
3. Offer a memorable anecdote/example.

4. Identify the main problem.

5. Identify solution(s) offered in the book.

6. Reveal the book's approach.

7. Explain other benefits readers get from the book.

8. Present the author's qualifications.

These can happen in nearly any order as long as the piece reads and proves effective. Plenty of books and articles exist on how to write essays (which is essentially what the overview is—an attempt to explain something), and those can help you see ways to present your overview material effectively. I won't try to teach you that skill here, but I will mention two things. (1) Make sure your lead rocks. You can use questions, analogies, quotes, surprising facts, anecdotes, myths, controversial data, or personal stories, as long as it grabs a reader's interest and refuses to let go. What's a great lead? If you had one sentence only to grab your audience, what would it be? Hint: that's your lead. (2) Spend some time reading over the overviews in the numerous proposal samples in chapters twelve through sixteen of this book. Seeing how it's done firsthand might prove more beneficial than reading a dozen how-to articles on writing terrific essays.

What's a strong lead look like for your Overview/About the Book section? Here are three examples:

- **Lead #1:** Car crashes are the #1 killer of children age 0 to 12 in America. Until now, that fact seemed just part of the deal for us having cars. No longer.

- **Lead #2:** In the highly readable For Dummies style, Dr. Ryan G. Van Cleave reveals how to successfully start *and finish* the most important story you know—your own! Now you can discover how to avoid the most common pitfalls, know which details to put in (and leave out), and create a clear vision for your life story.

- **Lead #3:** It's no wonder that when *The Simpsons Movie* debuted in theaters in August 2007, it was a worldwide hit, grossing more than $315 million in the first two weeks. Fans can't get seem to immerse themselves deeply enough into the hilariously disastrous lives of Homer, Marge, Maggie, Bart, Lisa, and the many residents of "America's crudbucket," Springfield. With fan-sponsored websites such as www.simpsonstrivia. com (and more than a dozen competitors) getting thousands of hits per month, it's clear, too, that there exists a demand for accurate, compelling *Simpsons* trivia—thus the need for *The Unauthorized Simpsons Quiz Challenge.*

Whether you name your book title at the start or hold that until later, all of these leads clearly promise what the book will be about. A few even start the sales sizzle already! A final note on overviews: How you choose to structure your overview might well come directly from how you structure your book. The next section covers this topic in depth.

HIT THE GAS

One of the ways you can speed up the writing process is to double dip. By that I mean to use something you wrote for one spot in another spot. Ninety percent of what I wrote for this book's introduction came from my proposal's overview. As long as you're not just mindlessly cutting and pasting things into multiple spots, this can be a great way to repurpose some of your best material. Take what you need and use it somewhere else. It's not cheating—it's reinforcing the main message(s) you want to drive home about your book.

LET'S TALK ABOUT STRUCTURE

One of the biggest problems I see with a proposal someone brings to me, saying, "No one's buying this. What's wrong with it?" is that the book's structure isn't sound. It's like trying to build a skyscraper on a sandy beach. Even if readers aren't 100 percent certain what's wrong, they sense the iffiness of it all. Structure has to have a logic to it. There has to be some sense of a larger design or framework present.

Let me share an example. A former neighbor of mine was a physicist. He also had that Robert Fulghum storyteller magic about him. He had stories about everything. They were funny, witty, and wise. After being bombarded with requests to write a book, he did. And like most first-time would-be authors, he wrote the whole thing and fired it off to six publishers. All sent back encouraging rejections. Frustrated, he came to me and asked for help.

I read the mess of papers he gave me. "What's the book about?" I finally asked, pushing the papers aside.

"The importance of physics in our daily lives."

"I don't get that from the stories," I said.

"But they're all about science!"

He's right—they were. But they were just a mishmash of anecdotes and experiences he'd had in science settings and with science colleagues. That's when we talked about structure and he started to get it. If each chapter doesn't have a clear purpose behind it (for instance, my third chapter for this book is about titles, and the fourth covers marketplace analysis, etc.), readers can easily get lost. Was his book a memoir? Essay collection? How-to? A book that doesn't quite know what it is becomes a near-impossible sell in the bookstore, so publishers simply pass for other books that offer clearer visions of what they are.

An editor taking my neighbor's manuscript to a pub board meeting wouldn't know how to pitch it, even if my neighbor had included an elevator pitch, concept statement, and overview that were about the importance of physics in our daily lives. In every other aspect of his life, my neighbor acts like a sponge—he learns everything he can about something before actually doing it. But when it came to writing, he just winged it and hoped for the best. You can't wing the structure of the book any easier than a layman could wing the answer to the following: "A ladder initially stands vertically against a wall. Its bottom end is given a sideways kick, causing the ladder to slide down. Assume that the bottom end is constrained to keep contact with the ground, and the top end is constrained to keep contact with the wall. Describe the envelope of the ladder's positions."

Without the foundational physics information (yes, all you word people, this involves math), the above problem is hard to solve. (FYI—the answer can be Googled at "physics Harvard ladder envelope solution." If you fear high-powered math, don't risk a peek at the answer.)

WORDS OF WISDOM

"I think the biggest mistake prospective authors make is proposing books that they cannot actually write. That might mean proposing a book so broad in scope that it would take an army of researchers years to complete, or requiring a depth of expertise that the author does not actually have. If you don't speak Norwegian, don't take on a project that requires archival work in bokmål dialects." — Jacob Appel

Had my neighbor embraced any of the following common book structure types and used his anecdotes to support chapters on specific individual points, he'd have been in the running for a book contract. Here's a list of proven nonfiction book formats that readers enjoy and my neighbor eschewed, including two real-world examples for each:

- **Books about mistakes:** We all make mistakes. No wonder we love books that reveal those and tell us how to avoid them. Let each mistake serve as a mini-chapter. *Nice Girls Don't Get the Corner Office: 101 Unconscious Mistakes Women Make That Sabotage Their Careers. The 25 Most Common Sales Mistakes … And How to Avoid Them.*

- **Books that teach you how to do something:** Who doesn't enjoy a good how-to book? Break up the "how to" into parts, and let those serve as chapters or sections. *How to Retire Happy, Wild, and Free: Retirement Wisdom That You Won't Get from Your Financial Advisor. How to Read a Poem and Fall in Love with Poetry.*

- **Books that offer questions and answers**: Q&A is another format that works for nearly any topic. Let each Q&A serve as a mini-chapter. *101 Great Answers to the Toughest Interview Questions. Why Doesn't My Doctor Know This?: Conquering Irritable Bowel Syndrome, Inflammatory Bowel Disease, Crohn's Disease, and Colitis.*

- **Books with numbers in the titles:** You know these. Heck, you've already seen a few pop up on this page alone. Start with #1 and just run through to the end. Consider, too, the order. (Perhaps go from most common to least common, or most important to least, and leave one of the vital ones toward the end for the big finale?) *365 Ways to Motivate and Reward Your Employees Every Day—With Little or No Money.* Or *I Can Read! 100 Tips for Beginning Readers.*

- **Books on how to hire:** Managers, CEOs, and administrators in all professions spend countless dollars on the hiring process. And for every bad hire, it costs a lot more to search, find, and hire a replacement. These books are sought out. Don't forget about the homeowner who has to hire someone, too! All of these have a similar structure—how to find, then interview, then negotiate, then hire, then work with a person. See how some of these handled it! *How to Hire A-Players: Finding the Top People for Your Team—Even If You Don't Have a Recruiting Department.* Or there's *Simplified Guide for Hiring Contractors:*

Get the Inside Scoop from a Contractor with Over 30 Years of Experience.

- **Book of interviews:** Find some interesting subjects, and you're off to the races. Typically, these are chronologically handled starting with your first question and ending with the subject's last answer. Don't be afraid to reorder the Q&A (or the order of the interviews) for maximum impact. *Interview with an Exorcist. Conversations with Millionaires: What Millionaires Do to Get Rich, That You Never Learned About in School!*

- **Anthology of stories:** If you prefer to do more gathering and researching than writing, consider putting together an anthology (meaning a book that compiles writings by authors other than yourself). Don't forget to think about the order of material. Some of my anthologies simply go alphabetical by authors' last name, but some are grouped by theme or subject. *The Scribner Anthology of Contemporary Short Fiction: 50 North American Stories Since 1970. Chicken Soup for the Soul: Angels Among Us: 101 Inspiration Stories of Miracles, Faith, and Answered Prayers.*

- **Books of biography (or memoir):** There's a huge market for telling the true stories of interesting people. If you don't consider your life noteworthy, tell someone else's. Most of these utilize a straightforward chronology, though some of the most interesting break it up to highlight key themes, moments, and subjects. *Seabiscuit: An American Legend. Happy, Happy, Happy: My Life and Legacy as the Duck Commander.*

- **Books of quotations:** Bring together what other smart people have said on a topic, and you have a book. It's a small one, typically, but these easy-read titles are welcome reading. Start with a great idea/tip, and then run through the rest. Consider grouping them by subject or mini-subjects for easier use (see chapter twenty for a sense of how this might look). *Success and Happiness: Quotes to Motivate, Inspire, & Live By. The Designer Says: Quotes, Quips, and Words of Wisdom.*

- **Books that collect your previous writing:** Spent a few years as a magazine columnist? Published some of your personal stories in literary magazines over the years? Collect those into a coherent story arc and let that be your book. *Philip Guston:*

Collected Writings, Lectures, and Conversations. On Architecture: Collected Reflections on a Century of Change.

Within each of these book formats, you still want to ensure there's some kind of progression from chapter to chapter. Big to small, out to in, first to last, top to bottom, oldest to newest, careful to crazy—the options are nearly endless. If you've got a bit of Sherlock Holmes in you, you can order the chapters by inductive or deductive logic. If you're more inclined to be literary, you can play with themes, story arcs, voices, and styles in your approach to structure. See if you can create a sense of building toward your conclusion. Books that have momentum are often called "page-turners." Can you make a page-turner out of a nonfiction book? An anthology? A book of interviews? It's possible, if done with consistency and logic.

Having a clear idea of how you plan to structure your book, with meaning and purpose, will give your overview—and your full proposal—the authority it needs to make it stand out.

CHAPTER SUMMARIES

Now it's time to take the book overview and structure concept and break that down into effective chapter summaries. These don't even need to be done in complete sentences if you choose. You can use fragments or a bulleted list with strong verbs for the moment. But by the time you submit your proposal, each chapter summary should be a paragraph or two long at most. Write much more than that and you're already starting to write the chapter, which is *not* what an editor wants in this part of the proposal. If you can't rein in your chapter summary at two paragraphs, you might have more than one chapter fighting it out there. If you feel like you're really adding fluff to get that summary done, you might not have enough material for a whole chapter.

One way to make sure that each chapter's function is apparent is to assign appropriate titles. I originally had different titles for many of the chapters of this book, but I ended up going with a very straightforward approach. I needed readers to feel like they could look at the table of contents and within seconds find exactly what they needed. Sure they could always hit up the index, but you shouldn't have to dig around in an index to locate the big stuff. Make your content completely visible via appropriate chapter titles. Make it clear in your chapter summaries as well.

Editors love chapter summaries because they show the author's thinking on a smaller scale. If an author can get the macro stuff right—like the elevator pitch and concept statement—*and* they can nail the micro stuff like what's in a chapter, what's to keep them from making an awesome book? As long as the quality and the content of the manuscript sample doesn't fire up any red flags, you're right where you want to be. You and the editor are partners working to make your vision become a reality.

The editor isn't your enemy. He's the best friend in publishing you can have. Unless your mommy owns Random House.

SOME FINAL THOUGHTS ON IDEAS, PURPOSE, AND STRUCTURE

When soliciting information and quotes from authors and experts to use in this book, I had one author (of many books) tell me that the writing of book proposals was "going the way of the dinosaur." It's all about self-publishing now, he assured me. And sure enough, he practiced what he preached. His first few books were with traditional publishers, yet the last one was indeed self-published.

Writing a book proposal involves the same level of research, planning, and trial and error that one should be doing on any of their books, self-published or not. And from the quality of most self-published books these days—that "dinosaur" quote author included—it's quite evident that this type of rigorous work is not getting done, to the detriment of many promising authors' careers.

Whether you're self-published or seeking a traditional book deal, and whether you're proposing a poetry anthology, a how-to on converting a garage into an in-law apartment, or a YA series featuring a boy wizard named Scary Totter, you should be (a) passionate about the project, (b) convinced that you can spend six months to a year working exclusively on this book, and (c) absolutely certain there is a clear audience for it. When you determine the answer to letter *c*, share that information with an editor so he can share it with the pub board.

Even if you're not quite ready with your idea, the rest of this book can still be extremely helpful to you. The more you understand about how good book proposals work, the more ready you'll be when it's time to write yours.

TOP TIPS TO REMEMBER

- An elevator pitch is your twenty-second sizzle pitch. Keep it concise and catchy! Try it on family and friends. Does it work? Solicit feedback whenever you can.

- Ensure that your book has structure, both overall and within each chapter, and that the structure/format is clear and beneficial to the reader.

- The editor is your friend, your advocate, your publishing partner. To paraphrase Jerry Maguire, your editor is out here for you. You don't want to know what it's like to be him out here for you. It is an up-at-dawn, pride-swallowing siege that he will never fully tell you about. So make sure you're doing all you can to help him help you.

- One to two paragraphs is plenty for a chapter summary.

- Even if you self-publish, writing a book proposal is incredibly helpful. It will show you where you need to improve your book, platform, or financial planning long before any of these can negatively affect your book's success.

FOR MORE INFORMATION

Heffron, Jack. *The Writer's Idea Book 10th Anniversary Edition: How to Develop Great Ideas for Fiction, Nonfiction, Poetry, and Screenplays.* Writer's Digest Books (2012).

See Appendix A for other helpful titles.

Chapter Three

SNAPPY TITLES:
HOW TO CREATE INTEREST FROM THE START

You wouldn't stroll into an important job interview wearing a dress shirt you found crumpled in the back of a dresser drawer, would you? Whether you're sweating it out in a job interview or wooing a prospective reader, you only have a single chance to make a great first impression. To that end, a title needs to be catchy and concise. It needs to grab hold and refuse to let go. With apologies to the late Barry White, your title needs to insist, "I'm your first, your last, your everything."

Let's talk specifics. Would you rather buy a copy of *Two Weeks to Incredible Sex: An Idiot-Proof Approach* or *You Can Have Better Sex Too!*? What about *The Confidential Guide to Making Your First Million* vs. *Making a Million Is Easy*? Same book. Same content. But in each case, one snares your interest far more easily, no?

Generating reader interest before the cover is even opened—that's one way a title can help your book (and your book proposal). A terrific title might not convince a browser to become a buyer, but a lousy title can make them pass you by and never return. Worse, a lousy title might get your book mis-shelved so that people who are actually looking for it can't find it at the library or at Barnes & Noble. Customers might be too busy to keep looking or too embarrassed to ask for help. The end result is the same—you've lost another reader. With the publishing landscape growing more crowded by the day, every individual reader matters.

Think about your last visit to a bookstore. Sure, your eye might be drawn to splashy cover art, but it's titles that really connect with people. The last two books I bought? *The Elfstones of Shannara* and *Wikinomics: How Mass Collaboration Changes Everything*. I picked up Terry Brooks' fantasy novel because the poet in me loved the sound of *elfstones* and *Shannara*. (I'm also partial to anything that reminds me of Tolkien, the first "adult" books I ever truly loved.) My inner child insists that I buy one fantasy book a month, so I was browsing the Sarasota Barnes & Noble sci-fi/fantasy shelves, wondering if I should finally read Douglas Adams' *The Hitchhiker's Guide to the Galaxy*, when my eyes fell on Brooks' fantasy book.

Elfstones.

Shannara.

There's something luscious about how the harsh monosyllabic *stones* is softened by the three-syllable word *Shannara*. But then I'm a poet, which means I get unduly excited about nuances of language and sound in ways my family doesn't understand. In any event, Brooks' 576-page paperback from 1982 called to me solely due to the title, and so I made the purchase in 2012. Not bad work for a thirty-year-old title.

And the *Wikinomics* title? It's clever. And I appreciate the heck out of cleverness since I fancy myself moderately clever. For those who aren't as familiar with wikis (web pages that can be edited by anyone who accesses them), Don Tapscott has a no-nonsense subtitle to clarify the book's purpose: *How Mass Collaboration Changes Everything*. What's the promise he makes? To discuss/explain/showcase "change" in relationship to "collaboration." And what will be affected by this change? He says "everything." It's no large step to move from "everything" to "everyone." Wow. That's quite a statement—I'll have to read a few chapters to see how this might relate to me.

WHAT CAN A GOOD TITLE DO FOR YOU?

My freshman composition teacher, Mrs. White, told me that a title has two functions: tell and sell. Having taught at universities for more than a decade myself, I know firsthand how tedious it is to read an endless stack of papers titled "My Summer Vacation" or "Edgar Allen Poe & 'The Cask of Amontillado.'" BO-RING! So she gave our class a dose of Newspaper Writing 101 and the tell/sell principle. It doesn't work for newspaper articles and freshman comp papers alone—it's sound advice for nonfiction books, too. In each case, the title broadcasts to the reader what the piece is going to be about. The title also sells the reader by making an explicit or implicit promise that there will be value in reading it. It's that simple and that complicated.

Thank you, Mrs. White!

INSIDER TIP

Fiction writers, too, need to make promises with their titles. Consider the title of Virgil Suárez's 2014 short story collection, *The Soviet Circus Comes to Havana & Other Stories*. What do you expect from the stories? Fidel Castro. Russians. Violence. 1960s. What do you expect from the following titles?

Stephen King's *Dr. Sleep*

Seth Grahame-Smith's *Pride and Prejudice and Zombies: The Classic Regency Romance—Now with Ultraviolent Zombie Mayhem!*

The promise you make in your title should be specific. Consider the following examples from Dan Poynter's *Writing Nonfiction*, where ads were run featuring two similar titles for the exact same book. The discrepancy in sales figures was astonishing. *The Art of Courtship* (17,500) versus *The Art of Kissing* (60,500). *The Art of Controversy* (negligible) versus *How to Argue Logically* (30,000). And *An Introduction to Einstein* (15,000) versus *Einstein's Theory of Relativity Explained* (42,000).

People have a driving need to get the inside scoop on something. The better-selling titles made a different kind of promise to the reader than the other titles—they said, "Here's *exactly* what we're going to talk about, and we're really going deep into this specific subject versus being wishy-washy about a number of things." In my own terms, it's the difference between a college student deciding between two classes: Introduction to Philosophy 301 (yawn) and Martin Heidegger: An Investigation of Truth, Being, & Existence (ka-POW!).

Grade worries aside, which college class sounds more intriguing to you?

SUBTITLES

The American journalist Richard Harding Davis claimed, "The secret of good writing is to say an old thing in a new way or to say a new thing in an old way." He might as well have been talking specifically about titles. Every fourth nonfiction book seems to be about losing weight, making money, or having sex. With so many titles out there competing for the same audience, how do you stand out? Richard had it right. Put some spin on it. One easy way to do this is with a subtitle.

A subtitle can punch up even these three tired topics. How about *Lose That Holiday Weight: A 10-Day Guide to Dropping 10 Pounds*? Wow, I'd buy that one. Consider *Money NOW!: A Wall Street Wizard Shares His Secrets for Building Massive Wealth*. That'd be a bestseller before the Kindle edition came out. And *Celebrity Sex: How to Make Your Man a Star in the Bedroom*. I'm not sure how someone could manage this one, but if they could? Yowzers. In all three cases, it's the subtitle that makes the real sale. Skip the subtitles and see the difference. *Lose that Holiday Weight. Money NOW! Celebrity Sex.* The first is boring. The second kind of silly. The third? It promises something far, far different than the version with the subtitle.

Powerful things, those subtitles.

When you've got a title like Richard Nelson Bolles' *What Color Is Your Parachute?* (it's not about skydiving, but it is the world's top-selling job search and career search book), it's easy to see why a subtitle is not just helpful, it's often an absolute necessity. Unlike titles, which tend to be short and punchy, subtitles can be any length and devote a lot of space to explaining. Thank goodness Bolles understood that, deciding on: "A Practice Manual for Job-Hunters and Career-Changers." Simple. Direct. And there's no way anyone who reads it could be confused about what they're going to find inside.

Another reason to use a subtitle is to differentiate books with similar (or exactly the same) titles. Marcia Muller has a private-eye thriller called *Vanishing Point* and Mary Sharratt has an English romance called *The Vanishing Point*. Jack Ketchum's *The Girl Next Door* is an occult horror book, while Paul Ruditis' *The Girls Next Door* is about Hugh Hefner's girlfriends. If you absolutely must go with a title that's close to your own, use a subtitle to make your book stand out.

A better option, though, is to go with a different, unique title rather than expect readers to scrutinize subtitles. Market confusion is never a good thing. You want to make sure that any PR you do is to sell your book, not somebody else's with the same (or a similar) title.

HIT THE GAS

For a nonfiction book title, go to www.amazon.com and find ten current how-to books whose titles appeal to you. Swap out their key topic-specific words for your own, and tweak the rest as needed. Select the best two options for now, call this your working title, and move on. Revisit the working title after you've written the rest of your proposal, and see if you can improve on it.

Examples for a book on fly-fishing.

Real Title: *The How of Happiness: A New Approach to Getting the Life You Want* (by Sonja Lyubomirsky)

Your Version #1: *The How of Fly-Fishing: An Insider's Approach*

Your Version #2: *The How of Fly-Fishing: A New Approach to Fishing Like a Pro*

Real Title: *How to Stop Worrying and Start Living* (by Dale Carnegie)

Your Version: *Stop Worrying and Start Fishing: Finding Inner Peace on the Water*

EXCEPTIONS TO THE RULE

Like every good rule, the tell/sell title rule has exceptions. Go ahead and take a chance with an "out there" title minus a subtitle if you want, but just remember that for every exception, there are probably ninety-nine others that follow the rule. For my money, I'd rather play the better odds. Want to be a renegade? Publish a book or two first, and then see how far you can convince a publisher to bend.

Self-help and how-to books in particular must use effective subtitles to motivate people to pick the book up. You're aiming at large audiences, and they generally are coming from a state of lack. The book must promise to fill that lack with speed, economy, quality, systems, or information. To (badly) paraphrase a line from *Field of Dreams*, "If you subtitle it, readers will come."

Give them the essence of the book in the title. Make them say, "God, how did I *ever* live without this book?" That's the sign of a great title. And if you need that extra nudge to clarify the who, what, when, where, or why, use a subtitle to get the job done.

TEN TITLE TIPS

1. **Make sure your title is unique:** Search your prospective title on Amazon.com and in *Books in Print*. Sure, you can't copyright a title, but why possibly confuse people when there are plenty of good unique options still available? Plus, you don't want your book confused with Laurie Notaro's *The Idiot Girl and the Flaming Tantrum of Death: Reflections on Revenge, Germophobia, and Laser Hair Removal*, right?

2. **Be clever:** Consider twists on well-known expressions or even other titles, such as Judy Gruen's *Till We Eat Again: Confessions of a Diet Dropout*, or Chelsea Handler's *Are You There, Vodka? It's Me, Chelsea*. This can get corny, however (consider Biz Stone's *Who Let the Blogs Out?*), so navigate this route with caution, especially if you're writing about serious topics.

3. **Humor works:** Not all the time, but when it does, it does. Consider John Warner's tongue-in-cheek writing manual, *Fondling Your Muse*

and Claudine Wolk's *It Gets Easier! And Other Lies We Tell New Mothers*. And who wouldn't glance twice at Stephen Colbert's *I Am America (And So Can You!)*? Another accidentally funny title is Disney's cookbook for kids entitled *Cooking With Pooh*, which brings me to a caveat: If you're going to be funny, make sure it's intentional!

4. **Use a number:** Where? At the start of your title. Why? Search engines and online bookstores typically list *101 Ways to Filet a Fish* before *Ways to Filet a Fish*. Numbers come before letters. Take advantage of how listing search engines privilege numbers.

5. **Get double-duty from titles:** Think ahead to PR—you'll want a website as part of the standard promotion plan for any title, so is the URL for your prospective title available? I checked (and bought) www.weekendbookproposal.com and www.theweekendbookproposal.com before sending this proposal to literary agents. It was worth twelve bucks to hold those domain names for a year. What about workshops? Would your book title serve as a catchy moniker for a lecture series, writing workshop, or DVD? If you've lucked into the perfect name, trademark it and make your millions. (Think Chicken Soup for the Soul, Guerilla Marketing, The Worst-Case Scenario, The Girlfriend's Guide to _____, or the _____ for Dummies series.)

6. **Keywords, keywords, keywords:** To see if words and phrases in your prospective title (and subtitle) are commonly sought after, test them yourself with various Internet search engines. A great keyword phrase will pull up ten times the traffic of an okay one, which will help immensely with online sales. For a book on pet death, you might Google "pet loss grieving" (784,000 results), "pet funerals" (496,000 results), "sympathy pet loss" (322,000 results), and "pet death grieving" (483,000 results). While those numbers all seem impressive, Google points out that "pet death children" pulls more than 7 million results—more than three times as much as the next highest phrase, "pet death quotes." Slanting your book to include children might make sense since there seems to be significant interest in this subject. As a result, sample titles might be: *Pet Loss & Children: A Survivor's Guide*; *Absent Pets: Helping Children Say Goodbye*; and *Coping With Pet Loss: A Conversation for Children*.

7. **Keep it short:** The longer your title is—the longer any part of your book is—the harder it has to work to justify its length. Try to keep

titles under seven words (some editors and agents claim five words is the max).

8. **Add immediacy:** Try the words *now* or *one week* or *48 hours*. Quantify the time needed to create change. Get people excited about the possibilities of short-term or immediate results.

9. **Left brain/right brain titles:** See if you can appeal both to people's creative side and their logical, factual side at the same time. An example: *Cadillac Desert: The American West and Its Disappearing Water.*

10. **Keep it positive:** Negative titles simply don't sell well. Instead of *Don't Get Ripped Off: A Guide to Buying Used Cars*, try *Getting Deals on Used Wheels: A Used Car Buying Manual.* Spin your title into a positive if you can.

BE FLEXIBLE

A few months ago, a Tampa man asked me to ghostwrite a memoir about his involvement in South American drug cartels, where he stole $2 million from a Colombian drug lord, gambled it all away, and changed his identity before he moved to American to outwit assassins. The title for this high-powered adventure tale? *Bang Bang.*

> **Me:** What about *Murder in Colombia: A Memoir*? Or *The Confidential Guide to Cartels: An Insider Account of the Colombian Cocaine Industry*? Maybe *Left to Die: A True Story*?
>
> **Him:** It's *Bang Bang.*
>
> **Me:** Titles really can affect sales. Are you sure this one is going to help sell copies?
>
> **Him:** It came to me in a dream. I just *know* that's the title of my book.
>
> **Me:** Oooo-kaaaay.

Anyone this obstinate about a title—a momentous selling tool for any book, but especially memoirs—was going to be a pain to work with throughout the entire writing and publishing process. Who knew what other things he was convinced he knew best about? Worse, less than a third of titles make it from proposal to finished book. Agents, editors, and marketing people love to change titles to make them better. This guy? He said he'd sooner cut off his toe than change the book "as he knew it had to be."

Dreading the nuclear meltdown he'd have when an editor insisted on a different title at the eleventh hour, I wished him luck and passed on what would've been a fairly lucrative job. As of this writing, this former drug runner and thief had burned through three other ghostwriters and was still spamming listservs and classified ads for help "writing the book the way I need it to be written."

Sometimes, it's a very, very good thing that the original title doesn't end up on the actual book cover. Here are some examples of well-known books that ended up with better titles than they started with.

At This Point in Time = All the President's Men

Before the Anger = Roots

The Birds and the Bees = Everything You Always Wanted to Know About Sex but Were Afraid to Ask

A Jewish Patient Begins His Analysis = Portnoy's Complaint

Incident at West Egg = The Great Gatsby

Bugles Sang True = Gone with the Wind

The Summer of the Shark = Jaws

Bar-B-Q = The Postman Always Rings Twice

What Your Mother Couldn't Tell You and What Your Father Didn't Know = Men Are from Mars, Women Are from Venus

TWENTY SECRET TITLE WORDS

Part of making a title pop off the page is to use powerful language that makes people respond. Consider using one or more of these secret, high-octane, attention-grabbing words in your nonfiction book title.

Best

Example 1: *The Best Year of Your Life: Dream It, Plan It, Live It*
Example 2: *The 10 Best Decisions a Parent Can Ever Make*

Complete

Example 1: *The Complete Manual of Things That Might Kill You: A Guide to Self-Diagnosis for Hypochondriacs*
Example 2: *Dr. Pitcairn's New Complete Guide to Natural Health for Dogs and Cats*

Confidential
Example 1: *Film School Confidential: The Insider's Guide to Film Schools*
Example 2: *Party Confidential: New Etiquette for Fabulous Entertaining*

First
Example 1: *Family First: Your Step-by-Step Plan for Creating a Phenomenal Family*
Example 2: *Your First Quilt Book (Or It Should Be!)*

Free
Example 1: *Free Lunch: How the Wealthiest Americans Enrich Themselves at Government Expense (and Stick You with the Bill)*
Example 2: *Mortgage Free!: Innovative Strategies for Debt-Free Home Ownership*

Guaranteed
Example 1: *8 Minutes in the Morning: A Simple Way to Shed Up to 2 Pounds a Week Guaranteed*
Example 2: *101 Team Games for Kids: Guaranteed Fun for All Ages*

Mastery
Example 1: *Mastering the World of Psychology*
Example 2: *Mastery of Your Anxiety and Worry*

New
Example 1: *A New Earth: Awakening to Your Life's Purpose*
Example 2: *Anticancer: A New Way of Life*

Original
Example 1: *The Original Beauty Bible: Skin Care Facts for Ageless Beauty*
Example 2: *Original Instructions: Indigenous Teachings for a Sustainable Future*

Perfect
Example 1: *Sex and the Perfect Lover: Tao, Tantra, and the Kama Sutra*
Example 2: *Seven Perfect Days in Northern California: A Guided Driving Tour*

Powerful

Example 1: *Speak Like Churchill, Stand Like Lincoln: 21 Powerful Secrets of History's Greatest Speakers*

Example 2: *Blogs, Wikis, Podcasts, and Other Powerful Web Tools for Classrooms*

Quick

Example 1: *Quick Meals for Healthy Kids and Busy Parents: Wholesome Family Recipes in 30 Minutes or Less From Three Leading Child Nutrition Experts*

Example 2: *Quick Calculus: A Self-Teaching Guide*

Risk-Free

Example 1: *Natural Flexibility: The New Risk-Free Alternative to Stretching*

Example 2: *The Money Tree: Risk-Free Options Trading*

Secret

Example 1: *You Can Be a Stock Market Genius: Uncover the Secret Hiding Places of Stock Market Profits*

Example 2: *The Secret Lives of Men and Women: A PostSecret Book*

Sex

Example 1: *101 Sex Positions: Steamy New Positions From Mild to Wild*

Example 2: *The Sex-Starved Marriage: Boosting Your Marriage Libido: A Couple's Guide*

Simple

Example 1: *Clinical Physiology Made Ridiculously Simple*

Example 2: *How to Write a Query Letter: Everything You Need to Know Explained Simply*

Steps

Example 1: *Breakthrough: Eight Steps to Wellness*

Example 2: *Writing Fiction Step by Step*

Transform

Example 1: *The Art of Extreme Self-Care: Transform Your Life One Month at a Time*

Example 2: *Ten Lessons to Transform Your Marriage: America's Love Lab Experts Share Their Strategies for Strengthening Your Relationship*

Win

Example 1: *How to Win Friends & Influence People*
Example 2: *Groundswell: Winning in a World Transformed by Social Technologies*

Worry-Free

Example 1: *Low-Stress Investing: 10 Simple Steps to a Worry-Free Portfolio*
Example 2: *The Allergic Traveler's Passport to Worry-Free Vacations*

STILL NEED A TITLE? TRY THIS

See if one, two, or all of these help you find the best title for your book.

- **Option 1:** Sum up the main idea of your book in three words. Use that as your exact title, or as a key part of it (or a subtitle). Examples: "Get Rich Quick" or "Lose Weight Fast" or "Have Better Sex" or "Learn Algebra Shortcuts."

- **Option 2:** Use a thesaurus to find at least three synonyms for every noun and verb in your tentative title. Play around to see which combinations sound best.

- **Option 3:** Look through your book proposal or manuscript for a catchy phrase, image, or idea that might serve as a title.

- **Option 4:** Use the Idiot-Proof Method of Titling. If you're writing about selling gourds on eBay for extra pocket money, try *Selling Gourds on eBay: How to Make a Little Extra Cash.* If you're writing about the fall of the KGB since the Cold War, try *The Fall of the KGB Since the Cold War.*

- **Option 5:** One-up a competing title. Instead of Viki King's *How to Write a Movie in 21 Days*, try *Write a Blockbuster in Two Weeks Flat!* Instead of the multi-author *The Non-Runner's Marathon Trainer*, try *Marathons Made Easy: A Guide for Amateur Runners.*

WORDS OF WISDOM

As Mark Twain said, " The difference between the almost right word and the right word is really a large matter—it's the difference between the lightning bug and the lightning." The same is true for titles. Here are some examples: Which side is the bug and which is the lightning? (If you're unsure, check these titles in Amazon.com and ask yourself "Why did the agent, author, and editor choose this title over any other?")

Napoleon Hill	
Use Your Mind to Make Money	Think and Grow Rich

Barbara Kingsolver	
Animal, Vegetable, Miracle	Eating Where You Live

Maria Shriver	
Just Who Will You Be?	It's Never Too Late

Eric Weiner	
Happy Where We're At	The Geography of Bliss

Virginia Woolf	
A Room of One's Own	How to Be a Writer

SOME FINAL THOUGHTS ON TITLES

Best-selling fantasy writer Lawrence Watt-Evans says, "The one real true unbreakable rule: Don't Bore the Reader. Everything else is just hints and suggestions on how best to achieve this." That's as true for the title as anywhere else in a book. Whatever you do, don't be boring. *How to Milk a Cow* is functional, but it lacks the pizzazz of *Udderly Yours: A Hands-On Guide to Modern Cow Milking* or *Milking Made Easy: 10 Steps to Dairy Success*. If you're boring, you're not going to survive in this business.

Be weird. Be long. Be short. Be anything except boring, and you'll be in decent shape. After all, most authors change their titles four times before sending a proposal out, so whatever you're settled on now probably won't last anyway. Settle on a title (for now) and move on!

TOP TIPS TO REMEMBER

- Keep titles under seven words. Cleverness counts. Humor, too.
- Emphasize a book's value. List a dozen target audience's values, needs, fears, and desires. Make sure this title addresses one or more of them.

- Run it by the book experts: librarians, booksellers, and other writers/editors. Go ahead and try your friends and family, too, but take their feedback with a grain of salt. Many will "LOVE IT!!!" just because it's yours.
- If you don't get chills, it's probably not the *best* title. Write a few until you get the right one.

FOR MORE INFORMATION

Bodian, Nat G. *How to Choose a Winning Title: A Guide for Writers, Editors, and Publishers.* Oryx Press (1989).

See Appendix A for other helpful titles.

Chapter Four

MARKET ANALYSIS:
WHICH READERS—AND HOW MANY
OF THEM—NEED THIS BOOK?

Book publishing companies are in the business of making money. It's an ugly, commerce-centered reality for some writers to face, but there it is. Once you come to grips with that reality, the point of this chapter becomes stunningly clear. You *must* carefully consider the potential audience for your book and its potential for profit. Who's going to plunk down ten bucks for an e-version (or even more for a print copy) of what you want to write? What about $25 for the hardcover?

Remember that you're asking a publisher to invest in both you and your book. What will the potential payoff look like? What's the bare minimum they can expect in return? What's the pie-in-the-sky high end? Ninety percent of books lose money for the publisher. Can you offer enough evidence and support to suggest you'll be on the winning 10 percent? What evidence can you offer that'll satisfy the bean counters doing the P&L (profit and loss) numbers?

Even with a modest advance—say $10,000—a publisher is actually investing at least $50,000 when you consider the production costs, freelance copyediting, marketing, warehouse, etc. A publisher buying a book isn't making a personal decision, but rather a serious, well-considered business one. Be business-like in how you convince them that it's a sound business decision that has many possibilities for a return on that investment.

VISIT THE BOOK GRAVEYARD

Here's an assignment for you as you consider your book's audience and marketability. Visit your local Dollar Tree or any of those other dollar stores. Hit up the book section, which many writers call "the book graveyard," because it's where books go to die. All the books there—from no-name publishers to midlist publishers to the biggest of the big New York guys—couldn't find a substantial enough audience to merit taking space any longer on a publisher's warehouse shelves. It costs money to warehouse a book. And other books are clamoring for shelf space, too.

So what they do is put a big black Sharpie mark on the spine or over the UPC (to stop people from buying them for a buck and then returning them for full price at B&N), and they sell them by the pound. Yes, just like you buy a good porterhouse at the market, the dollar stores pay pennies on the retail dollar per pound of "miscellaneous cookbooks" or "mass-market paperbacks." Even after you factor in the cost of shipping, that's still cheap enough for them to make money despite selling these books at 80 to 95 percent off the full retail price. Ouch.

Clearly, the publisher isn't paying your royalties on these books that are "remaindered." And the dollar stores aren't paying you for each sale either. Thus, you have a graveyard of books with a weak or nonexistent audience.

Okay, here's the assignment, which plenty of writers do regularly. Pick up a few of these cast-off books and ask yourself: *Why did these books fail?* What is it about them that didn't connect with an audience such that a publisher gave up on them? It's possible that the publisher overestimated the interest and printed a gazillion too many. But was there a significant market to begin with?

If you can answer those questions, you'll have a clear object lesson in what *not* to do with your own book. Embrace that knowledge and incorporate it into your own book proposal to decrease the odds your book will one day join the ranks of those celebrity memoirs, breathy romances, uberliterary novels, and odd nonfiction books that just didn't make that love connection with enough readers.

Note: A fate worse than being remaindered is having your book pulped. This means that your book is recycled for the paper value because the publisher foresees absolutely no retail value of any type. The Publishers Association reported that 61 million books were returned unsold to publishers in the UK in 2008, and another 16 million came back from overseas outlets. The number of books being pulped annually in the US? Industry insiders suggest the number might be as high as 40 percent of the total books printed, well more than twice as many as the UK is pulping annually.

SO, WHO *ARE* YOUR READERS?

Start with your mom, dad, spouse, and immediate, everyday family. Then expand this list to any aunts, uncles, and cousins who you can guilt-trip into buying a copy. Great—you've sold maybe a dozen copies to people who are buying it merely because they know you. Maybe more if you include co-workers and neighbors. Now the real work starts. Who *else* is going to be persuaded to buy the book?

That's the problem. Now you have to get creative.

WHAT ARE THE PRIMARY AND SECONDARY MARKETS?

Your primary audience is the ideal group of people who'd love to read your book. If your book is a Florida orchid-growing how-to, the primary audience becomes Floridians who grow orchids. If your book is a memoir about a forty-something using her renewed Catholic faith and positive thinking to create weight loss and overall health improvement, then the primary audience is health aficionados. But it might also be Catholic women's groups. And perhaps priests. Most books have a clear primary audience, though books that cover a lot of ground (like the latter example) might have more.

Your secondary audiences are the groups of people beyond the obvious primary audience. For that orchid book? Secondary audiences might be gardeners in Florida or the entire Southeast. Landscapers. Organic farmers. Member groups of the American Orchid Society. Botanical garden gift shops. For that memoir? Any Catholic church. Catholic parenting groups. Fitness clubs. Fans of *The Secret* and *The Law of Attraction*. Active forty-somethings and senior citizens. And so on.

Books should always have quite a few reasonable secondary markets. Make sure to mention them, even if they seem fairly small. The primary market should be doing the heavy lifting, yet secondary markets that bring in a couple dozen or a few hundred sales add up quickly.

You will eventually encounter the phrase "niche market" if you Google "book publicity." A niche market is simply a way of describing a small but clearly defined potential book audience, such as openly gay elementary schoolteachers in Texas, ham radio operators in North America, or female Korean War veterans. While these members might not be as numerous as most primary markets, they tend to be active and eager for books seemingly designed for them. Thanks to listservs, blogs, and websites dedicated to specific audiences, these members are often easier to reach than other demographics.

Publishers like niche markets because the rate of response (in this case, sales) is usually much higher than it is for other primary or secondary markets.

Ever hear of "special sales"? That's the term for bulk book sales beyond the online and brick-and-mortar bookstores. Some examples? Getting your history of the greeting card book picked up by Hallmark and sold on a rack by the register in every one of their 2,600 stores. Convincing the president of Carnival Cruise Lines to buy copies of your nautical memoir for all 37,000+ employees as a Christmas gift.

Some publishers and authors dislike special sales because they're often sold at huge discounts—sometimes up to 75 percent off retail. But these folks are shortsighted. Just do the math. If authors end up making fifty cents per sale and Hallmark buys five copies for each store (2,600 stores × 5 copies × 50 cents), that's $6,500. The publisher is, of course, making much, much more. Sell that same book to the Carnival Cruise Lines employees, and now you're talking $18,500! How many book signings and readings would it take to equal the same amount when you're making 10 percent off the retail price of $14.95 for each book sold?

If you see real potential for these special sale outlets, list them. Even if a publisher decides it's not worth the effort, they'll likely be impressed by your lateral thinking and marketing creativity.

BRAINSTORMING YOUR POTENTIAL AUDIENCES

To get clarity on who your potential audiences might be, use the following checklist to generate some ideas on how different pools of readers might connect with your book:

- ethnicity
- gender
- age/generation
- work
- education
- marital status
- geography/setting
- social class
- health
- religion
- organizations/memberships
- hobbies/interests

- pop culture
- theme/lessons
- problem/solution

Don't be afraid to go beyond this list. It's just a way to get you started. And remember that women account for nearly 80 percent of book sales, so any book that targets women is already ahead of the curve.

Need more suggestions for finding ways to build an audience for your book? Here are bonus ideas that will whet your thirst for the concepts chapter six will cover:

- your existing or past customers
- customers of your competitors
- attendees of your seminars, speeches, or workshops
- readers of magazines about your topic
- readers of blogs about your topic
- watchers of TV shows/films about your topic

INSIDER TIP

Some marketing gurus recommend authors create a persona of the ideal target audience for your book. Put simply, describe the person who will be interested in and buy your book. Come up with responses to all of the brainstorm bullet points above for this ideal reader, and you'll start to understand your audience better than ever before. What do they really care about? What motivates them to act? What turns them off? What might they want from your book? What don't they want from it?

Another thing marketing gurus often do is get out in the field and test the market. They scour Craigslist ads for services people routinely want. They use Google Trends, Google Insights, and Facebook ads to gauge potential interest in a subject. They even do focus groups to get the skinny in person on how people react to things.

Use this information to fine-tune the idea you already have, or use it to come up with a fresh idea from scratch. Either way, you'll be that much closer to that book contract by pitching a strong product and having a good sense of its audience interest and potential.

DON'T FORGET LIBRARIES, SCHOOLS, AND THOSE IVORY TOWERS

There are 120,000 libraries in the United States, 98,000 of which are school (K–12) libraries. Are you listing that data in your marketing information? I sure did when I pitched my young adult book, *Unlocked*, about a high school janitor's kid whose new best friend is rumored to have a gun inside his locker. Do you think gun violence—or the potential for it—is part of what kids today want to read about? You'd better believe it! That book went on to win a gold medal in the Florida Book Awards. It also became a book that sold well at independent bookstores where employees often offered book recommendations. Plus I regularly get fan mail from kids who told me a librarian recommended *Unlocked* to them. How cool is that?

If you've written a book about veterans of the Korean War, did you mention the 265 armed forces libraries or the 1,006 government libraries? What about a book that deals with Native American concerns? There are 160 Bureau of Indian Affairs libraries, after all.

Another great thing about libraries is that they want durable copies, so they buy hardcover if that's an option, which is awesome for authors. Ten percent of a $25.95 hardcover is a ton more than ten percent of a $7.95 paperback. So don't forget to mention some library statistics in your marketplace analysis.

Whether you're talking university or community college class adoptions or the 3,700 academic libraries, there's gold in them there hills. While there's not much I can do to generate sales to academic libraries, I can actively pursue class adoptions. Offering free thirty-minute virtual (Skype or otherwise) visits to classes that adopt any of my books has proven a wonderful tactic in generating sales. To that end, I list course titles that seem like a good fit for my book. I never know how many I can land, yet when I do land one, it's twenty-five sales at a time. And I often get invited back again and again because the professors have new kids every semester and it's easy to re-teach the same material rather than creating new lesson plans.

Elementary, middle, and high schools also require a lot of mandated reading. If you can tie into an established curriculum or connect with an educational organization, you're going to hit it big. For instance, Virgil Suárez and Delia Poey's anthology *Iguana Dreams: New Latino Fiction* was picked up by the American Librarian's Association and a few other nationwide education groups. The result was tens of thousands of extra sales.

TWO MARKETPLACE ANALYSIS EXAMPLES

Marketplace Analysis Example 1: Ryan G. Van Cleave's *Memoir Writing for Dummies* (Wiley, 2013)

Commentary: While I'm perfectly aware of the primary and secondary markets for this title, I chose to list this with bullets because it filled the page nicely. I also put these in order of importance starting with the best audience fit first. You don't have to come out and say which is the primary audience and which is the secondary, though you certainly can if you choose to. For this book, I didn't go that route.

The Audience

Because *Memoir Writing for Dummies* is delivered in the clear For Dummies style, the information will be easily utilized by a wide population of readers, including:

- retirees (especially the 76 million baby boomers controlling over 80 percent of the nation's personal financial assets and more than 50 percent of the discretionary spending power)
- the 326,000 writers who subscribe to various trade magazines[1]
- university professors and experts who want to bolster their reputation and credibility
- professional speakers who want to take advantage of their existing platform
- creative writing instructors
- people who've grown frustrated by using the other memoir "how to" books but still haven't been able to write their own memoir
- people who've never written anything but who are interested in writing their own memoir
- the entrants of National Novel Writing Month (2007 alone saw 100,000+ entries)[2]

---

1. Note: I had a separate page with writing magazine subscription breakdowns, which is where this number came from. It's important to include references and sources.

2. This is a bit of a stretch, but it's not completely ridiculous. Plus that's a big number of entrants who aspire to be book-length writers. Surely a few of them might switch to memoir at some point.

- people who've written short creative nonfiction and want to graduate to full-length books
- parents
- grandparents
- co-workers, friends, and family members of writers
- co-workers, friends, and family members of those who haven't written but want/need to write and publish a book

Marketplace Analysis Example 2: Jennifer Armstrong's *Mary and Lou and Rhoda and Ted: And all the Brilliant Minds Who Made* The Mary Tyler Moore Show *a Classic*

Commentary: This section is excerpted from the proposal included in chapter twelve and is styled a little differently from mine above. Write yours to suit your needs.

About the Market

The Mary Tyler Moore Show boasted more than 20 million loyal fans in its heyday—all of whom are now a prime book-buying audience, baby boomers. But more importantly, the show also remains relevant in current pop culture four decades after it began and has gained legions of new, younger fans along the way, in addition to influencing many of the women who dominate pop culture today. Thus pop culture fanatics and empowered women alike—such as the 3.8 million viewers who tune into *Oprah* daily and the 2.7 million subscribers to *O, The Oprah Magazine*—will revel in its behind-the-scenes look at the construction of an enduring feminist TV icon and her impact on our lives.

In just the last few years, *The Mary Tyler Moore Show* stars Cloris Leachman and Betty White have enjoyed a resurgence in popularity among younger audiences. Leachman delighted fans with her antics on *Dancing with the Stars* and now steals scenes weekly on Fox's cult hit comedy *Raising Hope*; White's stardom has reached perhaps its highest levels ever, with her role in the blockbuster *The Proposal*, a successful Facebook campaign for her to host *Saturday Night Live*, and her current role on TVLand's *Hot in Cleveland*. Their continuing popularity, too, will help to increase interest in a book about the show that made them stars.

There are several major outlets for *Becoming Mary Richards*: (**Note to the reader:** This was the original title at the time this proposal was written.)

- **Bookstores:** Women's studies shelves and pop culture shelves
- **Book groups:** Female-focused groups will find plenty of fodder for discussion about feminism, television, sex, and censorship.
- **Online:** Fan sites dedicated to *The Mary Tyler Moore Show* will serve as a key outlet for continuous promotion; the author's employer, EW.com, and her women's site, SexyFeminist.com, can promote the book to their targeted audiences; the author's personal site, JenniferMArmstrong.com, can serve as a hub for book-related news; and there are opportunities on women's, pop culture, and nostalgia sites as well.
- **College bookstores:** Possible partnership with women's studies and media studies classes

FINDING AND USING THE RIGHT SOURCES

Having current and accurate information is one of the best ways to prove your point—that your book idea is valid, commercially speaking. Sure, you can use data mined from authoritative websites, organizations' PR materials, or even useful reference books. But another way to show that potential readers are out there is to list keyword phrases that are commonly searched for online. You can easily do this by making an account with Google AdWords and using their keyword research tools. How convincing would it be for you to suggest there's a strong audience for your book on families dealing with a dog's death with the following information?

- "loss of a pet"   90,750 global monthly searches
- "death of a pet"   74,250 global monthly searches
- "grieving for a pet"   9,900 global monthly searches
- "death of a dog"   165,000 global monthly searches
- "loss of dog"   111,000 global monthly searches
- "dealing with grief"   18,000 global monthly searches

Remember that Google only handles two-thirds of the total Internet searches that occur every day, so whatever information they have, the real number of total Internet searches is roughly one-third higher. (I already did that for the above statistics by multiplying the Google numbers by 1.5.)

Feel free, too, to deliver the statistical information in whatever method makes the most sense. Pie charts, graphs, or bulleted lists might well be the easiest way to visually demonstrate to publishers what you need them to know.

INSIDER TIP

Most people think that editors make the yes or no decisions at a publishing house. That's no longer a certainty. With the massive turnover of editors that's happening today, many are replaced by young people straight out of graduate school or internship programs, and because of this a power shift has occurred. Old editors with a long track record could bank on their reputation to insist on taking a book simply because they believed in it. But a newcomer who has little or no track record and is in fear of losing her job by taking on a book that turns out to be a financial stinker must get everything signed off on by the marketing and sales people. See the material at the start of chapter two on pub boards for more on this.

After all, if the marketing and sales people don't think they can sell a book, what publisher would be crazy enough to take the book and hope it wildly outperforms expectations? To make this point even more clear: The marketing and sales people need to be convinced, or there's no deal, period. Chapters four through seven also concern topics that are in their wheelhouse—there are several—so don't be skimpy with the argument you put together for your book.

Cynical writers might go so far as to suggest that many of the marketing and sales people are also just like those young editors: fresh out of school or an internship and having little to no idea how to do their job well. In short, it's the onus of the writer to show them via the book proposal exactly how to do their job. You might wish it were the editor's job to locate potential readers and the marketing people's job to create all the sales opportunities, but that simply isn't the norm.

SOME FINAL THOUGHTS ON MARKETPLACE ANALYSIS

About assessing a prospective book's marketplace viability, literary agent Peter Rubie says, "Ask yourself this: 'Do I honestly believe that ten thousand people will buy a trade paperback version of my book?' If the answer is no, then this is either a small press book or a magazine article." The other thing I'd add is that a book with that small of potential readership could also be a good book to self-publish. Since it's now so amazingly cheap and easy to self-publish, it's financially sound to self-publish a book that realistically might only sell two hundred copies. A traditional publisher would lose thousands of dollars on a project like that.

Am I crazy for suggesting self-publishing to readers of a book on writing book proposals to get you book contracts from traditional publishers? Maybe. But to be honest, some books are better suited for the small stage of self-publishing. If that's the realistic fit for your book, no worries—just keep thinking of new ideas until you have one that should get you the sales needed to land a big fish like Random House, Viking, or Norton.

Once you're ready to write up your marketplace analysis for your big-fish publishers, be sure to be thorough and to use hard data to support what you claim. You're making an argument here. Make sure your argument is well supported, thorough, and clear.

TOP TIPS TO REMEMBER

- Clearly define your primary market and at least six viable secondary markets. Be realistic about the size of each market. Don't just say the half-million readers of *The Boston Globe Magazine* will read your dating advice book. You have to say that their section "Connections" (prior to May 2012, this was called "Coupling") is all about romance and dating.

- Consider creating a persona for your ideal audience. Read Amazon reviews of competitors' books to learn their needs.

- Use hard facts and data to make your case.

- Remember that women typically account for 80 percent of book sales.

FOR MORE INFORMATION

Howard-Johnson, Carolyn. *The Frugal Book Promoter: How to Do What Your Publisher Won't.* Loretto, PA: Star Publish (2004).

Levinson, Jay Conrad, Rick Frishman, Michael Larsen, David L Hancock. *Guerilla Marketing for Writers: 100 Weapons for Selling Your Work.* Cincinnati, OH: Writer's Digest Books (2001).

See Appendix A for other helpful titles.

Chapter Five

TAKING ON THE COMPETITION:
WHAT MAKES *THIS* BOOK SPECIAL?

In chapter four, we talked about making sure you had a clear, sizable target audience for your prospective book. Okay, done. Check. Knocked that baby out of the park. You've got readers lined up from here to Pluto. But now you need to *prove* that your book will motivate those potential readers to buy your book versus a competitor's book that's a little (or a lot!) like yours.

For instance, when I decided to buy my first house, I went to Barnes & Noble and picked up one—one only!—book on the subject. I can't recall how many others were on the shelf next to the one I picked up (probably a dozen or more), but I'm 100 percent sure of this: I didn't buy any of those. I think I chose the one I did because the author seemed well-credentialed, the cover and title were appealing, and the back-cover copy promised clear answers to the challenges of buying a home. Sounded like a perfect fit with my needs, so why would I need more books on that topic, right?

See the problem? The more specific the niche your book fills, the less likely a reader will buy more than one book on that topic. If for some reason I became obsessed with coin collecting, I might buy a couple of books on the subject to learn all the foundational stuff a numismatic (yep, the fancy word for it) needs to know. *Coin Collecting for Dummies, The Coin Collector's Survival Manual,* and *The World Encyclopedia of Coins & Coin Collecting,* maybe. But if I wanted a book on how to sell coins online in my spare time? That's a subcategory of a niche market (coin collecting in general), so I probably don't need more than one book on that. The further you specialize, the better your book needs to be so it's the one readers choose over any others.

So how are you going to convince a publisher that your book is special? Different? Noteworthy? Reader-friendly?

It comes down to being clear about your book's features and benefits. But the way to do that is in the context of seeing what's already available in print—your competitors.

WHAT EXISTING TITLES COMPETE WITH YOURS?

It's best to start by gathering the information already out there, so early on in your proposal, include a list of the top four to six books that in some way compete with yours. Don't be scared to admit that similar books already exist. Editors expect that. In fact, if you can't find any books that are similar to yours, editors will be leery of taking your book on. The assumption is, if it's a viable market, someone would've already tapped into it. So name your main competitors.

What information for each competing book should you include in that list?

- bibliographic information
- brief description of the book
- the book's selling points
- the book's weaknesses
- your overall conclusion

While you absolutely have to find flaws or missed opportunities of some type in those books to justify writing your own better book, you still should be respectful and honest in your appraisal. It's probable that your target publisher published one or more of the competing books. That happened to me with this title. Writer's Digest already had a book on writing book proposals—*How to Write a Book Proposal* by literary agent Michael Larsen. Worse (for me, not the publisher!), the book has sold over 100,000 copies and multiple editions have been published. But I thought I could distinguish mine from his by emphasizing a few distinctive features. Later in this chapter, I'll share how I did that.

Even if the publisher you're pitching isn't responsible for one of the competing books, you still need to watch it. Editors move from job to job. A lot. It wouldn't be all that surprising for the editor you're pitching to have been involved with a competing book at a different publishing house in his previous job.

This happened to a writer friend of mine who was hawking a CEO leadership book to a major New York publisher. My pal got a bit overzealous in his section on competing titles—one might say he did a hatchet job to the competition. His comments were accurate but harsh. You know the rest of this story. The editor at the perfect publishing house for his book—a place that needed a book just like his—was the same acquiring editor for that other title in her previous job. That book was one of her crown jewels in her mind, and she had become friends with its author over the years. My friend couldn't have known all of this when he trashed that book for missing key points, being poorly structured, and using lousy examples throughout. Needless to say, that editor passed on his project. It was only by pure luck years later that he found all of this out from an editorial assistant at a book release party. Talk about bad luck!

But the main point is clear—be kind in your criticism of the competition. The writing world is a small, small place. Don't badmouth other writers, agents, publishers, or books. That's not to say you have to lie about loving them! Just don't go out of your way to be the hatchet person chopping up the publishing world. Leave that to the jerks. Despite being one of the greatest American writers ever, Edgar Allan Poe had a lot (and wow, I mean a *lot*) of haters because he regularly trashed writers in his print reviews. Thanks to the increasingly public world we live in because of Twitter, Facebook, and the Internet in general, you need to be diplomatic at all times because your harshest comments will be passed around and spread like avian flu.

BUT THERE REALLY *IS* NO COMPETITION

Sometimes in the process of researching competing books, though, you find that there simply aren't any other books that do exactly what you're proposing. What then? I mentioned earlier that this could be a bad thing. But what if it's actually good news? What if it means that you're simply the first to the dance floor? That's an enviable position to be in. It does mean that you want to move very fast, however, because others might come up with a similar idea, and being first is a great handle for your media releases and PR campaign. It's the difference between "This is the first book on using Facebook to get out of bankruptcy!" and "This is the eleventh book on how to make money selling on eBay!"

To offer one example of this, consider California midwife Peggy Vincent, who wrote a book proposal for *Baby Catcher*. There had recently been a best-selling novel on the same subject titled *Midwives*, but no recent nonfiction books on midwifery were available. The success of that novel, though, helped Vincent convince Scribner there was enough interest in the subject to offer her a six-figure advance. She was the first to the dance floor, sort of. (The novelist beat her there.)

The lesson? You are always competing with other books. Always.

ARGH! MY BOOK'S ALREADY BEEN DONE!

Be open to the possibility of re-slanting your book's topic in order to better fill the niche you've come up with by scrutinizing the direct competition. Let me put this more clearly: If someone else has already published your exact idea, don't try to pretend yours is different. Make tangible changes to your book's angle in order to make it different. Don't fall hopelessly in love with what you first envisioned. The goal is to create a book proposal for a salable book that agents, editors, and readers will love. Be open to adjusting your vision to better achieve that goal.

This isn't selling out or surrendering, but rather overcoming a challenge presented by the existing marketplace. Experiment with the various marketplace lenses through which you might view your topic to achieve a fresh look at things.

HIT THE GAS

When it comes to talking about competing books, let others do the work for you. How? In your description of those books, quote directly from the dust jacket or back cover. Quote from print or online reviews to show strengths and weaknesses. If you find enough authoritative sources, you might not have to actually read the competing books (though you'll want to do so carefully once you have that book contract).

This might sound wacky, but don't make your book *too* different than the others. Jodi Lipper, author of the Hot Chick Book Series (*How to Eat Like a Hot Chick*, *How to Love Like a Hot Chick*, and *Live Like a Hot Chick*) and experienced ghostwriter and book doctor, explains this phenomenon. "Editors are often focused on fitting each book into a specific niche. This is a moment when being unique and different is not a good thing. Editors will often reject a book by saying, 'I don't know what it is,' which means it doesn't fit into a box with other similar books. If it doesn't fit clearly into an established genre, it doesn't have a chance. But at the same time, the book proposal can't feel obviously redundant, like it's treading over the same old material in the same way. Writing a proposal that fits neatly into a genre while standing out is a huge challenge that often spells the difference between success and failure."

COMPETING TITLES SAMPLES

Competing Titles Sample #1: Carol Ross Joynt's *Innocent Spouse: A Memoir*

Commentary: It's interesting that she starts by comparing her memoir to movies, but if Vincent could compare her nonfiction book about midwives to a novel, why not compare a memoir to a movie? Plus these are well-known movies, so if that's the best way to frame your story, do it. Note, too, how at the end of each of the book comparisons Joynt deftly switches from talking about the competition and instead talks about her own book's strengths. She also writes in the third person to give a professional distance to her assessments.

> *Innocent Spouse* is, of course, a story that's unique because it's my memoir. However, stories about love, self-sufficiency, grief, marital secrets, and starting over are universal. In fact, there have been many successful movies that revolve around these very themes. They include: *Bounce*, starring Gwyneth Paltrow and Ben Affleck; *Men Don't Leave*, with Jessica Lange; and *Alice Doesn't Live Here Anymore*, in which Ellen Burstyn gave an unforgettable performance as a widow and single mom to her young son. The same issues that made these films so emotionally gripping translate well to the page. Compelling books that explore similar themes include:
>
> 1. *The Year of Magical Thinking* by Joan Didion (Alfred A. Knopf)
>
> *Innocent Spouse* is *The Year of Magical Thinking*, absent the opportunity for magic. Both memoirs are stories about the grief a wife experiences after the sudden death of her husband. Both are stories where the widow is plunged into chaos. But *Innocent Spouse* is a story of blunt reality—a decade's worth—for a widow with no time to ponder the deeper meaning of her husband's death because she must battle for her survival, and that of her young son's, in the wake of all her dead husband left behind—beginning with a bankrupt bar and a multimillion-dollar criminal tax fraud case. Still, like

Didion's memoir, *Innocent Spouse* is a story that resonates with self-discovery (and some humor) as a woman tries to make her way in the world without her much-loved spouse, who was also her best friend.

2. *Personal History* by Katharine Graham (Alfred A. Knopf)

The first time they met, Katharine Graham told Carol Joynt "we have a lot in common." Carol was flattered but drew an important distinction. "Your husband died and you inherited a newspaper empire. I inherited a bar." Mrs. Graham said, "It's not as different as you think." She was right. In both cases, the widows had to walk into the boy's club environment of their late husbands' businesses and make them their own. In *Personal History*, Katharine Graham made *Innocent Spouse* into something bigger and better than it ever was. In *Innocent Spouse*, Carol Joynt struggles to keep her husband's bar alive while also coping with a criminal tax fraud case, and a decade of other challenges. Both women also raised children as single parents.

3. *Postcards from the Edge* by Carrie Fisher (Simon & Schuster)

When life gives you lemons, don't make lemonade—write about it. That's what Carrie Fisher did in the semi-autobiographical *Postcards from the Edge*, a story, like *Innocent Spouse*, about a woman who must put her life back together after being knocked down.

(Note to the Reader: She included other titles in her proposal, but you get the point.)

Competing Titles Sample #2: Ryan G. Van Cleave's *Memoir Writing for Dummies*

Commentary: I limited my list to four, and I ranked them according to recent sales figures. Instead of writing full sentences and paragraphs about the other books like Joynt did for *Innocent Spouse*, I used a much simpler method.

The following four titles (ranked by current Amazon.com sales figures) come closest to providing competition: (1) *Old Friend from Far Away: The Practice of Writing Memoir*; (2) *Writing Life Stories: How to Make Memories into Memoirs, Ideas into Essays, and Life into Literature*; (3) *Writing the Memoir: From Truth to Art, Second Edition*, and (4) *Writing & Selling Your Memoir: How to Craft Your Life Story So That Somebody Else Will Want to Read It.*

1. *Old Friend from Far Away: The Practice of Writing Memoir* (Natalie Goldberg, Free Press, 2009, 336 pages, $15)

DESCRIPTION: "An innovative course full of practical teachings, and a deeply affecting meditation on consciousness, love, life, and death, *Old Friend* welcomes aspiring writers."
STRENGTHS: Many good endorsements. Friendly tone. Many exercises and writing prompts. Author has written a memoir.
WEAKNESSES: Long on writing prompts, short on follow-through of turning that material into memoir. Repeats many ideas from her other books (monkey mind, fast-writing, etc.). From a reader: "Maybe I just feel frustrated because I know a few people who ought to be writing their memoirs. This book won't help them."
CURRENT AMAZON SALES RANKING: 22,000

2. *Writing Life Stories: How to Make Memories into Memoirs, Ideas into Essays, and Life into Literature* (Bill Roorbach with Kristen Keckler, Story Press, 2008, 304 pages, $16.99)
DESCRIPTION: "This book is full of innovative techniques that prove real stories are often the best ones."
STRENGTHS: Well organized. Many good endorsements. Friendly tone. Author has written a memoir.
WEAKNESSES: More of a discussion of his own creative writing classes. Exercises are "too silly" at times.
CURRENT AMAZON SALES RANKING: 44,000

3. *Writing the Memoir: From Truth to Art, Second Edition* (Judith Barrington, The Eighth Mountain Press, 2002, 224 pages, $14.95)

DESCRIPTION: "Her common-sense approach strives to temper the emotional honesty of the genre with the integrity of artistic skill." STRENGTHS: Ambitious. Includes good samples from Alice Walker, Annie Dillard, and Virginia Woolf. Author has written a memoir.

WEAKNESSES: Too prescriptive. Some readers find the tone discouraging versus affirmative. Spends too much time on basic writing mechanics.

CURRENT AMAZON SALES RANKING: 55,000

4. *Writing & Selling Your Memoir: How to Craft Your Life Story So That Someone Else Will Want to Read It* (Paula Balzer, Writer's Digest Books, 2011, 240 pages, $17.99)

DESCRIPTION: "There's more to writing a memoir than just writing your life story. A memoir isn't one long diary entry." STRENGTHS: Well organized. Plenty of good endorsements. Conversation writing style throughout.

WEAKNESSES: Written by a literary agent versus someone who has actually written a memoir.

CURRENT AMAZON SALES RANKING: 123,000

MY BOOK VERSUS LARSEN'S

Another example I can offer you is how this very book you are holding is different than Michael Larsen's *How to Write a Book Proposal*, which was also published by Writer's Digest Books. Here's what I said about his title in the Competing Titles section for *The Weekend Book Proposal.*

1. *How to Write a Book Proposal* (Michael Larsen, Writer's Digest Books, 2011, 280 pp. $15.99)

CURRENT AMAZON.COM RANKING: 21,000

DESCRIPTION: Updated edition full of advice, ideas, and suggestions on how to write a successful book proposal.

STRENGTHS: Authoritative voice—Larsen is a noted agent and author. Also includes self-promotion ideas. Explains promotions, partners, and plans more clearly than competing books.

WEAKNESSES: Ideas overlap often and sometimes work against the organization of the book. Some suspect advice (such as to include your own cover art, illustrations, and marketing plan for paperback editions). Too few sample proposals, as noted by an Amazon reviewer: "Larsen was great on explanation and details describing what each section required and why, but was light on examples."

Here are the main ways in which my book truly differs from Larsen's. My book offers many ideas ("Hit the Gas" sections) on how to write a book proposal fast, and my book also addresses a far wider range of book types (anthologies, textbooks, novels, memoir, etc.) than does Larsen's or any other book proposal writing how-to title. Of course, there are other less prominent things that I think make my book stronger, such as the inclusion of agent/editor interviews and the bulleted "Top Tips to Remember" list at the end of each chapter.

Clearly Writer's Digest Books agrees that our books are similar but distinct. A screenwriter friend of mine says this is how films are made, too. "They want the same, only different. They want *Die Hard*, but not exactly another *Die Hard*."

That's a good description of the relationship between my book and Larsen's then. Same but different.

YOUR BOOK

Okay, we've dealt with the books other people wrote. Now let's deal with *your* proposed book. The way to talk about it, as I mentioned before, is in terms of its features and its benefits. By that I mean the good things it delivers to a reader and the method in which those good things are delivered.

YOUR BOOK'S FEATURES AND BENEFITS

To talk about your book's features is to talk about the actual stuff on the page. The chapters. The appendices. The end-of-chapter questionnaires. The pie charts. The illustrations. It's the *what* of what will make up your book.

To talk about your book's benefits is to talk about the takeaways a reader gets thanks to the features that deliver them. Increased knowledge. A specific skill. Self-confidence. Understanding. It's the *why* of your book.

Let me offer an example using this book. The main benefit of my book is (and this is right from my elevator pitch): "Whatever your book-writing goal, *The Weekend Book Proposal*'s mentor-in-a-box, easy-to-follow approach will help you write a winning proposal in as little as forty-eight hours!" The benefit is your new ability to knock out a quality proposal faster than you ever could before. Simple as that. There are some other benefits that you might receive, too, such as: a better understanding of the publishing world, learning how to correctly spell *foreword*, and discovering how to create your author platform.

The features of my book that deliver the above? The "Hit the Gas" tips. The "Insider Tips." My modular chapter approach. The wide variety of proposals included.

Make sense?

Readers might not understand the importance of a book's features until the end benefits—the takeaways—are revealed. It's important to reveal those benefits as clearly as possible in your proposal. People don't buy a book—they buy what the book can do for/to them.

HIT THE GAS

Want to find the most important benefits of your book fast? Pretend to have a potential reader standing right in front of you who keeps asking the question, "So what?" Respond to those "So whats?" until you find a benefit from your book that makes her say, "Okay. I get it."

This book will teach you to write fast. *So what?*

Writing fast allows you to write more proposals per year. *So what?*

Writing more proposals translates into having more opportunities to land a book contract, which is a primary goal for a would-be writer. *Okay. I get it.*

WHAT FEATURES OR BENEFITS MAKE YOUR BOOK SPECIAL?

Here's the tricky part. Now it's on you to think through what features or benefits your book has that the competing books don't (or at least the ones they haven't done as effectively as you will). Here are a few possible ideas:

- **Thoroughness:** If your book is the most comprehensive, authoritative book on a certain topic, you're in great shape.

- **Timeliness:** Think about all the Y2K books or 2012 Mayan prophecy books that flooded the shelves before a specific calendar date. Dealing with the context of your book—the place and time—can help persuade your audience.

- **Access:** If your book provides special access to something or someone people want to know more about, that's a real value.

- **Skills:** Are you teaching something useful, like how to safely shed two pounds a week by doing yoga in your office chair at work? I wouldn't know how to do that without reading your book (and perhaps getting more flexible—ouch!).

- **Knowledge:** Are you making readers more knowledgeable? Are you promising to raise their IQ? Despite having no evidence to support the idea that they raised the intelligence level of children, the Baby Einstein DVDs sold like crazy when they came out. Why? Every parent wanted their kids to be as smart as Albert Einstein. (There's a lesson on good titles, too.)

- **Entertainment:** Pleasure is a popular benefit. If you're proposing a novel, this might be your main benefit.

INSIDER TIP

Pros know that one of the best ways to find out how to make your book stronger than the competition and ensure that you include useful features and desirable benefits is to use Amazon's reviews. The following Amazon reviews about my competition were extremely valuable as I prepared my proposal for this book.

re: *Write the Perfect Book Proposal: 10 That Sold and Why, 2nd Edition* "was extremely thin on guiding you through the process of creating your own proposal. Each chapter—corresponding to each section of your proposal—runs a mere one to three pages."

re: *Thinking Like Your Editor: How to Write Great Serious Nonfiction and Get It Published*: "Rabiner wrote this book primarily for academics trying to break out of ivy-covered walls and the university press. It's not for those of us writing what Rabiner calls 'narrative nonfiction.'"

re: *The Fast Track Course on How to Write a Nonfiction Book Proposal*: "It could use an update to address the digital age."

DISTINCTIVE FEATURES SAMPLE

Ryan G. Van Cleave's *Memoir Writing for Dummies*

Commentary: There are really three things here. One is the numbered list I used to articulate the features *Memoir Writing for Dummies* had to distinguish itself from the competition. The second is the conclusion. The third is a kind of back-cover copy marketing tool. Taken together, you can see what I'm planning to do with this book and how I'm going to do it.

DISTINCTIVE FEATURES

1. Foreword by an industry insider such as Koren Zailckas, author of *Smashed*, or Steve Almond, author of *Candyfreak*.[1]

2. Written by a best-selling memoirist and award-winning author of seventeen other books who has taught creative writing at seven different colleges and universities, as well as in prisons, community centers, and at-risk youth programs.

3. Author has relationships with numerous top memoir writers and will incorporate original craft-oriented quotes to help readers trim the writing curve.

4. Content delivery is predicated on clear information and step-by-step modular guidance that's delivered in the highly readable For Dummies style.

5. Trademark For Dummies value add-ons:
   - cheat sheet
   - navigational icons
   - top ten lists
   - cartoons
   - sidebars

6. Regular updates to the book as needed, using new information from the author's own workshops and writing, as well as more current examples, new references, and updated technologies.

7. THE VAN CLEAVE MARKETING CAMPAIGN,[2] which made *Unplugged* a June 2010 Amazon.com best-seller in three different categories (selling four thousand copies in less than thirty days).

---

1. We ended up not going with the foreword since that's not the norm for this series.

2. Some PR folks think that to make your publicity campaign distinctive, you should give it a name. That's what I did here.

CONCLUSION: THERE IS NO SIGNIFICANT COMPETITION

At a cursory glance, the market for books on writing one's life story may appear to be covered—but the majority of books available are seriously **lacking in two major ways:**

1. Most assume that writers and memoirists aspire to create *Literature*. (Wow, that lofty of a goal can be intimidating!)

2. Most overcomplicate the process and burden readers with too many rules, tips, and assignments.

In short, *Memoir Writing for Dummies* differs from the competition in three clear ways:

1. **Focus:** This book will clearly address the most-asked questions would-be memoir writers have *right now*.

2. **Authority:** This book is written by a best-selling memoirist who has taught successful memoir-writing classes at multiple colleges and universities. Plus, the For Dummies series lends its own unique brand of credibility.

3. **Style:** The author uses easy-to-understand language; key concepts are illustrated with vivid text and clear definitions.

FINAL THOUGHTS ON TAKING ON THE COMPETITION

Don't think that you can skimp on the competition and special features sections. You may be able to influence an editor with information about all of the competing books you're mentioning (or purposefully not mentioning). But if things advance to where a book contract is a real possibility, they'll do their own research and begin to see for themselves whether or not your book holds true value over the others. If you manipulated the facts or ignored other books to make your book seem stronger, they will find out. In many cases, editors are specialists in certain areas, meaning they might already be familiar with all the competing books. You'll have to be extremely thorough in explaining how the features and benefits of your book should earn you some shelf space alongside those competitors.

TOP TIPS TO REMEMBER

- Do your research on competing titles. Keep researching until you have at least ten books that might be competitors. Take three and outline their main features and the benefits they provide. Use this process to help you create your own Competing Books section.
- Be accurate yet respectful in revealing their shortcomings.
- Showcase your book's distinctive features and benefits. Identify the "why now" for your book, and reveal how your book is the same, but different.
- Three main motivators for purchasing a book are rational, emotional, and social. Tap into at least one of these.

FOR MORE INFORMATION

Morgan, John. *Brand Against the Machine: How to Build Your Brand, Cut Through the Marketing Noise, and Stand Out from the Competition.* Wiley (2011).

See Appendix A for other helpful titles.

Chapter Six

PUBLICITY CAMPAIGNS:
WHAT CAN I DO TO HELP SELL COPIES?

F. Scott Fitzgerald didn't have to explain to his editor, Maxwell Perkins, how he planned to move copies of *The Great Gatsby*. You and I? We sure do. It's called our author platform. Taken together, all the things you do to generate publicity equal the size of your platform. (Hint: Shoot for a big one!)

If we can't convince the team of decision makers at the publishing house that enough copies will sell to offset their costs (which can often reach $50,000 even for a modest book), it all ends. Worse, we're not talking about lifetime sales of the book—they want sales NOW NOW NOW. Let's put this another way: If you can't create a sales spike in the thousands within the initial months of your book's release, most New York publishers will label your book—and you—a disappointment. Should two or three different books of yours become disappointments, you might be permanently labeled a bad bet by *all* of the big houses. I've seen it happen with very good writers who wrote very good books that no one worked that hard to sell.

On the plus side, university and indie presses are often ecstatic with 1,000 sales in the first few months—their costs are less since they rarely offer advances, do much PR, or get your books into tons of stores. Since they don't put anywhere near as much money into each book up front, they're making money with those 1,000 sales.

So let's talk about how you can be your own best sales and marketing team and how you can plan that out in your proposal's Publicity Strategy section.

BUT WHAT WILL PUBLISHERS DO? I DON'T WANT TO DUPLICATE THEIR EFFORTS!

Not wanting to duplicate what a publisher is planning to do makes perfect sense. But you need to know what a publisher will do, and what they do differs from publisher to publisher. (P.S.—You should always have their publicity commitments in writing as part of the contract, or they won't feel compelled to follow through.) Here is a list of what most publishers will do for your book in terms of publicity.

- send out ARCs (advance reading copies) to magazine, news-paper, and select online reviewers

- send out promotional copies to contributors and, possibly, a select list of influencers that you provide for them
- give authors a small supply of promotional copies to use strategically
- send out a media release to relevant media
- post information on your book on the company website
- include your book in their seasonal catalog
- send out purchasing information to libraries
- enter your book in a regional/small contest or two

If you're really lucky, or if you receive a big advance, they might do the following for you:

- pay for print, radio, TV, or Internet advertisements for your book
- set you up with a multicity author tour for readings, book signings, and media interviews
- work to get you major media attention, such as an appearance on *The Today Show* or an article in *USA Today*
- offer media coaching so your interviews and appearances go smoothly and make you sound smarter than you probably are
- work with a professional photographer to create a set of publicity photos in various formats
- help create a reader's guide for your book
- help get your book adopted in classrooms
- enter your book in major contests

For most writers, much of the PR burden will eventually fall onto the author's shoulders. But because you don't have to do most of these PR things now, it's easy to think big as you plan and write your proposal. So do so! One of those big ideas might be enough to push your proposal into the "Yes!" category. Be creative, bold, and unique with your PR suggestions.

A word of warning: Don't promise more than you can deliver. Don't say you're going to hire a freelance book publicist and take yourself on a ten-city book-signing tour through the Midwest if there's a chance you might not actually do those things. Work up your best guess for a budget, and see how many things you can do for what you're prepared to spend in both time and money. Adjust accordingly.

You will need a media kit at some point in your future. While you don't have to use your media kit right away (you're certainly not going to include one with your proposal), go ahead and start putting it together. Many of the parts of a media kit can be used in your proposal, your website, and your query letter, so making a media kit is doing double duty.

What goes in an author's professional media kit?

- **Professional photo:** A head shot is the way to go. Color or black and white? Your call, as long as it's clear and professional looking.

- **Two- to three- paragraph bio:** Write this in the third person. Be sure to include information such as:

  - Where were you born?
  - What inspired you to start writing?
  - What educational experiences have you had?
  - What other books or professional writing have you done?
  - What relevant hobbies or interests do you have?

- **Details on your most recent published book (also called a "sell sheet"):** Include the following:

  - full title
  - publisher
  - release date
  - distributor information
  - PR contact at your press
  - high-resolution scan of your cover
  - full synopsis of your book
  - one-sentence description of your book

- **Short sample directly from the book:** A teaser page or two is plenty.

- **Endorsements/testimonials:** Don't go crazy with these. A single page is enough.

- **Reviews:** Excerpts of glowing reviews of your book are always welcome. Don't hold back. Include them all.

- **Awards:** If your book has won something, note that prominently.

- **List of previous media appearances:** Even if it's a local access cable interview or a ninety-second gab session on local NPR, include it.

- **Media pitch/topics:** What subjects can you fluently discuss that are relevant to your book? What's your book's angle/promise?

- **FAQ or short Q&A:** Ask and answer these questions yourself in the first person or third person, whichever feels more natural. (Reporters love having good questions that they can ask you. Not all of them have time or the inclination to read your book in advance of an interview).

- **Media release:** Include the latest media release about your book. I don't go into media releases here since most publishers like to write these themselves. If you want information on them for your own benefit, read Zach Cutler's article, "8 Tips for Writing a Great Press Release" (Huffington Post, 11/13/2012) or Google "sample media release" to find dozens of real-world examples that you can use as models.

- **Your contact info:** Include this prominently within the document, and include some kind of contact info on every page as a header or footer. Your book's website URL is a fine option.

- **Social media/Internet links:** Provide a list of any relevant links that showcase you as a great interview subject and someone worth speaking with. (If you don't have a good video showing your interview skills, get a good high-resolution digital camera and have a friend interview you on tape. Edit it, add intro and closing credits, and then post it on YouTube as your interview sample.)

Make sure you have this available in both print form and as a PDF (not a DOC file) that has all images at 300 dpi or better. For your print version, use a clean two-pocket folder, preferably with cutouts where you can insert a business card. You should also print a very nice label with your name and your book's name to use on the front.

Always keep your media kit updated. Always keep a digital copy prominently available on your website. Always use the media kit when trying to generate some publicity for yourself and your book. Always have a few hard copies of your media kit handy; you never know when you might need to hand someone a copy.

For examples of media kits that sometimes break the rules but are still quite effective, please visit:

- www.michaelhyatt.com/platform/media
- www.worrysolution.com/press-kit/
- www.carlyphillips.com/media-kit/
- www.fourhourworkweek.com/blog/media/
- blairpub.com/mediakits/judy_goldman.php

INSIDER TIP

Plenty of people are still talking about an "author press kit" or a "press release." Don't. The word *press* brings up images of old grainy black-and-white movies where reporters run around in funny hats with a little slip of paper sticking out that reads: *press*. It's a term from the old print age. Be part of the digital age. Use the phrase "author media kit" and "media release."

Since it's easy to embed video and sound into a digital media kit, the word *media* is even more appropriate, no? (And there's another idea for you, albeit one that doesn't reproduce in print form.)

SOCIAL MEDIA

If you don't have a Twitter, Facebook, Pinterest, and LinkedIn account already, get them (as well as any new high-traffic social media sites that seem like a ripe opportunity to connect with potential readers). To be a successful author in the twenty-first century means that you're actively engaged with social media to engage with your fans (present and future).

If you're overwhelmed by so many social media opportunities, set up your accounts, but regularly use only one or two of them. Update the others every three to four weeks. Some, such as Twitter and Facebook, or a blog and an Amazon Author page, can be linked so an update on one appears on another, making managing your various online tools a little more time efficient.

Here are some useful ideas experts offer on social media.

"Social media isn't the end all be all, but it offers marketers unparalleled opportunity to participate in relevant ways. It also provides a launch pad for other marketing tactics. Social media is not an island. It's a high-power engine on the larger marketing ship." — Matt Dickman, technomarketer. typepad.com

"Activate your fans, don't just collect them like baseball cards." — Jay Baer, Convince & Convert

"To utilize social media tools effectively and properly, you must absolutely generate spontaneous communications in direct response to what others are saying or to what is happening in that moment. Be yourself. Be conversational. Be engaged." — Aliza Sherman, co-founder of Conversify, alizasherman.wordpress.com

"Social media can be a bit like a bunch of people with megaphones blurting out their messages one-way. People will cover their ears (unsubscribe) and tune that out. Use social media to 'listen' to and learn more about your audience." — Brian J. Carroll, CEO of InTouch, startwithalead.com

WEBSITES

If you haven't bought the name of your book as a URL, do it immediately. Invest the $10. If the publisher later asks you to change the title, fine, do it. At that point, you've either got the book contract or are about to, so the $10 is a fair loss. But the last thing you want is for your book to have to go with a URL that's lengthy, uses hyphens, or is in other ways too confusing to be remembered easily because the obvious domain name choice is taken.

Do I even need to say that you *must* have the .com for your URL? The .net, .org, and .info version of the same thing just isn't going to be taken as seriously, much less remembered. People will by default always go to the .com option first.

Once you have the book contract in hand, you should have two websites that are promoting your book. The first is your own professional/home website. Your forthcoming book will be prominently displayed there along with a "Buy it now!" link to Amazon, BN.com, and Powell's (plus any other indie bookstore you choose to support). Truly savvy authors will have those links connected to affiliate accounts so you get a referral for each book sold via that link.

The other website you absolutely need is your book's dedicated website which has your entire media kit along with other information about and from the book. Both websites should have a clear contact page where people can either e-mail you, call you, or snail mail you.

If you can think of any unique content you might include on your book's website, mention that in your publicity section. Having a book website is the bare minimum. Using it effectively is a pro move. Show that you have firm ideas about how to drive traffic and convert visits to sales.

RADIO AND TV

It's not enough to say that you're happy to do radio and TV interviews. Of course you are. Do you have a specific contact with a producer that might earn you a spot on a large radio station or TV show? Do you have a specific way of pitching your material that might hook their interest? Is there a specific show that's a perfect fit?

These interview spots are often shorter than you'd like—two to three minutes. It's hard to get everything in, so practice, practice, practice. Memorize the three main points you want to convey, and smoothly get those out.

Also, don't try to sell your own book during interviews. The host will push it for you. You'll look like a pushy jerk if you yell, "Buy my book!" in the background as you go to commercial. Don't withhold and say, "Well, that's in my book." Share some of what's in the book and then say, "I offer a good deal more on that in my book."

MAGAZINES AND NEWSPAPERS

Again, if you have contacts or any type of in with print media, mention it. If not, offer to make a comprehensive contact list of appropriate journalists at the most relevant periodicals for your book. Some Google sleuthing, poking around on Twitter, Facebook, or LinkedIn, or visiting the magazine section of a book store will help you flesh out this list.

Unlike TV and radio, where the lead time might be hours, magazines work months in advance. Newspapers? Maybe a week. This means you need to plan or you'll miss your window of opportunity.

SNAIL MAIL

Do you have a huge Christmas card list? Is your old-school Rolodex near the bursting point? If so, consider promising a postcard campaign to promote your book. Every recipient on your list knows you, so the conversion rate will be much higher than it would be for cold calls to strangers. I recommend using postcards versus full-size paper mailings simply because it's more economical postage wise, and because postcards are inexpensive to create. Use a service such as www.zazzle.com, www.vistaprint.com, www.uprinting. com, or www.1800postcards.com to buy bulk custom postcards cheaply. Put your entire book cover on the front of the postcard, and on the reverse side include a very short endorsement or two as well as ordering information. That's all you need. Handwrite a personal note if you want to go the extra mile. Address it, slap a stamp on it, and throw it in the mailbox.

Give the publisher an estimate of how many people your snail-mail campaign can reach. If you can come up with more than one thousand, that's pretty darn substantial.

NEWSLETTERS

One of the differences between published writers who constantly whine about lack of sales and published writers who don't is that the latter typically use an active newsletter to communicate with their fans. A newsletter is a way to create relationships and inform potential buyers of new products. It's a way to announce special deals (like signed copies), giveaways, or upcoming events.

How do you get people onto your list? Offer a freebie on your website (a sample chapter from your book, a Top 10 list, or even a print or podcast interview). To get that freebie, people have to input their name and e-mail address. You could have an autoresponder send them the freebie if you don't want to use fancier software. If you want to invest a bit in software that's designed to handle newsletters as well as e-mail/social campaigns, try www. constantcontact.com, www.verticalresponse.com, or www.mailchimp.com. I've used all three, and each has its strong features.

READINGS, SIGNINGS, PRESENTATIONS, AND WORKSHOPS

This is one of the main ways for an author to get the word out about a new or forthcoming book. Give free talks at indie bookstores. Speak on your topic at schools and community centers. Offer workshops to help give people hands-on experiences. Do a freebie reading at a children's hospital. In short, find ways to present, present, present.

Your promotional plan needs to include the different cities in which you intend to offer these types of events during the first year after publication. This is where you can include any firm commitments, such as conference talks, classroom visits, or other confirmed reservations. I urge you to give a firm number and to include the location of those events, too.

If you've never participated in any of the above mentioned events, start now. Contact the rotary clubs, the church groups, the book clubs, and the community centers. Offer to give a very short talk for free. Work your way up to hour-long or ninety-minute programs. The more time you spend in front of people speaking and reading excerpts, the more comfortable you'll become doing these things.

Offer a giveaway drawing after your event (such as a signed copy of your book, or someone else's, or another type of small prize like a $10 Starbuck's gift card) to anyone who signs up for your newsletter. Have a form that they can fill out at the event, and you'll keep building your newsletter list, too.

BOOK TRAILERS

Having a video advertisement for your book is becoming the norm since people want information conveyed succinctly and interestingly. That's what the book trailer does! Unless you have crazy-good digital skills, enlist some help to make sure the production value of your book trailer is first-rate. Having cheesy music, still frames, ordinary fonts, and cheapo graphics—as many book trailers do—signals amateur hour. That's not the right type of message to communicate about your book. If the production is done properly, you never notice it—you simply see/hear the message clearly.

For some solid examples of book trailers, visit:

- www.booktrailersforreaders.com
- ilovebooktrailers.wordpress.com/book-trailers
- or Google "Tim Ferris: How to Create a Viral Book Trailer"

Or visit YouTube and search for "book trailers" to see oodles of examples, ranging from good to meh to horrible.

PARTNERSHIPS

If you don't have a huge platform to sell your work, can you create a partnership with others who do have a larger audience? One of the most recent books we took on at C&R Press, my nonprofit literary press, was a book by John Stephens, an Atlanta businessman whose son had been killed by a drunk driver. What made this book stand out from all the other tragic memoir queries we received over the last year was that he'd established a relationship with Mothers Against Drunk Driving, one of our nation's most successful charities. It's hard as a publisher not to sit up and take serious note of a book that has the promotional support of a nonprofit organization with over 2 million members.

When I wanted to reach the widest audience possible for my memoir, I partnered with dozens of authors, experts, and companies who had a clear self-help message as part of their own mission. That message coincided well enough with my own that I literally had hundreds of thousands of people learn about my book on the day of its release via tweets, Facebook posts, e-mail newsletters, website messages, and other forms of digital contact. This is the same strategy that Tim Ferriss used to make *The 4-Hour Workweek* and his other books massive hits from the start.

BLOG

Blogging is a fantastic way to generate a loyal following. It requires a real commitment from you because you have to be consistent in your postings and continue to offer something of value to your audience. Stick with it, though, and a blog can become so successful that you get a best-selling book out of it. That's what happened to the authors of *Fail Nation: A Visual Romp Through the World of Epic Fails, 1,001 Rules for My Unborn Son, Sh*t My Dad Says, PostSecret: Extraordinary Confessions from Ordinary Lives,* and *Grammar Girl's Quick and Dirty Tips for Better Writing.*

If starting and maintaining your own blog seems like more than you would like to take on, consider guest blogging for other people's blogs.

OTHER PR IDEAS

Here are a few more ideas you can try. See if any suit you.

- **Offer giveaways:** Will you use Goodreads (the world's largest website for readers and book recommendations) to host a giveaway for your title? Or will you create your own contest/ giveaway?

- **Suggest secondary products:** Is there an opportunity for a calendar? A Beanie baby? A line of clothes? A board game? An app? A workbook?

- **Match a publisher's financial PR commitment dollar for dollar:** If you have the cash for this, sometimes offering to go halfsies on PR efforts is enough to shake loose a few extra bucks from the publisher. Consider specifying how you'll use this money, whether to buy a national print advertisement or a radio ad or to hire a top freelance publicist to augment what the in-house PR folks can do.

- **Write op-eds, letters to the editor, or articles on your topic:** Generate buzz for your book by getting your name—and your ideas—out there in advance. Make sure that your byline mentions your forthcoming book. Include a publication date, too.

- **Create tip sheets or short filler items:** Send these liberally to periodicals. You might get a free mention about you and your book!

- **Connect your book to a holiday:** There's a holiday for everything, so find the right one(s) and let the media know how your book relates. Another option? Create your own holiday. Use www.holidayinsights.com/moreholidays/index.htm or Google around to see what's already out there. Creating and promoting "Video Game Addiction Awareness Week" did wonders for the sales of my book *Unplugged.*

- **Create promotional items:** I'm not a huge fan of promo items for the sake of having promo items, but if you can find something that syncs well with your book, consider investing in it. Steer clear of the obvious choices that end up being thrown away, such as buttons, stickers, pencils, and erasers. See if you can make your promotional item truly memorable.

BRING ON A PRO!

Consider making a commitment to hiring a freelance book publicist. Just like literary agents do, the professionals have contacts they've worked with before. This means they can get results fast! If you want an avalanche of attention in the media, a freelance publicist might be just what you need. If one of your goals is to establish yourself as a subject expert, a good publicist can not only promote your book but simultaneously present you as an expert available for interviews, quotations, and one-on-one (or group) consultations.

They can get expensive, however, and most require a three-month minimum commitment to take on a new project. They're often more effective than in-house publicity people because they have fewer projects to manage at once, they have to justify their rather high fees, and their reputation is on the line with every client. You can really make them work hard for you. The results, though, aren't guaranteed. If a publicist guarantees results, run.

HIT THE GAS

Why be the only one working on your PR campaign? Enlist the help of competent friends or family members to take on tasks they can manage such as creating mailing lists or searching for relevant bloggers. Even if you give yourself a full six-month jump on PR once the book is under contract, you'll find there is always more to do. Plan for it by creating your team.

One way I got help in the past was by bartering my services as a writer and editor with a freelance book publicist who needed some help in those areas. She got things she desperately needed, and I got hundreds of my media releases sent from a PR pro (releases coming from a pro are always taken more seriously than those that arrive from an author or a nobody). She also had expensive subscription lists that gave her the contact names at plenty of places that weren't on my list.

PUBLICITY CAMPAIGN SECTION EXAMPLE

Here's the "Publicity Campaign" section I used in my proposal for this book, *The Weekend Book Proposal*. While I'm willing to do everything listed below, the publisher wants me to focus on the items that seem likeliest to have the most impact. Fair enough. Now that I've got a book contract signed, the publisher is boss.

Part IV—Launching Your Dynamite Publicity Campaign

Mail Campaign/The Publishing I.Q. Test

To presell *The Weekend Book Proposal* among volume buyers, I recommend mailing out a short, easily completed book publishing/proposal-writing quiz to show how some traditional ideas are, in fact, proposal killers!

Included might be a short pamphlet or trifold flier with relevant statistics and quotes from *The Weekend Book Proposal*, including book order forms. Other options for mailers include a Top 10 list of staggering book publishing statistics or a short Q&A, similarly angled. These last two options could be done on a postcard featuring the book's cover and ordering information.

Ancillary Print Products

Possible products include: (a) *The Weekend Book Proposal* Boxed Gift Set, (b) *The Weekend Book Proposal* Day-by-Day

Desk Calendar, (c) spin-off articles on specific elements of book proposals to be distributed via e-book platforms, and (d) *The Weekend Book Proposal Workbook.*

New Writer's Digest Products

I am open to generating book proposal–related articles for *Writer's Digest* magazine or creating webinars, seminars, tutorials, or boot-camp programs to reach the vast network of people who utilize *Writer's Digest* as their go-to source for the best writing information out there.

PR Consultant

I will investigate hiring a PR firm (ideally, the same PR firm that Steven Almond used to catapult his professional reputation with the publication of *Candyfreak: A Journey Through the Chocolate Underbelly of America*) to have them work with the publisher's PR department to make *The Weekend Book Proposal* the standard for would-be writers and seasoned writers honing their craft.

Companion Website

The active web presence at www.theweekendbookproposal.com could include a blog where I will regularly share tips and tricks for those writing their book proposals. Also included could be samples of annotated proposals above and beyond those in the book to ensure that this book will be able to help writers in any genre.

Another option is to have a yearly contest—anyone who has bought the book can enter (for free) to have a proposal critiqued by me.

The Weekend Book Proposal Workshops

Using skills developed during my years as a university professor, I will develop a writing workshop specifically designed to get people to find book-worthy ideas and then write winning book proposals about those ideas.

To market the book, I will use samples from *The Weekend Book Proposal* (primarily the end-of-chapter questionnaires and the reproducible worksheet in the appendices) and get people writing during the session. The workshops could easily be presented in shopping malls or community centers in short one- or two-hour formats. This calls for a tie-in with area booksellers to sponsor the workshop. I will help develop a mail sales kit to assist retailers in promoting the writing workshops.

After bookstore writing workshops, I will hold a signing that will increase sales of *The Weekend Book Proposal* as well as increase overall traffic to the retail location. I have held writing workshops in shopping malls before, and many of the host booksellers agreed to future formal signings and presentations thanks to the success I encountered. While the outcome of these workshops is to generate awareness of *The Weekend Book Proposal*, I can also provide attendees with a powerful skill—the ability to use language more effectively in their own lives.

Product Placement
I will contact Barnes & Noble executives Mary Ellen Keating (Senior V.P. of Corporate Communications and Public Affairs) and Jaime Carey (Chief Merchandising Manager) to discuss product placement (B&N) as a specific replacement for every generic use of "bookstore" in *The Weekend Book Proposal*. Possible compensation for this product placement could be: (a) the purchase of a certain quantity of books by B&N for corporate/gift giveaways, (b) agreeing to carry *The Weekend Book Proposal* in all B&N stores for at least one year, (c) free two-week front store displays for *The Weekend Book Proposal*, (d) a foreword or blurb by senior B&N executives, (e) a financial arrangement, or (f) some other win-win agreement.

Radio
Having done a number of radio interviews in the past (local NPR, book shows, talk shows), I have numerous contacts in the industry. I will make myself available for any and all radio show opportunities as well as pursue national venues to speak about *The Weekend Book Proposal*, including programs on the following topics: literature, writing, lifestyle, entertainment, and general interest.

TV

Since 81 percent of Americans "have a book in them," talk-show format TV is an ideal vehicle to promote *The Weekend Book Proposal* and get regular people excited about sharing their own stories in print. An accomplished interviewer myself, I know what it takes to create a good interview, so I'm able to make the most of any chance to speak about the book. To this end, I will make myself available for any television opportunities, whether it's *The Today Show* or local public television.

"Internet Buzz"

Modeled after Tim Farris' successful *The 4-Hour Workweek* "Internet buzz" campaign, I will use my own blogs and my connections with other bloggers/Internet gurus to publicize *The Weekend Book Proposal*. I will also maximize the book's online visibility (with the help of my large network of writer friends as well as the bloggers/Internet gurus mentioned above) through MySpace, Facebook, Second Life, myyear-book, LinkedIn, Pinterest, Bebo, Studivz (Germany), Mixi (Japan), YouTube, Flickr, Twitter, and Zooomr, to name just a few networking and media-sharing sites that can creatively and memorably promote books.

"Monkey in the Cage"

To show that winning book proposals can be written in forty-eight hours, I can do the entire process online at the companion website. This will include answering the worksheet questionnaires, showing my notes, and posting the various stages of my proposal-in-progress as it develops over forty-eight hours. Robert Olen Butler did a similar online event at Florida State University where he allowed people to witness him writing an entire short story based off a postcard (www.fsu.edu/~butler).

YouTube Book Trailer

I will construct a book trailer for *The Weekend Book Proposal* and feature it on the book website, my personal website, my professional website, my blogs, and YouTube. Like most successful online book trailer videos, this one will have a sense of humor about it and be succinct (and truthful) about the promises this book makes.

Underground/Alternative PR
I will get Las Vegas writer Jarret Keene (a former FSU classmate and current alternative magazine writer/editor who authored *The Killers: Destiny Is Calling Me* and *The Underground Guide to Las Vegas*) to interview me about *The Weekend Book Proposal*. It will then be syndicated to alternative A&E weeklies, plus create another general interest article about this topic specifically for traditional online and print venues. As a stringer for *People* and other mainstream magazines, he might create coverage for *The Weekend Book Proposal* in those more traditional publications as well.

Newsletters
I will use my nonprofit press's newsletter (1,200+ names of writers) to promote *The Weekend Book Proposal*. I will also acquire the mailing lists of regional writing organizations and literary presses to help connect with writers who are hungry to break into the publishing world.

Contributors of My Other Books
I keep a mailing list of the 400+ writers whose work was included in either of my two creative writing textbooks and my numerous literary anthologies. I will request that they share *The Weekend Book Proposal*'s information with students, colleagues, and other writers in their network.

Pre-Publication Blurbs
To give *The Weekend Book Proposal* academic credibility, I will personally send review copies to distinguished professors of creative writing, journalism, business, and technology to request blurbs. I will also use my large writer network to obtain blurbs and word-of-mouth PR. A representative sample of these names is included in Part VI.

Here are some ways to jump-start your publicity campaign. Few of them are the sort of thing I'd mention in your proposal, but that doesn't mean I'd skip doing them. See for yourself.

1. Create a Facebook fan page for your book.
2. Create business cards with your book's information, and hand them out like free candy.
3. Poll your readers, and carefully listen to their thoughts and ideas.
4. Start commenting on other people's blogs.
5. Host a Q&A session on Google+.
6. Link your websites to those of other writers and experts.

SOME FINAL THOUGHTS ON PUBLICITY CAMPAIGNS

Ensure that your publicity plan is as big as your goals are for your book, though don't bite off more than you can chew. If specific publicity responsibilities for you get into your contract, you're stuck doing it no matter the cost, financial or otherwise.

One thing you can do that will alert publishers that you're serious is include a statement that says you're eager and quite open to doing whatever you can to help promote the book, and to that end, you're willing to respond to any suggestions the publisher has to generate publicity and sales. Say it in your own words, but that's the gist of the message. Believe it or not, more than a few authors feel their job is done once the final manuscript is turned in.

It isn't, and only the foolish think otherwise.

Finally, remember that this is your book and it's your publicity campaign. Don't feel compelled to do things that feel wrong for your image of the book or yourself. The publicity campaign may be unique and creative, but make sure it's unique and creative in a way that reflects you and your book.

TOP TIPS TO REMEMBER

- The publisher will do some of your publicity, but the lion's share is on you.
- Effective publicity doesn't have to cost a lot.
- Be clear that you're willing to work hard.
- Spell out any financial commitments you're willing to make.
- Use partnerships to reach audiences beyond those you already have access to.

- Consider using a book trailer to publicize your book.
- Don't overcommit on your campaign.

FOR MORE INFORMATION

Katz, Christina. *Get Known Before the Book Deal: Use Your Personal Strengths to Grow an Author Platform*. Cincinnati, OH: Writer's Digest Books (2008). See Appendix A for other helpful titles.

Chapter Seven

AUTHOR BACKGROUND:
WHO AM I TO WRITE THIS BOOK?

Great question! If you're a big-name author, you have an edge here (although if you're a big-name author, you're probably not reading this book because you already have more books under contract than you can shake a red pen at). I'm guessing that you're a first-time book-length author or an early- to mid-career author looking to crank things to a higher level, right? Throw some gas on the coals of your publishing career and see if you can get those flames roaring? This chapter is going to hit on all the things you need to do in order to sell yourself well, whether your name already appears on the spine of books or not.

WORDS OF WISDOM

Jodi Lipper, author of the Hot Chick Book Series (*How to Eat Like a Hot Chick, How to Love Like a Hot Chick*, and *Live Like a Hot Chick*) as well as an experienced ghostwriter and book doctor, explains: "The author's bio is incredibly important. For nonfiction, perhaps the most important thing about the proposal is the author's platform, which includes not just their bio but their media contacts, experience in the media, and social media platforms ... it will be an uphill battle to convince the publisher that the story/book is so compelling that the media will come calling without any experience or celebrity."

Remember that even if you have an amazing idea and a dynamite book proposal, you might still lose the deal if you don't present yourself as the single best candidate to do the job. I know this is the case. I've lucked into a situation before where someone else pitched an idea and the publisher wasn't wowed enough by the author's credentials, so they passed. By sheer luck, I pitched something close to that first idea, but my credentials (and how I presented them) did the trick. I got the book deal. The other author? I'm guessing she never knew how close she came to scoring big with a major publisher. (I only know this story because I became pals with the acquisitions editor. Plus a few apple-tinis in a Manhattan bar with the right person can do wonders for getting the 411 on the publishing world!)

YOUR WRITING BACKGROUND

On a blind date, do you stroll right up to shake your date's hand and announce, "Osteoporosis runs in my family, I snore loud enough to scare the neighbor's cats, my farts are truly toxic, plus I have the world's third largest collection of Smurf drinking glasses"? Of course not. While you're probably a terrific person despite these problems/faults/challenges/quirks, if those things are all your date knows up front, you're surely getting an "Oh my, I think a migraine is coming on. I need to hibernate. Maybe until June. Goodnight." And then a door will slam in your face. She'll be inside, peering at you fearfully through the peek hole, praying to God you leave and forget her address. She might even call the cops on you.

Don't announce that you've never been published.

Don't confess that you've never taken a writing class or that you did but you got a C minus or that you earned (gasp) an incomplete because you never finished the final assignment.

Don't lead with *any* reason to say no to you.

Now, there are a few things you might be tempted to include when selling yourself, but instead of them helping you, they often earn an automatic rejection. Avoid these at all costs:

1. Claim that you're going to outsell Stephen King (or Malcolm Gladwell or the King James Bible).

2. Misrepresent your writing/publishing/academic history.

3. Lie about your background in any way.

4. Use any of the following phrases, or anything even close to them:
    - "I've been writing since I was three."
    - "My mother thinks this is the best book I've written so far."
    - "This book will be a hit with every reader, regardless of age."
    - "This story will make a *great* movie!"
    - "Oprah will love this."

You might feel that way in your heart, but resist the temptation for that kind of honesty. Just don't do it. Reread the dating example above as many times as you need in order to see how this kind of first impression will play out with publishing professionals. Considering the flood of submissions publishers enjoy, they have a defense mechanism in operation—it's called "look for reasons to reject everything." Use your bio to highlight your best features, not your worst. Don't give them a reason to say anything but a resounding yes!

Now, if you do have previous training in writing or some of your writing has been published somewhere—anywhere—awesome! That's terrific information to include. Having something you wrote that's been published says a few things:

- You can complete a written piece.
- You can edit/proofread it to a professional standard.
- You understand how to submit work to a publisher.
- You have worked successfully with a publisher in the past.
- You take yourself seriously as a writer.
- You're building a writing career.

All of these seem like valuable things to communicate to a prospective publishing partner, no?

If you don't have professional writing credentials, you might decide to take a bit of time to generate some. Considering how many print and online opportunities there are these days, it's easier than ever to get something accepted for publication. Begin with local publication opportunities to start racking up credentials.

HIT THE GAS

A great way to grab a few writing credentials F A S T is to write letters to the editor (also called "LTTE" or "LTE") to publications that print such a feature. These shouldn't take you long to write since they are typically about 200 words long. They're usually in response to a piece that's already been published, although they could also be about a topical issue of interest. Land one or two of these babies and you can honestly say, "My writing has appeared in *Hyde Park Herald* and *Chicago Defender*."

YOUR EDUCATION

Here's where you say you went to Stanford (unless, like me, you didn't!). If you went to a number of different colleges and universities, don't give the entire laundry list. Give the last one and/or the most prominent. If your education stopped at high school or before, leave that out of the letter entirely. Now calm down—I'm not saying you're a dud because you didn't go to college. People like John D. Rockefeller, Richard Branson, Bill Gates, Dave Thomas, and Henry Ford all did quite well without college, I realize. But it's just too easy for an editor who's never met you to have a negative reaction to your not having what's considered to be the bare minimum of education. (If your book is about succeeding without a college degree, however, by all means, lead with that fact.)

A word of warning: Academic writers are trained to write stuffy, dense, reader-unfriendly works. So if you have advanced degrees, make sure that your entire proposal reads like you're writing for actual people versus Socrates. Keep the massive, convoluted sentences and exotic vocabulary to a minimum. You're writing for the twenty-first century audience, not William Shakespeare.

Education, though, is more than just degree programs. Consider beefing up this area of your bio by taking classes at the local community college. You can find first-rate online classes through Writer's Digest University (www.writersonlineworkshops.com), Stanford University Continuing Studies (continuingstudies.stanford.edu/courses/onlinewriters.php), and the Gotham Writers' Workshop (www.writingclasses.com). If you go any of these routes, they're worth mentioning.

I learned to write from *Writer's Digest* magazine and many of their how-to books from the early 1990s. While that was an important part of my educational experience—in some ways, more crucial than my degrees—I leave this out of my author bio. I choose to let my writing speak for itself.

For the proposal for this particular book (which I only submitted to Writer's Digest), you better believe I included the above info prominently!

RELEVANT BACKGROUND INFORMATION

You might be inclined to add that you raise Yorkshire terriers or that you hold three *Guinness Book of World Records* records relating to bubble gum blowing. Good for you. Just don't put it in your author bio because it's not relevant (unless, of course, your book is on raising/hoarding dogs or bubble gum blowing, or if it's a memoir on your life quest to get as many world records as humanly possible).

If you truly think something is interesting albeit a bit off the topic of your book, fine, just include no more than one of those factoids to give your life a little color. Such an addition might make you stand out from a slew of other authors' proposals. It also might make sense if you don't have much to say by way of education or writing background. You have to say something, right? I get that. Just don't go overboard with hobbies, interests, and skills. This isn't a job résumé or dating profile, after all.

If you choose to add a nice detail for flavor, see if it can also—on some level—suggest something that might help your cause as a writer. For instance, if you're a freelance web designer, then you must be pretty creative and industrious. You also probably know how to use the Internet to promote yourself and your book. And if you say you get in at least three rounds of golf a week at the best country club in San Jose (Silicon Valley), it's reasonable to assume you might have an in with high-tech innovators and dot-com entrepreneurs. If you're writing a book about the dot-com bubble bursting, then this is crucial information to share.

INSIDER SECRET

Write your author bio fairly early in the proposal process. Why? Giving an honest look at your bio against the proposed book will tell you that yes, you're the right person for this book, or no, this isn't a great fit. If it's the latter, you might need to hold off on this particular book until you improve your qualifications (or grab a more qualified co-author).

ADDITIONAL INFORMATION

What else might you include in your bio? Anything that could convince the publishing community that you are a professional writer as well as the right person to write this book right now. Simple as that. Awards, memberships, or skill sets are just a few things that might merit inclusion. I've been a member of American Mensa for decades, but I can't recall ever using that in a bio. But if I propose any book relating to brainpower, puzzles, or critical thinking, I sure will.

To give just one example of how information beyond what I've mentioned above might be pertinent, consider what Jan Cullinane used in her author bio for *The Single Woman's Guide to Retirement: Everything You Need to Know* (see chapter twelve for the rest of this proposal). She led with a full-color author photo and concluded with an extensive listing of her speaking appearances.

V. About the Author

Jan Cullinane has distinguished herself as an expert in the retirement arena. *The New Retirement: The Ultimate Guide to the Rest of Your Life* (Rodale, 2007 and 2004) has been widely acclaimed, and the first edition reached the number two rank on both BN.com and Amazon.com (right behind *Harry Potter*). *The Chicago Tribune, Publishers Weekly,* and *Library Journal* have given the book outstanding reviews. Michelle Singletary, personal finance columnist ("Color of Money") for *The Washington Post,* chose *The New Retirement* as a book club selection and recommended its purchase for holiday gift giving. The book is endorsed by the NEA, AARP, and Motley Fool. This new book will utilize the same breezy, positive, helpful style. Cullinane also presents seminars on various topics of retirement through her company, Retirement Living from A to Z. (Please see below for a list of presentations—many of these are recurring events.)

Cullinane is the Retirement Expert for the NABBW (National Association of Baby Boomer Women), a contributor to *The Ocean Breeze* and *Vibrant Nation,* and a retirement consultant. She has a B.S. and a Master's degree from the University of Maryland, and is ABD (all but dissertation) from Rutgers, The State University of New Jersey. She taught extensively at the college level prior to writing *The New Retirement: The Ultimate Guide to the Rest of Your Life* (Rodale).

Her media events include:

PRINT:
Wall Street Journal
USA Weekend magazine
Forbes.com (article/quiz and interview with John Dobosz)
Cincinnati Woman Magazine
The Cincinnati Enquirer
Suburban Press
Retirement Weekly (CBS MarketWatch)
The Washington Post
Albany Times Union
Daytona Beach News-Journal
Columbus Dispatch
Ocean Breeze
Star-Ledger
Healthy Wealthy-n-Wise

50plus Online Magazine
Ideal Living
Plan Ahead Get Ahead
Body and More
The Augusta Chronicle
Jewish Exponent

TV:
Fox and Friends
KOVR (Sacramento)
WCPO (Cincinnati)
WGHP (Greensboro)
WTAP (Parkersburg)
WBOC (Salisbury)
WFIE (Evansville)
KSFY (Sioux Falls)
WQOW (La Cross-Eau Claire)
WDTN (Dayton)
WSIL (Carterville)

RADIO:
KYW (National through CBS)
WBIX (Boston)—*Your Money with Chuck Jaffe*
WMKV (Cincinnati)
WRRS (Cincinnati)
WICH (Norwich)
WEAA (Baltimore)
KTOK (Oklahoma City)

INTERNET:
www.smartmoney.com
www.basilandspice.com
www.personallifemedia.com
www.retirementrevised.com
www.greatretirementspots.com
www.forbes.com

SPEAKING ENGAGEMENTS:
Wells Fargo Advisors
Deloitte & Touche LLP
Ameriprise Financial

Fifth Third Bank

AARP

Royal Caribbean's *Navigator of the Seas*

Realty Presentations, Inc.

United Way

AARC (American Association of Retirement Communities)

Ford Motor Company

Public Library of Cincinnati and Hamilton County

Well, what do you think? Was it a good idea to include all of that "additional information" beyond the basics? If you were an editor, would you feel that Cullinane was the right person to write this book right now?

ONE BIO DOES NOT FIT ALL

We all have strengths and things we can put in a bio, but one size does not fit all. To see what I mean, let's consider an author I've brought to my college numerous times to speak with students about writing and editing. He's Las Vegas-based writer Jarret Keene, and he covers a lot of book topic areas, from poetry to biographies to guidebooks to anthologies. Here's a bio he used to land *The Killers: Destiny Is Calling Me* (Manic D Press, 2006).

> In addition to having been close friends and bandmates with members of the now multi-platinum-selling The Killers, author Jarret Keene covered the rapid rise of the group during his three-year stint as arts and entertainment editor for *Las Vegas CityLife*. From The Killers' humble beginnings as the house band for a local transsexual dive bar to their eventual friendship with Jay Z, Keene saw and heard it all. Keene is also the author of the poetry collection *Monster Fashion* and the alternative travel guide *The Underground Guide to Las Vegas*. He lives in Las Vegas.

Sounds like he's the best guy for the job of writing a candid unauthorized biography/photo book on that band, wouldn't you say? And now here's how he pitches himself for a quirky fiction anthology entitled *Dead Neon: Tales of Near-Future Las Vegas* (University of Nevada Press, 2010).

> For twenty-seven years, nothing happened to him. Finally, he earned a Ph.D. in English from Florida State University and, bored of Chaucer, moved to Las Vegas to chronicle the city's underground music scene. He has written for every kind of

media (*Spin*, BBC Radio, Godzilla fanzines) and has written and edited every kind of book (*A Boy's Guide to Arson, Las Vegas Noir*). His primitive nuclear doom metal band Dead Neon terrorizes local dive bars.

Again, doesn't that sound like a match made in literary heaven? It seemed like it to the University of Nevada Press, who gave him and co-editor Todd James Pierce the contract. Jarret didn't even mention his Ph.D. in English in the first bio because it didn't matter all that much. For a tell-all biography of a band, it's all about access. For the second book, the Ph.D. made more sense—it was a university press, after all. They understand and appreciate the rigor of a doctoral program. They trust Ph.D. holders to be thorough, organized, and deadline savvy.

HIT THE GAS

Create a boilerplate bio ASAP, and keep it handy at all times. When you need a bio for proposals or PR purposes, it's a simple cut-and-paste job plus some tweaking particular to your intended audience and *voilà*, you're done. (Just remember to update that boilerplate bio info as your successes arrive or the facts of your life change.)

SOME FINAL THOUGHTS ON AUTHOR BACKGROUND

Now isn't the time to be modest. Cast yourself in the best light possible for this particular book proposal. Be clear, be concise, be honest, and consider running your bio by a few friends or relatives for some feedback. You never know where you'll get an "Oh, what about including ..." idea that's perfect for your bio.

TOP TIPS TO REMEMBER

- Keep your bio relevant and current, and emphasize your strengths.
- Don't confess your weaknesses.
- Write it in third person, unless the book is very personal (like a memoir).
- Use active verbs—avoid *is/are/were* as much as possible.

- Bolster your bio by writing for the local newspaper, speaking for a local group, or offering a free workshop in a local school or library.
- Make sure to have a one-sentence, one-paragraph, one-page, and 1,000-word long bio on hand.

FOR MORE INFORMATION

Beckwith, Harry and Christine K. Clifford. *You, Inc.: The Art of Selling Yourself.* Warner (2011).

Katz, Christina. *Get Known Before the Book Deal: Use Your Personal Strengths to Grow an Author Platform.* Writer's Digest Books (2001).
See Appendix A for other helpful titles.

Chapter Eight

MANUSCRIPT SAMPLES:
THE LOWDOWN ON SIZE, STRATEGY, AND SIZZLE

Now that you've invested a good bit of time thinking about your book, why it's needed, who it's for, and why you're the slam-dunk choice to write it, it's time to consider the writing sample. It should go without saying (but I'll say it anyway) that agents and editors don't want to deal with an author whose writing sample delivers any of the following messages:

- I don't know how to edit.
- I don't know how to revise.
- My chapter summaries have no relation to what I'm actually writing.
- I enjoy *microscopic fonts*!

Your writing sample is your opportunity to prove beyond all doubt that yes, you can write at a professional level and take the idea from your chapter summaries into a nice-size chunk of prose that's impressive, easy-to-read, and evocative. That's a tall order, which is why I devoted an entire chapter to the manuscript sample.

INSIDER TIP

If you've never worked in a publishing house, you probably won't know this: Many editors read the sample chapter first. If it's a winner, they read the rest of the proposal. If it's a clunker, then it's "next manuscript" time. All that good work you might've done with the marketing campaign, elevator pitch, and chapter summaries doesn't even matter. The sample needs to be a showstopper.

HOW MUCH IS TOO MUCH?

When I applied to graduate school for fiction writing, nearly every university's creative writing program requested twenty double-spaced, typed pages. Why that number? Because nearly anyone can produce two to five well-written pages, given enough time (and help). But to sustain it for ten, fifteen, or even twenty pages showcases some real talent. So the standard became twenty.

And that's why I recommend submitting at least twenty double-spaced, typed pages of sample manuscript material. Mahesh Grossman, author of *Write a Book Without Lifting a Finger* and president of AuthorsTeam. com, says, "I usually have the authors I work with submit an introduction and a chapter. The introduction should be at least ten pages and tell the story of how you became an expert on your topic and why you are writing your book. The sample chapter should be at least eighteen pages. The truth is, however, that you need to make the chapter long enough to include everything necessary to convey how to do what you're talking about, or to tell the complete story."

Of course there are exceptions to the page count rule, such as my illustrated humor book (see the entire proposal and three-page manuscript sample in chapter twelve). But a good rule of thumb is twenty pages.

WHICH PART OF THE BOOK SHOULD I SEND?

Many people will say to just send the first chapter(s) of your book as your manuscript sample. That's what a reader at a bookstore will likely encounter first, so let the editor start the same way. That's fine. Certainly, if you can't hook a reader with those initial pages, you likely won't later (even if for some masochistic reason, readers read on past the beginning that they didn't like).

I didn't include the first chapter with my proposal for this book. Heck, it wasn't even the second chapter—it was the third chapter that I sent (which during the post-contract writing and revision process became chapter two). What was my thinking? I had all of my ideas for this chapter laid out clearly in my head and on paper. I knew I had lots of strong tips regarding book titles. Most importantly, this was the chapter I had already worked out clearly in my mind. I was jazzed to write it.

Something obviously went right because here I am writing this, and there you are reading it. And I didn't touch any of the other twenty chapters until after I had signed a contract I was happy with (another good reason to get a strong literary agent—have them negotiate better terms in contracts!). That's the way to do it. Proposal, then contract, then write the whole blasted thing.

INSIDER TIP

Professional writers don't feel religiously bound by rules. If the "send the first chapter" rule doesn't make sense for their particular proposal, they ignore it. For instance, if your book is a tell-all, maybe include the juiciest chapter. If your book reveals the true shooter of the JFK assassination, maybe that's the chapter to include.

You're welcome to break any "rule" you choose. Just make sure that the reasons for breaking it are significantly stronger than the reasons for the rule in the first place.

Warning: While you do want to send your best material, don't cherry-pick bits and pieces from many chapters. That gets schizophrenic and confusing. Include full chapters or at least self-contained sections that start strong and end even better.

YOUR ENGLISH TEACHER WAS RIGHT: GOOD WRITING AND PROPER GRAMMAR *DO* MATTER

Typos, misspellings, and other grammatical snafus all announce that you're not a very careful (or competent) writer. You either don't know how to write well or you can't be bothered to do it. There's no place for shoddy work anywhere in a book proposal, but in your sample? The sample should exhibit the absolute *best* writing that you can produce. You're not constrained by bullet points or marketing jargon or anything else—this is you communicating as only you can communicate. It should be smooth and error-free. It should have a sense of style and flair. Above all, it should have a sense of story to it, even if it's straight-up nonfiction. Stories produce experiences, create an emotional impact, and transform information into meaning. Plus stories are more often remembered (and less often resisted).

INSIDER TIP

"People who cannot distinguish between good and bad language, or who regard the distinction as unimportant, are unlikely to think carefully about anything else." — B.R. Myers, contributing editor for *The Atlantic* and opinion columnist for *The New York Times* and *The Wall Street Journal*

"If you still persist in writing, 'Good food at it's best,' you deserve to be struck by lightning, hacked up on the spot, and buried in an unmarked grave." — Lynne Truss, author of *Eats, Shoots and Leaves: The Zero Tolerance Approach to Punctuation*

"You can be a member of all the romance writers associations, take part in all of the networking available, or win the latest romance award ... but guess what? None of that makes a difference if you don't *write* something people want to *read*. The greatest editor in the world won't make your book a bestseller if it isn't something people care about. So forget all of the fluff that clouds your purpose: writing!" — Kathryn Le Veque, one of Amazon's top-selling historical romance authors

Make sure your writing ability and use of grammar are up to the task of helping you tell powerful stories through your writing. If your proposal is a bit dry but your writing sample sings, you might get that book contract. If your proposal screams "bestseller!" but your writing sample is lifeless, you might end up out in the cold.

HIT THE GAS

Since the writing sample might be the largest part of the entire proposal package, here's where writing fast helps a ton. So let me offer two tips on writing fast.

1) Crank up the Metallica. If you don't like Metallica, pick something else with a kicking beat that's 120 beats per minute or faster. Many people find that they start typing to the beat versus the slow *tap-tap-tap* they normally do.

2) As my wife constantly tells our young daughters, "Use your words." By that, I mean don't type your book—that's old school. Speak them aloud. Look—most of us type about 40 wpm (words per minute), but we can easily speak at 100 wpm or more! (To give you a sense of the upper end of this, auctioneers can handle 250 wpm, and the world's fastest speakers can top 600 wpm). Get a copy of Dragon NaturallySpeaking or some other speech recognition software and "type" your book by speaking it aloud.

WHAT'S THE "SECRET SAUCE"?

Just like McDonald's has their secret sauce to give the Big Mac a little oomph, a little something special, you should consider giving your manuscript samples something special. What might this be? Charts, graphs, illustrations, questionnaires? Sidebars? Checklists? Time lines? Interviews? Quotes? Something else entirely?

For my nonfiction books, I often include magazine-style sidebars as part of the sample material. For my illustrated humor book (again, the entire proposal is in chapter twelve), I used graphics and sidebars. I'm willing to do anything with a manuscript if it helps the piece stand out and doesn't come across as gimmicky. What type of special sauce can *you* add to your sample material?

Lena Dunham believes in the special sauce, too. Her sixty-six-page proposal for *Not That Kind of Girl: A Young Woman Tells You What She's Learned* earned her a $3 million+ advance from Random House in October 2012. To give it the right look and vintage feel to mirror Helen Gurley Brown's women's advice book *Having It All*, she hired New York studio CHIPS to design her proposal and New York artist Joana Avillez to illustrate it. Talk about going all out to make an impact on an editor! (The book went to auction with a minimum bid of $1 million.)

Warning #1: While it might be a great idea to suggest that the chapter you're including has three tear-out origami swans or other such bonuses, someone has to pay for that if the book makes it into production. Try very hard not to find ways to increase the production cost of the book (such as including color photographs or using extensive die-cut pages). No one wants to make or buy $80 books.

Warning #2: Don't spend a fortune hiring professionals to help you design your book proposal unless you're superwealthy and/or stunningly sure it will make the difference between a nice book contract and a Lena Dunham book contract.

HIT THE GAS

"The key to writing quickly is to know where you're going. If you were planning a family vacation, you'd choose a destination and then map out a path to get there. Yet many writers start writing without a clear finish line in mind—and the result is endless meandering to no purpose." — Jacob Appel

SOME FINAL THOUGHTS ON MANUSCRIPT SAMPLES

Whether you write your manuscript sample before, during, or after you've written the rest of the proposal, you must make sure that it delivers on the promise the proposal makes. The proposal is a business document. The sample? It's a literary document. Even if it's a business leadership book, a biography of Winston Churchill, or a memoir, readers expect a literary (read this as "storytelling") quality that's more than just an information exchange.

While you should be able to write an entire draft of your proposal within forty hours, you might well want to set your sample material aside for a bit and come back to it with fresh eyes before sending it in.

TOP TIPS TO REMEMBER

- Don't automatically include chapter one as your sample. Pick your sample material based on the most interesting/useful/exciting/shocking things you have to offer.
- Ensure your sample is well written, well edited, and compelling. Enlist some smart writer friends or hire a freelance writer (or editor, book doctor, or writing coach) to offer an opinion.
- Cookbooks, list books, and other unusual book types might require a very different style (and size) of sample.
- Any graphics or illustrations that you include need to be professionally done.
- Twenty pages or so of your book is a good rule of thumb for sample size. (A writing teacher of mine once said a book proposal writing sample needs to be like a woman's skirt—long enough to cover what you need to but short enough to be interesting.)

FOR MORE INFORMATION

Truss, Lynne. *Eats, Shoots & Leaves: The Zero Tolerance Approach to Punctuation*. Gotham (2006).

White, Fred. *Where Do You Get Your Ideas?: A Writer's Guide to Transforming Notes Into Narratives*. Writer's Digest Books (2012).

See Appendix A for other helpful titles.

Chapter Nine

ENDORSEMENTS:
WHICH BIG-NAME PEOPLE WILL ENDORSE YOUR BOOK?

If the answer is "none," you're missing out on a huge (think dinosaur huge) opportunity.

This chapter is one that other books on writing book proposals simply don't cover as extensively, if at all. Why is it here? Because one of the main goals of this book is to show you how to create *successful* book proposals, and using celebrity or fame to add value to your proposal is a tactic that most writers don't consider. My thought about it is this: Why work so hard selling yourself when you can let someone famous do it for you?

Enter the world of endorsements (also called "blurbs"). Get enough quality endorsements, and it almost doesn't matter if your book proposal has a few flaws. Endorsements are contagious. If enough influential people say your book is going to be great, literary agents and editors get excited because they can more easily envision future book sales, and book sales are what it's all about.

Connecting celebrities to your book (or book proposal) gets people to pay attention. It adds instant credibility. It also often leads to increased media exposure. What acquisitions editor wouldn't like those things?

Forward-thinking writers ask for blurbs—or at least a commitment to give a blurb—in advance so they can include that information in the book proposal. Most writers wait until the book is under contract and has been fully written before asking for blurbs. Sure, this works, but all those nifty blurbs don't have a chance to help you get a book contract or a larger advance.

Here's a dirty little publishing secret—95 percent of people who give blurbs don't read the whole book. Many, in fact, don't want or need to see more than a sample chapter. Some don't even want to see that much when a synopsis or summary will suffice.

With that in mind, approach your list of hopefuls now. If they ask to see the book, send a sample and a synopsis. Almost none will come back and insist on the whole book.

WHY DO BLURBS MATTER?

Throughout the world—but especially here in TMZ America—celebrities have power. Like it or not, what they say gets listened to more than what's said by regular Joes and Janes. A strong blurb by Stephen King on your debut horror novel will sell thousands more copies than it would have sold without it. A great blurb by Bill Gates on a business how-to will give you a similar bump. Same thing with Oprah on anything—for writers, her famous book club was thought to be the literary equivalent to winning the lottery. The phenomenon of being in her book club even has its own name: the Oprah Effect. Without exception, each of the seventy books she recommended enjoyed a massive sales spike. Fordham University marketing professor Al Greco estimated the sales of the Oprah Effect during the six years it ran at more than 55 million copies. Divide that by the seventy books she endorsed and you'll start to get a better sense of the amazing power of celebrity.

That's why blurbs and endorsements matter.

Remember that a book proposal, first and foremost, is a sales document. Any evidence of surefire sales is going to increase your odds of getting that book contract.

Let's put it another way. If you were the decision maker at a publishing house, would you take a strong book from Writer X that has no endorsements or a similarly strong (or even slightly less strong) book from Writer Z with blurbs from a US Senator, a Fortune 100 CEO, and Donald Trump? DING DING DING, it's a knockout for Writer Z.

THINK LIKE AN EDITOR

Remember that many young editors fear losing their jobs for taking on a book that's a sales stinker. Do you think it might be easier for them to accept and support a book that's already been supported by influential people? It's yet another aspect of the herd instinct of publishing.

LOCATE EXPERTS IN YOUR FIELD

While it's great to have Tom Hanks or Tom Brokaw praising the merits of your manuscript, don't neglect experts in your field. If you're writing a book about the world of art forgeries, a quote by Mark Landis—one of the most successful art forgers of the last one hundred years—would (ironically) go a long way to support the authenticity of your book. Now, the average literary agent wouldn't know Mark Landis from Marky Mark, but a quick Internet search that pulls up his Wikipedia page and the January 11, 2011

New York Times article on him will reveal that his words have sincere weight for this particular topic. You can find experts readily at major research universities, too.

Need some help on finding the right expert for your book's topic? Try any or all of the following:

- www.prnewswire.com/profnet
- www.helpareporterout.com
- www.findanexpertonline.com
- www.rtir.com
- www.guru.com
- www.guestfinder.com
- www.expertclick.com
- Google keywords relevant to your topic plus *blog* to find the main bloggers in your niche.
- Google keywords relevant to your topic plus *Twitter* or *Linkedin* to find even more experts.

MAINTAIN HEALTHY NETWORKS

Okay, okay, it's great in principle to say I need endorsements from celebs to say my work is super bueno, you might be thinking, *but how do I connect with the rich and famous? I have to actually talk to them before they can offer these awesome blurbs.*

Great question. And connecting with the rich and famous is harder than connecting with experts. Experts want to be found. They actively seek out opportunities like yours. Celebrities don't want to be found. Most actively avoid opportunities like yours. In fact, most surround themselves with layers of people whose job it is to keep people like you away.

One of the easiest ways to get past those layers of defense is to take advantage of the "small world syndrome." If you have an active presence and following on Twitter, Facebook, or other forms of social media, you are likely only one person removed from more celebrities than you can imagine. For instance, I played in MLB Hall of Famer Carlton Fisk's Celebrity Golf Classic a few years back (there's even a picture of the two of us on my website under the About section). Because I did a nice write-up on his event for a magazine, he'll remember me, which is good since I still have his private e-mail and cell phone number. I also did some reviews of fantasy books for a Las Vegas magazine, and those jobs necessitated me talking at length to mega-writers Terry Goodkind and R.A. Salvatore. I have uncirculated contact information for both of them, too.

People don't often brag about their famous friends/acquaintances. I sure don't. I've included the examples above only to show that any positive connection you may have had in the past with someone of influence can help you later down the road. I'm not going to funnel every writer I know to the three celebs I listed above nor the many other celebs I've met and hobnobbed with over the years of doing writing conferences and other events. But if the request was sincere and the book was a fine match with a celebrity I knew (like the book was primarily about a cause the celebrity openly supports), I'd strongly consider it.

So ask around. Someone you know might know someone who knows an expert or a celebrity who is a perfect fit for your book. Put a sincere request out on Facebook. Tweet away. E-mail your friends, family, and colleagues. It's a smaller world than we think, and you can use that fact to your advantage to bypass a celebrity's posse and reach them directly.

HIT THE GAS

Instead of trying to figure out how to get the contact info for Michael Jordan on your own—trust me, you'll never find it simply by Googling—use a service like www.contactanycelebrity.com. They have an online version that you can try out for free, and they have a yearly *Celebrity Black Book* that has over sixty-seven thousand addresses.

There are other options that you can use to find celebrity contact information such as www.fanmail.biz and www.thehandbook.com/celebrities. Google around, and you might find even more choices.

HOW TO ASK FOR BLURBS

When you first reach out to these people, don't start by asking for a book blurb. Start by proving you're not some know-nothing yokel—reference an award they've received, a book they've written, how you are personally connected (if you are), or something else specific about them. Once you've established some kind of relationship with the expert, *then* you can politely ask for a single quote to use in your book. Never assume they will say no—if they're going to say no, let *them* do it. And even if they pass on giving you a full blurb, any nice quote can add real value to your book. And trust me—most experts will answer one to three questions for free if you ask nicely. They recognize the value of free PR. Being quoted in magazine articles and books further establishes their credibility and keeps their name on the tips of people's tongues when it comes to their specific area of expertise. I do it all the time for marketing, writing, publishing, teaching, and the digital world—my areas of strength. Basically, an expert's inclusion in your book is like putting money in their bank account.

Some experts on contacting and working with celebrities suggest handwriting a letter to give it a personal touch. Certainly, it'll stand out against all the other e-mails and typed correspondence. A few also recommend jazzing up the envelope with drawings, stickers, etc., but I think that will come off as either juvenile or gimmicky.

Still, whether you choose to handwrite your letter or not, do keep it short and to the point. One page is the absolute maximum. And any snail-mail correspondence *must* include an SASE (self-addressed stamped envelope) with enough postage for a response. Yes, 98 percent of the letters you send out will be thrown away. But I guarantee you that not making it easy for them to respond will equal a much lower return rate than the normal lousy return rate. Celebrities are frankly too busy to be expected to work hard to comply to a single fan's request. Make it so easy for them to respond that they can't help but respond.

One thing I've done in blurb requests? I wrote the blurbs for them. I said that I knew they were terribly busy, so I suggested a few blurbs that they could choose from, though they were of course welcome to write one on their own! I hesitate to say how many chose the premade blurbs—it was a *ton*! Why? Many celebrities aren't great writers. It might take them twenty minutes or more to write two or three sentences of endorsement. And even then, they may feel self-conscious about sticking their name to something that might be less than professional. So when offered to take credit for a smart-sounding, professionally written blurb, many leapt at the chance. A bonus is that it's supereasy for them to say, "Go with #2."

BLURB REQUEST SAMPLE LETTER

Here's a version of a letter I used to get blurbs for my memoir, *Unplugged*. Some of the big-name folks who offered words of endorsement after receiving a letter like this included Pulitzer Prize–winner Alice Walker, radio host Tom Joyner, and South Carolina Senator Ernest Hollings.

Now, I fully recognize that I said never just cold-call someone to request a book blurb, which is what I did in my sample blurb request letter below. The return rate on a letter like mine is far lower than the slow-play strategy listed above. I was in a deadline crunch when I sent my letters out, so I simply sent hundreds and played the numbers. It worked fine, though it cost me a good deal in postage (which I still considered a fine investment).

Dear XXXX[1]—

I recognize that your time is valuable (and overtaxed), so let me keep this as brief as possible. A 2007 study by the AMA reports that more than 5 million American kids (ages 8–18) may be addicted to video games. With 114 million adults regularly playing Wii games, online games like World of Warcraft, and social networking games like Farmville or Mafia Wars, experts suggest that the number of addicted adults might be far higher.[2]

My book, *Unplugged: My Journey into the Dark World of Video Game Addiction* (by HCI, the same publishers who do the Chicken Soup for the Soul series), is the first memoir about video game addiction. Playing video games cost me a tenure-track university job, my financial future, my friends, my dignity, and very nearly my life. I'm committed to keeping this from happening to others.

My request is this: I would like to partner with you in order to raise awareness about video game addiction in America.[3] China, South Korea, and some European countries have already labeled video game addiction as their #1 public health issue. Here in America, too, it's quietly reaching epidemic proportions.

Some possibilities on how to achieve increased public awareness:

- Offer a quote for a press release on video game addiction.
- Send a Twitter, Facebook, or MySpace message about the growing problem of video game addiction.
- Create a PSA.
- Offer a blurb for *Unplugged*.

---

1. Of course this was the celebrity's full name, first and last, correctly spelled. I don't like saying "Dear Tom" (inappropriately familiar) or "Dear Mr. Hanks" (too stiff), so I go with "Dear Tom Hanks."

2. Note how I make this more about a cause than about me or my book.

3. To draw attention to what my one specific request was, I bolded this sentence. I also went on to offer various options on how they could support my cause.

I'm open to hearing any ideas you have on how we could partner up to make a difference. I know you're committed to having a positive impact on the lives of children and teens,[4] so this issue seems like one that you in particular would want to know about.

Thanks for your time. I look forward to hearing from you—

Ryan G.Van Cleave
[my full contact info plus e-mail and website URL]

P.S.—My editor and agent might go crazy if they knew I was doing this, but I've put a hidden PDF file of *Unplugged*'s first chapter on the official book site: www.unpluggedthebook.com. If you'd like to get a sneak look at these few pages, just click on the "$14.95 US" in the center of the main landing page (right above the picture of me). Let me know what you think.[5]

ENDORSEMENTS SECTION SAMPLE FROM A PROPOSAL

This section came right out of Jennifer Armstrong's proposal in chapter twelve of this book. Yes, she's name-dropping here, but remember, she spent nine years working for *Entertainment Weekly*. I wouldn't have much chance of landing these folks, but with nearly a decade of experience and contacts under her belt, this list seems eminently doable.

Endorsements

The following people, with whom the author is connected, may provide blurbs for *Becoming Mary Richards*:

- Tina Fey (*30 Rock, Bossypants*)
- Sarah Dunn (TV writer, *Murphy Brown, Spin City, Veronica's Closet*; also author of *The Big Love, Secrets to Happiness*)
- Mary Birdsong (actress, author, playwright; *Reno 911, 99 Cent Whore, Love, Loss and What I Wore*)

---

4. I adjusted this part to better match with whatever main causes the recipient openly supported. I primarily targeted people who championed young people, though. I thought I'd have the best chance of landing them versus others.

5. In my book contract, I had permission to do anything PR-wise I wanted with a single chapter, so this wasn't that illicit. I tracked the click-throughs, though, and nearly half of the folks who received my blurb request letter checked out a few pages.

- Gavin Edwards (contributor to *Rolling Stone* and author of pop culture compendium *Is Tiny Dancer Really Elton's Little John?*)
- Mickey Rapkin (*GQ* editor and author of *Pitch Perfect* and *Theater Geek*)
- Sheila Weller (*Girls Like Us*)
- Mark Harris (*Pictures at a Revolution*)
- Ken Tucker (*Entertainment Weekly* TV critic and author of *100 Things to Love and Hate About TV*)
- Patrick Sean Smith (executive producer/creator of *Greek*)
- Mark Schwahn (executive producer/creator of *One Tree Hill*)
- Aaron Martin (executive producer of *Being Erica*)

CAN I USE OTHER TYPES OF ENDORSEMENTS?

Absolutely. Anything that's given to you is fair game. E-mails from former students. Snail-mail letters from workshop attendees. If what someone sent you helps position you as an authority in your area or as a quality professional, hold onto that. You never know when you need to present yourself as a great teacher, a great workshop leader, a great parent, or something else.

GENERAL ENDORSEMENT EXAMPLE

When I was pitching *Memoir Writing for Dummies*, I wanted to make sure the For Dummies people at Wiley knew I was a pro in general and an effective communicator/teacher in specific. I included this page of general endorsements I've received over the years for my books, workshops, and speaking engagements. It's unlikely that you'll recognize any of the names here, but that's no problem—the sentiments are genuine and help offer social proof for my two goals above. (P.S.—Don't make up quotes for yourself or the names of people quoting you. It's easy to tell with a bit of Googling, and the fake ones just never sound authentic.)

If the For Dummies series used celebrity blurbs regularly (they don't), I would've taken the time to acquire some. In this particular case, these general words of endorsement and support helped make my case. And not one of them was specifically talking about the book I was pitching.

Endorsements

"I saw your interview on the evening local news—very VERY interesting and it caught my eye immediately!" — **Jessica Jenkins, Rockstar Presenters**

"I stumbled upon your memoir when researching a speech for class. It's very candid and very good … terrific story, man." — **Kameko Jennings (high school student)**

"I couldn't put *Unplugged* down for three days straight. I was up into the wee hours reading. It was like I was addicted to your words." — **Slatie Keynes, customer service rep (Vancouver, Canada)**

"I required formal responses to any of our five guest lecturers, and more of the students chose to respond to your visit than any other." — **Dr. Alma Bennett, MA Program in English at Clemson University**

"The presentation was excellent!" — **Dr. Kristine Petlick, psychologist (Stevensville, MI)**

"I can't thank you enough for your presentation this weekend. The kids are still raving about it." — **Robert Opitz, director of bands/Cherokee High School (GA)**

"You have a way of quickly getting to the heart of what matters." — **Steven Shepard, owner of Neo-Genesis Design**

"I'm glad Ryan Van Cleave has been willing to tell his story and [I] hope it helps many young men avoid similar patterns." — **Kurt Bruner, co-author of *Playstation Nation***

SOME FINAL THOUGHTS ON ENDORSEMENTS

Getting endorsements from people no one recognizes isn't helping the cause (unless they have credentials that are recognizable, such as NASA scientist or PETA president, or they represent your target audience, like the student and instructors in my list above). Shoot high and hope for the best. Plus give yourself plenty of time to get these endorsements before you start submitting your proposal. While you can write a draft of your proposal in a weekend, getting endorsements from high-powered people can take far longer. But land just three good ones and you'll look like an insider who's going places versus every other author firing off proposals and manuscripts.

TOP TIPS TO REMEMBER

- Publishing decision makers are influenced by blurbs, so don't neglect experts and authorities in your field. Make a Top 10 list and go after those people. Consider local experts as well.
- Keep blurb request letters short and error-free. Position yourself as a fan first and a blurb requester second.
- Avoid generic compliments—be specific in your praise.
- Keep a careful log of your request. Don't be afraid to follow up.
- Use other types of endorsements or support, if appropriate.

FOR MORE INFORMATION

McAuley, Jordan. *Celebrity Leverage: Insider Secrets to Getting Celebrity Endorsements, Instant Credibility, and Star-Powered Publicity.* Mega Niche Media (2010).

See Appendix A for other helpful titles.

Chapter Ten

THE PITCH:
GETTING A FOOT IN THE DOOR WITH
A DYNAMITE QUERY LETTER

Once you have a completed, well-edited, killer proposal, it's time to start selling. That means contacting literary agents or editors to showcase—or pitch—what you've got using a query letter. So read on to uncover more about the who, what, where, and how of pitching. (For a refresher on the parts of the book-writing/submitting process, revisit chapter one!)

WHY IS THIS CHAPTER HERE VERSUS AT THE BEGINNING?

This is a lesson I learned in two decades of teaching: If you give students a handout, no matter how much you insist they don't look at it, they will look at it the moment it touches their hands. They can't help themselves. Following this logic, it's possible that reading about ways to pitch your story might influence a terribly excited writer to start sending out queries before reading the rest of the book.

Resist this impulse.

Patience is one of the keys to success as a writer. So, too, is arming oneself with all the necessary information to be a success.

WHAT IS A PITCH?

Like I said at the start of this chapter, a pitch is what you do to briefly convey your idea to a publishing professional in writing, either through a hard copy letter or a digital one. Depending on an agent's or editor's specific guidelines, you will write a one- to three-page query letter. There was a brief period in history when writers, agents, and editors faxed such letters back and forth, but that's no longer the case. Stick to e-mail or hardcopy, depending on the specific requests of the agent or editor.

An effective pitch has three fundamental parts: two questions and one fact.

Question 1: Why me?

Question 2: Why you?

Fact: Here's what I'm offering.

Straightforward as that.

WHY ME?

You have a good deal of information on this thanks to what you learned in chapter seven. The trick is getting all of this information across in a paragraph or two max. Query letters need to be short. Many are no longer than a page, though a few run onto a second or third page if you're positive you have enough must-have material to warrant the extra potentially off-putting length.

To help assuage any concerns an agent or editor might have about your ability to produce the proposed book, mention any significant writing experience you have or relevant degrees. If you can't say much about either of those, then it's up to you to demonstrate your unique expertise by mentioning how your experiences make you the person for the job. You have to convince a stranger that you're a qualified author. Produce whatever evidence you need to in order to make that happen.

INSIDER TIP

Former Simon & Schuster editor Marcela Landres explains that not having a platform is the # 1 mistake that authors make. What is #2? "Describing their book idea instead of selling it. A proposal isn't the Cliff Notes version of the manuscript; instead, it's the equivalent of a trailer for a movie. A successful trailer doesn't comprehensively convey every plot point of a film so much as persuade folks to reach into their wallets and buy a movie ticket. Likewise, a successful proposal will make an agent think 'I can sell this' and an editor think 'I can buy this.'"

The same is true for a query. Sell your book; don't describe it.

WHY YOU?

Writers routinely skip this part. Why are you sending to Amy Boggs at the Donald Maass Literary Agency versus Jennifer at the Jennifer De Chiara Literary Agency? Amy likes fantasy, science fiction, Westerns, and historical fiction. Jennifer: spiritual self-help books, GLBTQ books, celebrity bios ("everything Hollywood," she claims), screenplays, and picture books. Amy does *not* want picture books. Jennifer does *not* want science fiction.

To pick agents' names out of a hat and submit to them is to put on a blindfold, spin in circles, and then try to hit a bulls-eye with a dart ... in a room that has no dartboard. You won't win with this reckless, unfocused strategy. Since you're then going to take the time to research each agency (or publishing house, if you're skipping the agent part, which I usually don't recommend), you might as well get credit for doing that work. It took me about eight seconds to Google a ton of info on Amy Boggs. I found out that she:

- worked on her school's literary magazine
- plagiarized Bruce Coville's *My Teacher Is an Alien* for a third-grade creative writing assignment
- is a graduate of Vassar College
- says "I don't want to sign any client just for a quick buck; I want to do business with them for the long haul."
- wants queries that make her "perk up and go 'Oh!'"
- recently sold Teddy Harrison's *Dragon Lord of New York* and Thea Harrison's *The Shadow Game*
- has an active Twitter account at @notjustanyboggs (where she refers to herself as a "sf/f nerd")

From all that I can see a half dozen ways I might show that I've bothered to read a few of the interviews she's done online and that we share interests. I might say that I'm a big fan of Bruce Coville's work, too. Or that I'm not a one-and-done author but someone looking for a long-term partnership with an agent. Or I might mention that my cousin, Ivana, graduated from Vassar six years back. Or I could reference something specific that she tweeted about.

Get the idea? Agents are people, too. They want to feel special. Yes, yes, cue the orchestra swells, but it's true. If you give them the impression that you specifically chose them, they can't help but be slightly prejudiced in your favor. That won't overcome a flawed submission, but it might be enough to push things along if you're at that 50/50 point.

If you can connect with them on some kind of personal level, it could be helpful. For instance, even if they decide to reject your submission, they might feel more inclined to provide some advice rather than give you the usual form letter. Those stinkers look a lot like this:

Dear Writer:

We read your submission(s) with care but find at this time that we are unable to offer you representation. Best of luck elsewhere.

XYZ Literary Agency

HERE'S WHAT I'M OFFERING

Now you need to deliver the BOOM. You need to sell the book idea like you've never sold anything before. Use your log line/elevator pitch right from your proposal for this part of the query letter. If you feel the need to say more than that (and you probably should), pillage your proposal's overview, though you'll have to shorten it to keep your query the right length.

Suggesting a word or page count also helps you stand out as a pro, as well as noting the specific genre (or subgenre) for the book (where it'd be shelved at a bookstore) and a "will be completed by" date (for nonfiction—your novel should be finished at this point). Use a single sentence to mention all three. Then use the rest of your "Here's what I'm offering" section to pitch that book. Think sizzle. Think highlights. Think benefits. Think: What's the #1 takeaway for readers?

It might be useful, too, to liken your book to another book or author that the recipient agent is sure to know—perhaps an author she worked with. Don't say that your book is just like the other book or, gasp, better than it. Say something like: "With the big-idea-made-simple style of Malcolm Gladwell's *The Tipping Point,* my book, *The Perfect Spouse: Proven Strategies to Create a Great Marriage,* will take Dr. John Gray's Mars/Venus concept to a new level through psychological insights, biofeedback, and herbal treatments." You get the idea. Position your book in such a way that your audience (the agent) can easily see the goals you have for it, in addition to who will read it and what editors will potentially be interested.

HIT THE GAS

Struggling to write this kick-butt copy you need to hook that agent? Read the back-cover copy from the books that are similar to yours. Mimic the style and interest-generating approach. Remember that you're not writing a complete synopsis in a query letter but rather a teaser. Give enough to make them yearn for more.

CONSIDER STRATEGY

So you have three things to communicate. How best do you go about doing so? Do you lead with an anecdote? A statistic? Should you explain the "why you?" bit first? One thing I hear again and again from agents: Don't lead with a rhetorical question, such as "Have you ever wished you knew what went on behind the curtains at the Grammys?" Instead, go with something more like "Please consider my 75,000-word nonfiction tell-all from the man who's seen every backstage secret the Grammys has had for the past two decades, from fistfights, to drunken groping, to paralysis from stage fright, to an 'unfortunate incident with a push broom'—Herman Hollywood, the production assistant, has witnessed the madness." Jeez. Now I want to read that book! Agent Jennifer De Chiara likely does, too.

For a nonfiction book, you might want to lead with your credentials. For a novel, you might want to lead with the story.

For anything else, take it on a case by case basis. But here's my strategy. Lead with the strongest of the three things. Work backwards so you end with the least important. Get in, get out, and hope you garnered enough interest for a request for more from you.

FOLLOW THE GUIDELINES

This should go without saying, but here I am saying it. If you're sending Jennifer De Chiara your book entitled *Hollywood Curves: The Story Behind Celebrity Plastic Surgery*, she specifically wants an e-mailed query (the e-mail address is right on her agency's website). In that e-mail, she wants to see a one-paragraph synopsis of the book and a one-paragraph bio. She also requires the entire proposal (including a single sample chapter) as a Word document attachment. That's all somewhat different than what other agents and editors want, but who cares? Send exactly what the agents say they want. Nothing more. Nothing less.

If you can't follow the posted guidelines that appear on an agency's website, you can't be trusted to listen to an agent's advice. No trust = no deal.

Do I need to add that you spell the agent's name correctly? Sending to an agent who has since moved on to another job is a surefire way to earn a delayed rejection. You're essentially sending it to no one. Only worse.

QUERIES VS. COVER LETTERS

A cover letter is not a query letter. A cover letter is about as simple as a letter gets. It's what you use to offer a bit of human interaction after your query letter earns you an enthusiastic "Send me the full proposal pronto!" Here's one that I made up.

[Date and Super Agent's Address]
Dear Super Agent:

Enclosed please find the full proposal for my 85,000-word nonfiction book, *Why Vampires Hate Garlic and Other Wild Facts: 101 Things You Never Knew!*, as you requested.

If you need anything more, please don't hesitate to ask.

Sincerely,
Budding Writer
[Budding Writer's full contact info]

Always mention that the material was requested, and include the full name of the project. Why? Requested material goes right onto an agent's desk. Including the full name of your project might jog their memory in case they forgot about you and your project, thanks to the zillion other moving parts that constantly clamor for an agent's full attention.

HOW DO I FIND AGENTS AND EDITORS?

Get thee to a marketplace guidebook like the Writer's Market annual *Guide to Literary Agents* or Jeff Herman's annual *Guide to Book Publishers, Editors, and Literary Agents*. (Other marketplace book options are detailed in Appendix A.) If you're attached to the computer by a digital umbilical cord, use www.publishersmarketplace.com or www.writersmarket.com and search away. A few other online sources include www.pw.org, www.agentquery.com, and www.absolutewrite.com/forums.

Another way to find good agents is to check out the websites of writers whose work is similar to yours. More than likely, they have the agent's name listed somewhere in case Steven Spielberg wants to buy the movie rights for their recent title for a billion dollars and needs to contact that agent immediately.

A third way to find agents is to ask around, starting with your writer friends. Keep in mind that asking about their experiences with agents is one thing and asking for a personal recommendation is another: It's like asking to lick the frosting on someone else's birthday cake. Don't expect a yes. To vouch for a writer by offering to make a personal connection with an agent is to put your own butt on the line. It's terribly embarrassing if it doesn't go well. And writers rarely recommend more than one person a year this way. Why should they use their one recommendation for you? Why should you expect them to? Just ask which agents they know have been receptive to new writers, which agents are easy to work with, and which ones to avoid. That's plenty of useful stuff in itself.

WAYS TO DELIVER THE PITCH

This is easy because there are only three commonly accepted ways to pitch. The first is via a written query letter. The word *query* comes from *inquiry* as in "to question." You're inquiring as to whether the publishing professional on the receiving end of your query letter is interested in seeing more of your project. This is the most common method, so we'll spend more time with this later in the chapter, including sharing examples of queries that scored big with agents and editors.

The second way to pitch? If your agent's or publisher's guidelines say they accept proposals, then that becomes your pitch. You're essentially bypassing the query stage. If the proposal is done well (and it will be if you take the advice in this book), you know that they had a real sense of what the book was before they made any type of decision. Just make sure you use a brief cover letter when you send in the proposal.

The final way to pitch? Live and in person. But you don't show up at a publisher's office or house in the Hamptons to do this. That's intimidating and a little creepy. Your best bet to have a brief face-to-face meeting with an agent or editor is to attend a writers conference (which will cost money) and sign up for a pitch session (which might or might not cost more money).

The *Writer's Digest* conferences feature a "Pitch Slam," which is where they bring in at least twenty agents or editors to meet with you in speed-dating fashion. To sell your project, you only get … wait for it … ninety seconds. But then you get ninety seconds of "unbiased, constructive feedback—and possibly, if you play your cards right, a request to see more of your work."

There are other conferences and writing boot camp–style events where editors and agents are accessible. To locate these, check out:

- www.newpages.com/writing-conferences
- www.awpwriter.org/awp_conference
- www.pw.org/conferences_and_residencies

TO PITCH SIMULTANEOUSLY OR NOT

Some books refer to sending a single proposal to more than one agent/editor as "multiple submissions," but this term is imprecise and misleading. The term "multiple submissions" really refers to the world of magazine and literary journal publication where a single writer submits multiple different things *at the same time* to the *same editor*. That's a multiple submission.

A simultaneous submission? That's when you send your thoughtfully revised, well-edited, and fully completed proposal to, say, Knopf, Random House, Norton, and Penguin all on the same day.

Is it a good idea to send to more than one agent or editor at a time? Probably. When you consider that response times are typically in months versus days, it might take years to land a perfectly viable project. Who has that kind of time? Yet if you go the simultaneous submission route, be courteous and be sure to mention in your query that you've sent a simultaneous submission. Some writers believe that the idea of someone else snapping up a winner before another agent or editor can is enough to psychologically add immediacy and value to your submission.

There have been times that I chose to send things out one at a time. For instance, when I'm so carefully targeting a specific audience that it'd be silly to move on without getting a response from that audience first. My *Memoir Writing for Dummies* book was like that—I wrote one query letter and one proposal, both geared specifically for the For Dummies line. It seemed such a natural fit that it didn't make sense to spend the time completely revamping the letter and proposal for another publisher until I'd heard from my #1 target.

SAMPLE QUERY LETTERS

If you're at all like me, you get a lot out of seeing real-world examples of things versus just reading about how stuff is done. With that in mind, here are four different successful query letters that showcase a variety of styles and strategies, which in each case began the path to book publication.

See what you can take away from each one, even if it's for a project in a completely different genre than you're planning to work in.

SAMPLE QUERY #1: Nonfiction

Christina Hamlett's *Screenwriting for Teens: The 100 Principles of Screenwriting Every Budding Writer Must Know*

Commentary: This query is short and sweet, but it packs quite a punch. Paragraph one presents a problem. Paragraph two is the solution, plus it makes mention of a foreword written by a prominent screenwriter. Paragraph three is a very effective "Why me?"

> **Dear XXXXXX:**
>
> It's no secret that teenagers comprise the largest movie-going audience in the world. Not surprisingly, many of them also have access to the tools, equipment, and resources to start writing and producing films of their own. Until now, though, the only how-to texts on the craft of screenwriting were written for adults. Until now, there wasn't a book that spoke directly to the interests, concerns, dreams, and frames of reference inherent in a high school student's world.
>
> *Screenwriting for Teens: The 100 Principles of Screenwriting Every Budding Writer Must Know* not only breaks down storytelling concepts into bite-size chapters but also provides readers with 300+ brainstorm writing exercises to get the creative juices flowing and prepare them for the realities of a film industry career. Ideal for classroom use, film camp, or individual study, the book has already been teen-tested to ensure its relevance and readability for the target market and comes with an inspiring foreword by screenwriter John Collee (*Master and Commander: The Far Side of the World*).
>
> My credits to date include 24 books, 118 stage plays for high school production, 4 optioned feature films, and screenwriting columns that appear regularly in online and trade publications

throughout the world. My reputation as an expert in developing curriculum and providing mentoring services to aspiring teen writers provides me with a substantive platform for marketing and media relations activities. Additional background can be found at www.authorhamlett.com.

I look forward to hearing from you at your earliest convenience.

Christina Hamlett

SAMPLE QUERY #2: Memoir
Lori Jakiela's *The Bridge to Take When Things Get Serious*

Commentary: I know this one well because it came to my nonprofit press. When my business partner saw it, he e-mailed me and said "Very serious query here." He was right. This query for a memoir is far more personal than most query letters, and necessarily so since a publisher really needs to get to live with the writing voice of a memoirist before making a decision. Lori offers a taste of her story here but then attaches a fifty-page sample, which is what our website guidelines recommended. The information about her other books and successful career as an educator is all icing on the cake. If the story didn't hook us, we'd still pass. We didn't pass, though.

One final addition. Can't you just sense from this letter that she's a good person? She is. And she's been one of the easiest to work with. There are too many prima donnas in the publishing world. Lori Jakiela is not one of those people who make me want to claw my eyes out every time they call with a new request, complaint, or "disaster."

> **Dear XXXX:**
>
> I hope you'll consider my memoir, *The Bridge to Take When Things Get Serious*, for possible publication with C&R's new Illumis imprint.
>
> *The Bridge to Take When Things Get Serious* is a memoir about a daughter—me—who learns that coming to terms with her difficult and terminally ill mother ultimately means coming to terms with herself.
>
> Here's a short version of my credentials and bio:
>
> My essays, op-eds, and poems have appeared in *The New York Times* (Modern Love), *Creative Nonfiction*, *Gulf*

Stream, The Washington Post, The Chicago Tribune, KGB BarLit, The Pittsburgh Tribune Review's magazines, *Pittsburgh Quarterly, 5 AM, The Pittsburgh Post-Gazette, Superstition Review,* and elsewhere. I'm the author of another memoir, *Miss New York Has Everything* (Hatchette 2006), and three poetry chapbooks. I have a full-length poetry manuscript—*Spot the Terrorist!*—scheduled for publication in April 2012.

My first memoir is out of print, though it's still available from the publisher (POD version) via Amazon and has sold just under 12,000 print copies to date, excluding e-sales. I teach in the undergraduate writing program at The University of Pittsburgh-Greensburg and in the low-residency MFA program at Chatham University. I've been nominated for a Pushcart Prize every year for the past ten years.

My newest manuscript, *The Bridge to Take When Things Get Serious,* is a contemporary, real-life version of Anna Quindlen's *One True Thing,* written in a style closer to David Sedaris. *Publishers Weekly* compared my last book to Chuck Klosterman, and Jonathan Ames called the book "wonderfully comedic, beautifully written."

I think our saddest moments can be the funniest, and our funniest are often the most tragic.

In 1999, it became clear that my mother, after her fourth heart attack, wouldn't be able to live alone. I was living in New York then, working as a flight attendant, running up credit card debt to survive. I was dating a cop I could barely stand. Almost all my dreams—being a poet, teaching college—were dead, but they were still my dreams. I didn't want to come home. I didn't want to care for my mother.

I'm an only, adopted child.

Of course I came home.

Of course I cared for my mother.

My mother, who desperately wanted me home, could barely stand me when I arrived. I was an intrusion. She was furious. She was tired of having heart attacks. She was tired of hospitals. She'd been warned to not slap her doctor, and that made her angry, too. When I finally found a job teaching college and had to leave the house, my mother spite-dragged a 25-pound ham up the stairs until she couldn't breathe. If I went out, she gorged on cheesy puffs and skipped her nightly meds. She rearranged furniture. She referred to our neighbor as her "good daughter."

This was just after my father had passed away. My mother was still grieving. I knew that. But it didn't make her any easier to be around. I was still grieving my father, too. In my more selfish moments, I grieved for my own life, whatever I'd given up, even the things I hadn't wanted.

And then, in the four years I spent as my mother's primary caregiver, everything turned. My mother survived Last Rites three times in those years. Then she got better. She got well enough to travel—senior citizen bus trips, bingo in Atlantic City. She took to wearing Ray Bans and having lunch dates and hopping yard sales on weekends. "I have my life," she said, "and you have yours."

But how does a woman approaching middle-age find a life when she's stuck in the house she grew up in, in a town she fled?

I got an apartment. I tried to be a better teacher. I did yoga and imagined being alone for the rest of my life, childless, waiting for my mother's next heart attack. I thought about getting cats. I'm allergic to cats. I missed New York until New York was all I could think about and even my cop boyfriend looked OK.

Then on accident, I fell in love and became pregnant and everything changed.

The Bridge to Take When Things Get Serious is the story of my mother's last years, and the beginning of my new life. It's the story of a woman who never wanted to be married or have a child having a child and getting married and doing all of this on her own unexpected terms.

Before my mother died, she was—happily, joyfully—a grandmother. When she left this world, I was with her in her bedroom. My husband was down the road, taking care of our son.

Being a caregiver in the United States isn't unusual—according to AARP's latest statistics, nearly 68 million people, most of them women, serve as caregivers for someone they love. But I think finding books about the experience is unusual. When I was caring for first my father, then my mother, I looked to books for help. I couldn't find many that dealt with the experience head-on. I read Simone De Beauvoir's *A Very Easy Death*. I read and watched *One True Thing*. I read Philip Roth's *Patrimony*. These books were helpful in the ways that memoirs are often helpful—they made me feel less alone; they showed me a way to go on.

This is what I'm hoping my memoir will do for readers, many of whom I imagine will be just like me—women in their thirties and forties, who have to balance their parents' lives with the demands and dreams of their own.

Platform-wise, chapters from *The Bridge to Take When Things Get Serious* have appeared in the Tribune Review company's *Caregiver* magazine, which has a distribution of 40,000 and an estimated readership of 120,000 in Western Pennsylvania.

Chapters have also been published in literary magazines and newspapers, including *KGB BarLit*, *The Washington Post*, *Tears in the Fence (U.K.)*, *Fourth River*, *Pittsburgh Quarterly*, *The Pittsburgh Post-Gazette*, *Superstition Review*, *Jenny*, *Waccamaw Review*, *Brevity*, and more.

As a freelance writer, I publish regularly in the Tribune Review company's magazines and in *The Pittsburgh Post-Gazette*. My "Here & Now" column, which ran in the Trib's *Westmoreland* magazine, received a 2010 Golden Quill award from the Pennsylvania Newspaper Association for best column writing, and a chapter from *The Bridge to Take When Things Get Serious* ("Elevens," published in *Pittsburgh Quarterly*) received an Honorable Mention for Best Writing. Another chapter, "Incisions," was just nominated for a 2011 Pushcart Prize by *Brevity* magazine.

Thanks very much for your time. The first fifty pages of the manuscript are attached. I hope you'll be interested in taking a look at my full manuscript.

Best,
Lori Jakiela

SAMPLE QUERY #3: Anthology
Ryan G. Van Cleave and Virgil Suárez's *Like Thunder: Poets Respond to Violence in America*

Commentary: This short query didn't offer much beyond a strong idea and a few possible sales avenues. The second paragraph probably helped us since it promised original material beyond the poems. When we generated some interest from this query, we constructed an eight-page proposal that listed potential contributors, defined specific subject areas the poems would cover, and created a stronger sense of audience. This book came out on January 1, 2002. Some people thought we were being tacky by trying to capitalize on

9/11. We ended up doing a last-minute change to the editors' note to talk about 9/11 and how this book was years in the making.

Dear XXXXX:

From Waco to Columbine, from Oklahoma City to Atlanta, violence in America has captured our daily imagination. Our intention is to challenge media oversimplification of this ever-increasing, disturbing social trend with an anthology that will bring together many American poets to address this issue of violence. This gathering is for those who've perished and those who've survived the ravages of violence, from domestic abuse to random shootings, from gang wars to religious fanaticism, from serial murders to acts of terrorism. A poetry that cuts to the truth. A poetry of witness. A poetry of survival. A poetry of remembrance. Contemporary poets reflect and meditate, rage and bless, as they speak out in their own voices about this growing social concern. In short, we want to put together an anthology of poetry that draws upon the sensitivity, tenderness, patience, and spirituality that point to the future of America.

Like Thunder: Poets Respond to Violence in America will be a reader-friendly anthology of no more than 250 pages, following an introduction by the editors and a preface written by a high-profile poet. Some of the poetry will be reprinted, but the majority will be solicited new work. All of the poets will also contribute a brief commentary and biographical statement to accompany their work, written expressly for this anthology.

Due to the timeliness of this topic, *Like Thunder: Poets Respond to Violence in America* can be ready for publication in the Fall of 2001. Course adoption possibilities for this anthology are extremely high as it appeals to a wide variety of curricular needs, from contemporary American literature to current issues in history, sociology, political sciences, and composition courses.

Feel free to share your comments, observations, and concerns regarding this project. We look forward to hearing from you at your earliest convenience.

Sincerely,

Ryan G. Van Cleave and Virgil Suárez

SAMPLE QUERY #4: Novel

Sarah Tregay's *Love and Leftovers*

Commentary: This particular query letter happens to be for a young adult novel, but this kind of query will work for any novel. After more than one hundred rejections for various projects, Sarah scored with this new query for a young adult verse novel with Danielle Chiotti of Upstart Crow Literary. Soon after, Sarah's new agent generated interest for *Love and Leftovers* at three publishing houses, ultimately selling it to Katherine Tegen Books, an imprint of HarperCollins.

> **Dear XXXXX:**
>
> Stuck on summer vacation in September, Marcie Foster tries to make the most of it, but ends up making a mistake so dreadful she can't even tell her best friend.
>
> It all begins when her father comes out of the closet. Marcie and her mom retreat to the family summerhouse on the coast, but Labor Day comes and they aren't going home anytime soon. Shedding a few pounds, her long hair, and her high-school Leftover reputation, Marcie starts at a new school and befriends JD, a soccer-playing jock with a Prince Harry grin. Lonely after the long summer away from home, Marcie falls into JD's arms.
>
> One problem: She has a boyfriend back home, Linus. Before she can summon the courage to dump him, her mom finds a box of condoms in her room and ships her back to Boise.
>
> Out of options, Marcie breaks Linus's heart with the truth about her actions. Her best friend, Katie, gets stuck in the middle, playing in the band with Linus, who sings mean songs about Marcie in front of the whole school. Angry, hurt, and without friends, Marcie gravitates toward a popular senior who tries to take things too far. Taking advice from her father's boyfriend, Marcie goes out of her way to be understanding. Little by little, she mends her friendships—even with Linus.

Love and Leftovers has been named a finalist in several Romance Writers of America chapter contests and placed second in the children's/young adult division of the 77th Annual *Writer's Digest* Writing Competition.

My work for younger children is published in *Stories for Children Magazine* and in *Creek Kids,* a local anthology.

May I send you my novel?

Sincerely,
Sarah Tregay

INSIDER TIP

"A quick indicator of whether I should keep reading or not is if the subject matter is to my taste or if the project is clearly a good fit for Putnam. For instance, Putnam isn't a mass-market imprint, so if what's being pitched is a mass-market kind of project, that's a fast no." — Stacey Barney, acquisitions editor for G.P. Putnam's Sons Books for Young Readers

WHAT IF THE REGULAR PITCH ROUTES FAIL?

No matter how many times writers, teachers, or how-to writing books recommend that you follow the traditional path to publication, I find more and more that one size does not fit all. Getting your project in front of publishing decision makers can be as straightforward as firing off an e-mail, sticking a letter inside an envelope and sending it off to New York, or chatting with an agent at a writers conference.

Those are fine options, sure, but there are other options you might choose to use. That's what this section is about—finding new ways to reach the right people in publishing. Some of these won't suit you or your project, but read through and be open-minded. Sometimes it takes bold action to reach your dreams. After all, it was Albert Einstein who said that insanity was "doing the same thing over and over again and expecting different results." If you're not getting the results you want despite having what you know is a solid book project, then this chapter might be the real takeaway for you.

Note: If you have an agent, don't do anything without your agent signing off on it first. Agents typically have their own way of approaching editors. However, if you're going it alone and want to snare an agent or editor with something unconventional, read on.

USE THE BACK DOOR

If the front door won't open—meaning the standard query letter and full-length proposal aren't netting results—try the back door. By that, I mean see if you can find a different mode of reaching publishing decision makers than most everyone else tries. Have someone from the mailroom hand deliver it to a decision maker on the tenth floor. If you can find the phone number for the editor and you have a gift for the verbal pitch, you can risk giving them a brief call. Or if your book is about something related to a gift, you can send that. Find any creative way you can to get your submission out of the slush pile and directly into the right person's hands.

GET CREATIVE WITH YOUR PROPOSAL "PACKAGE"

If you're looking to stand out, then *really* stand out. If you're hawking a cookbook, maybe send along a dozen of your secret-recipe red velvet cupcakes, too. If you're proposing a book on making a fortune with a metal detector, try sending along an old Spanish coin you found on the Gulf of Mexico and in your query, tell the story of how you found it and where it came from way back when.

Now don't go crazy with this. If it looks like a plain-and-simple bribe, you're toast. If it's something appropriate to your proposed book and it's not too expensive/big/ugly, you're probably okay including it if you think it might help your chances.

One final word of warning: Don't terrify the editors. There's an infamous story about how a thriller writer once sent a ticking package to a New York editor, along with a note saying something like "You have five minutes to live." Well, after the bomb squad came and everything returned to normal, it became clear that the overeager author simply wanted the editor to know what it was like for the protagonist of the story who experienced that same situation in the manuscript. Needless to say, that author did not get a book deal that day.

IGNORE THE GUIDELINES

Some writers claim that even if the guidelines say, "Submit queries only," you should send a query plus the full proposal. The theory is that it's a second chance to grab them. If the query isn't a full-blown yes, they might flip to the first page or three of the proposal and experience that hoped-for yes! The other part of this thinking is that if a query is successful, you'll be asked to send along a full book proposal. How much faster can you deliver it than have it already there in an editor's hands the moment after the query is read?

This isn't a tactic I use. If an editor requests more, 98 percent of the time they've e-mailed me to make that request. That means I can fire back whatever they require the same day. It might also be seen as pushy or annoyingly rebellious (or lazy) to just send it all at once. Yet I do run into authors at writing conferences who swear by this little secret.

MAKE THE SALE

No matter what method you try, don't forget to *make the sale.*

My father worked as a salesman for Amoco Oil (later, it became BP) for thirty-plus years, and while he regaled me with tales of his exploits of selling millions of gallons of oil and tons upon tons of wax (an oil byproduct), what stuck was this: Don't assume anything. Especially about the sale.

Take that mentality to your query letters. Go ahead and say it. "I'm eager to pursue the possibility of being represented by you." Or try something more casual, such as: "I'm a big fan of your work, [agent name]." Or really put it out there with "You're my #1 choice for a literary agent. I want you to represent me."

Another way to do this more subtly is to ask some version of the following at the end of your query letter. Never assume. Ask.

- May I send you the completed proposal along with sample chapters?
- May I send you some or all of the completed 80,000-word manuscript?
- I have the entire manuscript completed. Would you like it e-mailed or sent via regular mail?

FINAL THOUGHTS ON THE PITCH

Some writers would rather eat a box of live cockroaches than try to pitch in person or on the phone. For others, the reverse is true. Be honest about what suits you best, and then do the legwork to set yourself up for success. Pitching is just one step of a long process. Get it wrong, though, and it doesn't matter how good your proposal or manuscript is.

FINAL THOUGHTS ON RENEGADE-STYLE BOOK PITCHES

Warren Buffett—often considered the most successful financial investor of the twentieth century—often said that the best time to buy a stock was when everyone was selling. That's the mentality behind the second half of this chapter. Buck conventional wisdom. Work against trends. Don't be stymied by the thought, "Oh, this isn't how it's done." Every time I dismiss an avenue of reaching a publisher, I hear of a success story using that same method.

TOP TIPS TO REMEMBER

- There are three parts to the pitch: Why me? Why you? Here's what I'm offering.
- Model your query's book description after back-cover copy.
- Do your research to find good matches before submitting. Find ten agencies or publishers you think are a good match and rank them in order of most to least desirable.
- Follow submission guidelines to the letter.
- A no is a no whether it comes from a standard query letter or any other type of pitch.
- Unless guidelines specifically say otherwise, it's okay to simultaneously submit your queries and proposals.
- Keep a log of where you have sent query letters and how long you should wait for a response.

FOR MORE INFORMATION

Burt-Thomas, Wendy. *The Writer's Digest Guide to Query Letters*. Writer's Digest Books (2009).

See Appendix A for other helpful titles.

Chapter Eleven

NUTS AND BOLTS:
FRONT AND BACK MATTER, FORMATTING, AND MORE

After reading the previous ten chapters, you might be itching to write, write, write. Heck, you might've already written a pile of stuff because you were so excited. Either way is fine as long as you comb through this chapter before sending anything out. Why? Because this is where you learn a good deal about the vital details many writers get wrong or simply don't understand.

FORMATTING IN GENERAL

In its most basic sense, formatting refers to the margins you set on the page, the headers you use, where the page numbers go, etc. But formatting also has a lot to do with layout, or the way the thing actually looks on the page (or the screen). It matters. Take the time to artfully lay out your material so that it has a positive aesthetic quality.

Let me offer an example. After finishing up a year as writer-in-residence at George Washington University, I got the opportunity to head to Sarasota, Florida to be the creative director of a new film production company. One of our first projects was to develop a prospectus that would entice well-moneyed people to invest in our movie. We ended up spending thousands upon thousands of dollars—and countless hours—to produce a first-rate prospectus just to have a better shot of receiving funding (the movie equivalent of a book contract). Take a look at the finished product at www.ryangvancleave.com/about.html and click on "Film Company Prospectus." When we brought a full-size, bound color copy of this baby and placed one in every potential investor's hands, the effect was instantaneous. They immediately recognized that we were pros, and they started really paying attention.

But you don't need to spend thousands of dollars or dozens of hours to produce a fine-looking proposal document that will stand out from the rest. Just make smart choices about what you include, how you present it, and how well the entire package works together. Show it to people you trust, and solicit their honest feedback. Are they wowed? Where? Where aren't they wowed? Why not?

Use that information to make the presentation of your proposal as professional as everything that you wrote for it.

FORMATTING IN SPECIFIC

Let's talk hard numbers. For your entire proposal, use 1" margins all around (1.25" is fine, too). Both options give editors the space they need to handwrite notes.

Double-space everything, too, on your 8.5" × 11" white paper. And if you don't indent five spaces at the start of every new paragraph, you should be whapped in the head repeatedly with a Hillshire Farm summer sausage roll. Or at least that's the marginally effective threat I've been using on my nine-year-old for her school writing assignments.

As for fonts? Stick with something basic. I use Book Antiqua sometimes, but the main choices for editors are 12-point Times New Roman, Courier, or Garamond. All of these are very easy to read. After two decades of teaching writing, I have to confess—if students turn in a paper that uses a typeface that's smaller than 12 point, or if they use a font entitled something ridiculous like Crypt, Snowstorm, or Chalkboard, I hand it back to them. "Try again," I say. Many editors will do the same, only without the invitation to resend your work. They essentially give you an *F* and move on.

Don't staple anything. If you feel the need to yoke your pages together, use a pair of strong rubber bands or a good binder clip. No staples ever. Never. Why? If you could look at my fingers right now, you'd see a half dozen scars where I've been poked by staple prongs that weren't fully secured. One time, I bled so much on a paper on Geoffrey Chaucer I could no longer tell who wrote it.

Feel free to center headers, subheads, and titles if you want. The rest should be justified left. Don't full-justify the text to match what you see in books. That's the job of the designers once they're working on your manuscript. Until you have a signed book contract in hand, pretend the full-justify option doesn't exist. As a matter of fact, always pretend the full-justify option doesn't exist, signed book contract in hand or not.

PRODUCTION DETAILS

Every sample proposal in chapters twelve through sixteen includes information on production details—your proposal should, too. What numbers will you need to provide? Here are the main elements a publisher needs to know to work up prospective financial estimates on their end.

- **Length:** Make an educated guess of page count based on 250 words per page. If your book is already completely written, offer the word count rounded to the nearest thousand.

- **Delivery date:** Decide how long you need to write the book. Whatever you come up with, add three months because stuff happens. Trust me. If you're regularly the victim of Murphy's Law, add fourth months. If your life is best described as (a) a total train wreck, (b) hot buttered insanity, or (c) chaos on steroids with a Red Bull chaser, add five months to your estimate on how long you need to write the entire book.

- **Front matter:** If you haven't included this in your table of contents, you can put it here instead. Given a choice, I'd add this information to the table of contents so the book's size and scope is fully laid out there. I will give examples of what might be included in the front and back matter later in this chapter.

- **Back matter:** See what I recommended for front matter.

- **Illustrations and artwork:** For my *Memoir Writing for Dummies* book, I knew I needed a few simple illustrations to show how stories work. Not only did the publisher need to know that an in-house graphics person would have to create these, but extra space would need to be figured into the page count to make room for these illustrations.

- **Permissions:** Copyright law is tricky to understand so if there's any doubt that any material you're using might constitute more than "fair use" (which means you can use a tiny portion of something for free), then request a budget for permissions. This includes photographs, song lyrics, excerpts from other books, or any IP (intellectual property) owned by someone other than you.

- **Book size:** If your book requires a specific trim size (say it has to be 10" × 13" inches to accommodate crucial illustrations or graphs), mention it now. Bigger books require more resources to produce.

- **Resources needed:** If you need $1,000 to travel in order to interview three former members of a cult who are hiding in Nova Scotia, put that expenditure in there. A publisher might say, "No stinking way!" but you'll kick yourself if you don't at least ask. Other reasons to request money here might include purchasing access to special equipment, paying a VIP to write your foreword, or hiring a researcher. Some agents recommend you not including this information because a big number here might be offputting to an editor, and a very small number isn't worth quibbling over. Instead keep this figure to yourself and mentally deduct it from any advance offered to see what you're really going to earn up front on the book. If it's too low, counteroffer. Don't work for cheaper than you have to.

COVER PAGE

A proposal must include a single cover page, even if you're sending a query or cover letter along with it. It's just what the editors expect. So do it. Here's a real-life example that I used with my proposal for this book.

The Weekend Book Proposal
Every Writer's Guide
to Creating a Successful Proposal—Fast!

by

Ryan G. Van Cleave, Ph.D.

Represented by
Claire Gerus Literary Agency
Address 1
City, State, Zip
Phone: XXX-XXX-XXXX
Cell: XXX-XXX-XXXX

FRONT AND BACK MATTER

Front matter is all the stuff that can be included before page 1. Front matter material uses Roman numerals (i, ii, iii, iv, v, etc.) versus the Arabic numerals (1, 2, 3, 4, 5, etc.) that regular chapters utilize. Back matter is all the stuff that comes after the final chapter's final page. Back matter pages are also numbered in Arabic numerals.

Here are the most common possibilities for front and back matter as well as the order they should appear in your table of contents and manuscript. Don't worry, I'll explain each part in the following sections.

- Dedication
- Foreword
- Preface
- Introduction
- Chapter 1, Chapter 2, additional chapters as needed
- Afterword
- Glossary
- Acknowledgments
- Appendix
- Bibliography/reference list
- Index
- Author's biography (this could instead appear on the back flap of a hardcover's dust jacket)

DEDICATION

A dedication is the very first thing at the front of the book, right after the title page and publishing information (the page your publisher puts together that includes your publisher's information, the book's ISBN, copyright data, Library of Congress control number, etc.). It's a place where you offer public thanks. A dedication is far different than an acknowledgments page (more on that a bit later) where you thank everyone and anyone who helped along the way. A dedication is a profound, clear thank you to a profoundly important person/thing/group in your life or work.

Don't include this in your proposal beyond a mention in the table of contents if you choose. If you decide to put one in your book down the road (after you have a book contract, of course), here's what a couple look like. Note that they are generally centered and are written in *italics*.

From J.K. Rowling's *Harry Potter and the Chamber of Secrets*:

> *For Sean PF Harris, getaway driver and foul-weather friend.*

From Michael Savage's *Trickle Up Poverty: Stopping Obama's Attack on Our Borders, Economy, and Security*:

> This is dedicated to all of the men who gave their lives that we may have the freedom to write and read as we please.

FOREWORD

First, please note the spelling of this word—it's one of the most misspelled publishing lingo words there is. Please do get it correct in your proposal and your manuscript if you intend to include a foreword! I'm not even sure what a *forward*, *forword*, or *foreward* would be in terms of a book.

Now that we know how to spell it properly, what the heck is it? Simply, it's a brief section of the book located in the front pages (numbered in Roman numerals versus Arabic numerals). The foreword usually gives a sense of the book's story and what readers will get from the book (its benefits). It might focus on one chapter of the book, the whole book, or even the author's entire career. No matter how it's written, one thing always holds true about forewords—they're never anonymous and they often explain how the foreword writer knows the book author.

Not all books need forewords, which must add value to the book to be of any real use.

An especially good foreword can motivate someone to buy the book. If the writer of the foreword is famous enough, their fans might buy the book for the foreword alone. A foreword written by the right person might also help establish your credibility, as it did for my video game addiction book *Unplugged*—the foreword is written by Dr. Mark Griffiths (Professor of Gambling Studies at Nottingham Trent University and Director of the International Gaming Research Unit).

A foreword only really makes sense if it's written by someone with some clout, someone with the kind of name recognition you'd approach for a killer blurb. Blurbs are free. Forewords, in general, are not if you're getting one from a big-name person. Earmark $100 to $1,000 of your own money to pay them to write it. Publishers typically don't cover this cost, though you can certainly ask them to do so in the production details of your proposal.

Want to see a few examples of forewords?

- www.triplecrownleadership.com/foreword
- www.vrphotography.com/bookpromo.html
- www.paulmccomas.com/unforgettable

PREFACE

Unlike a foreword, a preface is written by the author and isn't signed. While plenty of authors use these two terms interchangeably, they're wrong. Don't be wrong with them.

A preface (from the Latin *praefatio*, meaning "speech before") comes after a foreword (if you have one), and it, too, is numbered in Roman numerals versus Arabic numerals. It's often the first thing a reader reads beyond the dedication, so it needs to be solid. Its function is to convince the reader that the book is worth reading. It might explain the reasons for writing the book. It might bring up some questions readers likely have about your topic, though it leaves the answers to be found within the book itself. It might reveal why you wrote the book or reveal your sources of inspiration. It might offer advice on how to read the book. It might also talk about the target audience you kept in mind while writing the book.

A preface is a fairly personal document. As such, not every book needs a preface. You might also see one called "Note to the Reader" or "Note from the Author" or something like that, but the function is still the same.

One more note regarding prefaces: They're short. Three pages max. So keep them tight, interesting, and relevant. If it turns into rambling, cut it.

Need to eyeball an example? Check out www.abookofages.com/preface.htm to see a fine one by Eric Hanson.

INTRODUCTION

An introduction is exactly that—an introduction to the rest of the book. It's located in the front and is numbered in Roman numerals versus Arabic numerals. Unlike the foreword or preface, the introduction (from the Latin *introducere*, meaning "to lead in") offers information that's essential to read in order to fully understand and appreciate the rest of the book. That's why it's the last thing included before the text. It answers the reader's unvoiced question about whether this book will be useful or not. One way to answer this question is to clearly offer the main benefit of the book (see chapter five for more on features and benefits).

An introduction is less personal than a preface, instead adhering more to the tone and style of the chapters to follow.

Many, many books have introductions. Here are a few examples from books you can likely find in your local library:

- Rachel Carson's *Silent Spring* (The 2002 edition has an introduction written by Linda Lear, who is not the author. Why didn't the author write the introduction? Carson died in 1964.)

- Thomas C. Foster's *How to Read Literature Like a Professor: A Lively and Entertaining Guide to Reading Between the Lines*

- Jennifer Homans's *Apollo's Angels: A History of Ballet* (the 2011 paperback edition)
- Janet Reitman's *Inside Scientology: The Story of America's Most Secretive Religion*

AFTERWORD

This short piece of prose—often 1,000 to 3,000 words—appears at the end of a book. Spelled *afterword* versus *afterward*, it's generally written by the author and is included in later editions of a book. What it covers is how the book was originally written, how it has affected the lives of the author and others, and how it has changed over time. Sometimes it's an opportunity for an author to share stories about how readers reacted to the book's content.

Unless your book is decidedly successful and has gone through multiple printings and editions, you don't need to worry about an afterword. If you'd like to see a good one, though, check out the newest edition of Malcolm Gladwell's *Blink: The Power of Thinking Without Thinking*. His afterword clocks in at twenty-two pages and adds stories and ideas that only came to him well after the book was in print.

Lawrence Krauss's *A Universe from Nothing: Why There Is Something Rather than Nothing* has an afterword from Richard Dawkins. The plan was for Christopher Hitchens to write a foreword, but he grew too ill to write it and eventually died. So Krauss had Dawkins write an afterword instead. It's very unusual for anyone other than the author to write an afterword unless the author is deceased.

GLOSSARY

This is just an alphabetical listing of key terms with short definitions. Since it's easier than ever to Google any terms a reader doesn't know, book glossaries are becoming less common. *The Weekend Book Proposal* originally had a twenty-page publishing glossary. As you can see, by the end of the revision and copyediting stages, that glossary shrunk to twelve pages, then to eight pages. Finally, a hard page count decision bumped it entirely out of the print edition and onto the book's website (www.theweekendbookproposal.com).

If you choose to include a glossary, make sure you're not plagiarizing the definitions. Explain them in clear, simply language in your own words. Readers will appreciate not having to slug through the ponderous definitions some dictionaries specialize in.

ACKNOWLEDGMENTS

Again and again, I hear the complaint: "I'm told to include an acknowledgment page, but I don't know what one is!" Or "I don't know how to write one!" Worry no more. Actual examples will follow a bit of explanation.

Let's start with a clear definition. An acknowledgments page appears in the very front (after the preface) or very back of your book and is your chance to publicly thank everyone who helped and encouraged you in the making of the book. It's an opportunity to express your gratitude. It's very personal, and the writing style should reflect that. Who decides where to put the acknowledgments page? Your editor, usually. If it's long (or boring), it goes in the back. It might also go in the back if there's already a ton of stuff in the front. More and more, readers want to quickly get to the first page of the book. Finding ways to reduce front-matter text is more common than ever.

This sample is from the final manuscript of my young adult book, *Unlocked*. It's short, simple, and identifies the key publishing people by name.

> **Acknowledgments**
>
> A successful book is always the product of a powerful initial vision, some careful re-envisioning and adaptation, and collaborative input from trusted sources. With that in mind, thanks to my wife for sifting through countless drafts of this book and for reminding me to "get back into the mind-set of a kid." A very special "Thank you!" is deserved by Caryn Wiseman and Mary Kole at The Andrea Brown Literary Agency—their help at a crucial point in this book's evolution was invaluable and spot on. Most of all, thanks is due to Mary Kate Castellani, who provided both the gentle support and tough-nosed editorial feedback that this book sorely needed.
>
> To the many others who helped along the way, a sincere and well-deserved "Thank you!"

When writing an acknowledgments page, don't forget the people who matter. Everyone remembers to thank their family, their friends, and their writing critique group members. But did you think about your agent? Your acquiring editor? Some of the marketing or sales people at the press? How about a researcher, an assistant, or a secretary?

I can't tell you how many times I've specifically named the people listed above to thank them for their hard work and support, only to later hear that they couldn't recall the last time an author mentioned them in a book's acknowledgments page. Wow! What an easy way to stand out and leave a great lasting impression with your important publishing partners.

INSIDER TIP

While an acknowledgments page is something you'll want to have in the manuscript you submit, pros don't send this in with their book proposal. Neither do they send in a dedication, index, or glossary. List these book parts in your table of contents if you plan to include them in the final manuscript, but save all the thanks and well-wishing for when there's something to thank them for—like turning in a manuscript that you've been contracted to write!

APPENDIX

My book has appendices, and if you're writing a nonfiction book, you might want to use them, too. These appear after the last chapter but before a glossary, index, or author biography. They're simply supplementary materials that some readers might want, but if readers skip them, they won't be missing anything dire. If it's just like its namesake, the vermiform appendix (a small tube in our bodies that we can live quite fine without, thank you very much) then why include it in your book? For the readers who *do* want that material, it can be a godsend. I recognize that a good number of my readers don't need sample syllabi; however, if you're a creative writing teacher at the high school, community college, or university level having such things might make your week.

Every additional page adds cost to the book, so include back matter only if you can justify it. To keep my book within budget, Writer's Digest Books moved the syllabi and a few other sections online to meet the page count goal."

BIBLIOGRAPHY/REFERENCE LIST

For those readers who want to know where to get more information on specific topics, you might include a bibliography or reference list. I included one for this book titled "Suggested Readings." It sounds less academic and formal than "bibliography" and "reference list" do. But no matter what you call it, some readers will see the pages of books they're "supposed" to read and roll their eyes in disgust. Include a bibliography only if your subject truly demands it. Scholarly books just about require a bibliography by definition. Most serious nonfiction ones do, too.

INDEX

This final bit of back matter is an alphabetical list of terms, names, words, or phrases of importance. Each includes specific page references so readers can readily locate the pertinent sections of the book.

This is a very tedious task. If you don't do it, however, the publisher will hire someone to do it for you. It's not cheap, and the person paid to do it might not be as familiar with your subject as you are, which means he might not do as thorough a job as you can do. So prepare to spend a long weekend making your own index after you've received the book contract, written the book, turned it in, received copyediting suggestions, made edits, turned the book back in, and then received a final typeset manuscript. At that point, the index is ready to be written.

SOME FINAL THOUGHTS ON THE NUTS AND BOLTS

Many of the things in this chapter might seem like no big deal. But the difference between a good proposal and a great one has a lot to do with getting *all* the little things right. Don't breeze through this chapter and think you're set. Confirm and reconfirm that you're working with industry standards. Use terminology correctly. Act like an insider instead of a newcomer.

TOP TIPS TO REMEMBER

- Your formatting—margins, font, and layout—must be visually appealing.
- Published writers include specific production details. Amateurs don't.
- All proposals need a cover page.
- Not every proposal needs front matter or back matter.
- Please don't misspell *foreword*. And get *afterword* correct, too (if you plan on having one).
- After you get your book contract, expect to create your own index.

FOR MORE INFORMATION

Sambuchino, Chuck. *Formatting & Submitting Your Manuscript*, 3rd Edition. Writer's Digest Books (2009).

See Appendix A for other helpful titles.

Part Two

SAMPLE
PROPOSALS

Chapter Twelve

THE NONFICTION BOOK PROPOSAL:
TWO ANNOTATED EXAMPLES

Far more than 80 percent of all nonfiction books are sold via a proposal. The truth is that you'll find more contracts made from nonfiction book proposals than all the other types of book proposals (chapters thirteen through sixteen) combined. That's both good news and bad. It's good because it means that agents buy a high volume of nonfiction books after seeing just the proposal every day. Awesome. At least you have a chance because editors are always buying books this way. It's also bad in that there's a high volume of nonfiction books being bought off proposals every day, which means it's easy for your proposal to get lost in the mix.

Carefully examine the following two successful nonfiction book proposals to see some of the ways in which you can stand out from the masses and secure that book contract. Both samples contain only certain parts of the proposal. Some are the same parts, but they're used in different ways. You might want to take ideas or techniques from the samples to customize the right proposal for you and your project.

SAMPLE NONFICTION BOOK PROPOSAL #1

Jan Cullinane's *The Single Woman's Guide to Retirement:*
Everything You Need to Know
(Wiley, 2012)

Commentary: This is one of the bigger proposals I've seen recently. It comes in at a whopping eighty-one pages (22,000+ words), so of course I'm only including a few excerpts from it. I'm excluding elements such as the About the Author section (which we discuss in chapter seven), a comprehensive sampling for praise and reviews for her previous book (we talk about endorsements in chapter nine), and the sample chapters, but this shows us the standard structure of most nonfiction proposals.

> **Outline:**
> I. Overview
> II. Target Audience
> III. Competitive Titles

IV. Marketing and Promotion
V. About the Author
VI. Reviews of current book, *The New Retirement*
VII. Chapter Outline
VIII. Sample Chapter

I. Overview

What group is 25 million strong and growing? It's single women in the United States over the age of 45.[1]

The Single Woman's Guide to Retirement: Everything You Need to Know is the only all-inclusive blueprint that covers every aspect of retirement to ensure the single woman's retirement is fulfilling, fun, and financially fit. Readers will discover:[2]

- Myths about single women and what the research really shows
- Should you retire? Answer three simple questions to know for sure.
- Where are the best places for single women to retire?
- Hot careers and how to get one, including working from home
- Meaningful ways to use your 168 hours a week (and avoid the single supplement when traveling)
- What to do if you become "suddenly single"
- How to save for retirement (or in retirement) so you can live the lifestyle you want
- Should you take Social Security early? Get long-term-care insurance? Get a reverse mortgage? Buy an annuity?
- How to deal with divorce, death, and dipping back into the (dating) pool
- Strategies to stay (or become) physically, psychologically, and spiritually healthy
- The best ways to handle boomerang kids and care for aging parents

---

1. Strong opening—editors like statistics, and this also suggests the scope of the potential audience.

2. The bulleted list here reads like the back-cover copy of the book. It seems to find multiple things that any one of those 25 million women over 45 might want to know about.

Best-selling author of *The New Retirement: The Ultimate Guide to the Rest of Your Life* and retirement expert Jan Cullinane weaves anecdotes and specific suggestions from single women throughout the book and includes the expertise of attorneys, certified financial planners, and CPAs. Technical information is presented in a nontechnical way and makes this humorous, practical, easy-to-read 350-page book more like a get-together of knowledgeable female friends sharing their specific, professional advice. Worksheets, quizzes, sidebars, and references round out *The Single Woman's Guide to Retirement* to make it the only retirement book single women will need.[3]

II. Target Audience

The general market for *The Single Woman's Guide to Retirement* is single women Boomers. If we look at Census figures, there are 2.9 million single women between the ages of 40–44; 3.2 million between 45–49; 3.0 million between 50–54; and 5.3 million between 55–64. The 14.4 million single women between the ages of 40–64 are the potential purchasers of the book.[4]

Ninety percent of women will be solely responsible for their finances at some point. Surveys (Transamerica, Hartford) find that single women feel unprepared and are concerned about retirement. The easy-to-understand writing about money and taxes that includes examples using single women will be a strong incentive for purchasing the book.

Single women are also the second largest group of homebuyers. The National Association of Realtors reports that single women are responsible for more than 20 percent of all home purchases, and they purchase one-third of all condos. These women who are purchasing homes will also purchase the book since locations specifically suited to singles are emphasized and are an important portion of the book.

---

3. Here's the page count along with a sense of the style. The phrase "get-together of knowledgeable female friends sharing" is an excellent way to communicate a light, breezy, but informative style. And in case a prospective editor thinks it's too breezy, the mention that it includes "worksheets, quizzes, sidebars, and references" answers that.

4. Look at how thorough and specific this information is. Here's an author who really knows exactly who the ideal readers are, and there are a lot of them. She's got the data to back that up.

The idea for this book originated with the many single women who approached me after my speaking engagements. They would share their concerns about where to live, fears of running out of money, not knowing what to do when they find themselves "suddenly single," and the general lack of information about single women and retirement. *The Single Woman's Guide to Retirement* will fill a big void.

Who buys books? The *2008 U.S. Book Consumer Demographics and Buying Behavior Annual Report* published by R.R. Bowker reveals that women purchase 65 percent of books; *American Demographics* states that 48 percent of book purchasing is by adults between the ages of 45–54; *USA Today* reports that households headed by someone with at least some college education and a higher than average annual income account for approximately 70 percent of book buying in the United States.[5] So these Boomer women who are educated and more affluent will buy *The Single Woman's Guide to Retirement.*[6]

III. Competitive Titles

There are no books specifically targeted to single women that address all aspects of retirement, according to Amazon. com, BarnesandNoble.com, and a general Google search. That is what makes *The Single Woman's Guide to Retirement: Everything You Need to Know* unique. There are books (I omitted self-published books or those not published in the United States) about women and reinvention, women and financial planning, women and aging, and professional women leaving their careers. None address single women and retirement in a holistic manner.

Books about women and money:

Women's Worth: Finding Your Financial Confidence. Direction$ LLC, 2010, $26.95

Peace and Plenty: Finding Your Path to Financial Security. Grand Central Publishing, 2010, $24.99

---

5. Editors know this already, but it doesn't hurt to have the statistics right there again to remind them.

6. Anything that you can do to highlight key points is useful, and **bolding** a sentence, phrase, or statistic is a fine choice.

Making the Most of Your Money Now. Simon & Schuster, 2009, $35.00

Women and Money. Spiegel & Grau, 2010, $9.99

Smart Women Finish Rich. Crown, 2002, $14.95.

Kiplinger's Money Smart Women. Kaplan Business, 2006, $15.95

Books about career women coping with the emotional aspects of retirement:

Project Renewment: The First Retirement Model for Career Women. Scribner, 2008, $20.00

Women Confronting Retirement: A Nontraditional Guide. Rutgers University Press, 2003, $22.95

Women Facing Retirement: A Time for Self-Reflection. Aslan Publishing, 2006, $16.95

Books about women and reinvention/transition/acceptance:

Inventing the Rest of Our Lives: Women in Second Adulthood. Viking Adult, 2004, $15.00

Fifty Is the New Fifty, Viking Adult, 2009, $25.95

Smart Women Don't Retire—They Break Free. Springboard Press, 2008, $24.99

Single Woman of a Certain Age. New World Library, 2009, $14.95

Books about women and aging:

The Next Fifty Years: A Guide for Women at Midlife and Beyond. Hampton Roads Publishing, 2005, $19.95

The Single Woman's Guide to Retirement: Everything You Need to Know is the first book to approach retirement and single women from the following multiple perspectives:[7]

- It recognizes the unique needs and desires of single women.

---

7. Another useful bulleted list. Check out how many strong verbs are here. "Utilizes," "recognizes," "describes." I'd have reworked a few of the last ones to find stronger verbs than "is," but that's a very minor point.

- It examines the research involving singles and retirement and analyzes and summarizes the studies to see what can be learned from them.
- It explores work and health issues, and lifelong learning opportunities, and it suggests travel and volunteer opportunities.
- It describes specific retirement locations especially good for singles, as well as how to age in place successfully.
- It lays out a blueprint for fiscal planning.
- It provides concrete suggestions for meeting others and deepening existing relationships.
- It includes stories from (real) single women.
- It is unbiased—the author does not have a financial stake in any of the suggestions. The goal is a "consumer report" approach to retirement for single women.
- It is easy to read, practical, specific, and interactive. It can be read cover to cover, or individual chapters can be accessed for specific topics. The use of subheadings, bulleted lists, quotes, and humor make it extremely reader-friendly.
- It utilizes experts in addition to the expertise of the author.
- It provides surveys, sidebars, worksheets, and references.

IV. Marketing and Promotion

Jan Cullinane is already a best-selling co-author of *The New Retirement: The Ultimate Guide to the Rest of Your Life* (Rodale), now in its second edition.[8]

Cullinane has an online presence—she is the Retirement Expert for the NABBW (National Association of Baby Boomer Women) and is a contributor to *LetLifeIn, Vibrant Nation,* and *TopRetirements.* Cullinane has a website and is on LinkedIn, Facebook, and Twitter. She frequently speaks on the (primarily) nonfinancial aspects of retirement, and would promote *The Single Woman's Guide to Retirement* through her speaking engagements. Clients include Deloitte & Touche LLP, Ameriprise Financial, Ford Motor Company,

---

8. Who doesn't want to sign an author who's already a bestseller in the same topic as the book she's pitching you?

The Federal Government, The Smithsonian, Wells Fargo Advisors, Wisdom Retirement, and RPI Media. She will aggressively promote the book through talks, radio interviews, TV appearances, and she has been quoted or interviewed in many magazines (please see "About the Author" for a list of media appearances). Thus, there is already a platform to promote *The Single Woman's Guide to Retirement.*[9]

For example, during the past twelve months, Cullinane has given talks for the high-wealth clients of Wells Fargo Advisors—twice in Cincinnati; for the ISCEBS (annual meeting in Charlotte); the MDRT (national meeting in Vancouver, BC); and talks in Chicago, King of Prussia, Parsippany, and twice in Long Island (for one of her clients, Wisdom Retirement), reaching a total of approximately 1,500 attendees.

Many financial services firms, insurance, and banking companies are now targeting women with seminars designed just for them—and many of those attendees are single women. The author will contact these companies to partner with them to promote *The Single Woman's Guide to Retirement* and discuss the nonfinancial aspects of retirement with their clients—she has already done this with firms with mixed (male and female) audiences, such as Wells Fargo Advisors and Deloitte & Touche LLP. Cullinane will also contact Internet sites that cater to single women (including single women travel sites) and home builders who are pursuing women buyers (second largest group of home purchasers) to promote/purchase the book as well. In addition, several contributors to the book have wide audiences who will publicize *The Single Woman's Guide to Retirement: Everything You Need to Know.* Cullinane has at least one client (she has signed a confidentiality agreement so cannot divulge the client) who could utilize many copies of the book. Cullinane has contacted Dr. Bella DePaulo, who has indicated a willingness to blog about the book (she's a social scientist/author/speaker/consultant and writes about "Living Single" at *Psychology Today*). Dr. DePaulo is happy to read the manuscript and consider writing a blurb,

---

9. This list of companies and clients is impressive. It's part author bio and part sales venues for this book.

as will Mark Miller (author, journalist, and blogger on The Huffington Post) and Anne Holmes ("Boomer in Chief" of the National Association of Baby Boomer Women, www.nabbw. com). Stephen Reily has offered to write a blurb as well as help publicize the book (founder and CEO of Vibrant Nation, "the leading online community for Baby Boomer Women").

National Unmarried and Single Americans Week is the third full week of September. *The Single Woman's Guide to Retirement*, which is already 80 percent complete, would be the perfect media hook for this event.[10]

Cullinane will reach out to all previous contacts—including John Dobosz of Forbes, Chuck Jaffe, Robert Powell, and Marshal Loeb of MarketWatch, and Kimberly Palmer and Emily Brandon of *U.S. News and World Report*. She'll contact all freelancers she has worked with, including Erika Rose and Meghan Streit.

All specific communities that are mentioned in the book as desirable places for single women to retire will be contacted—as with Cullinane's first book, realtors will purchase copies of the book to give to prospective home buyers/renters. In addition, the contributors of anecdotes will want to purchase copies for themselves and their friends and family. *The Single Woman's Guide to Retirement* will also be found in most libraries, as is *The New Retirement*.

New outlets for book sales would include mature women's clothing stores such as Chico's, Coldwater Creek, Talbots, and Ann Taylor, as well as gift and card shops.[11]

Cullinane also has several ideas for TV tie-ins (Retirement Living TV, for example, could do a series about single women searching for their ideal retirement location—highlighting

---

10. If you can connect your book to a specific date, time, or event, mention it. Reporters love to find new things to talk about for those, so the author is right—there's a strong media hook built in already.

11. Everyone knows you can buy books at Amazon.com and BN.com, as well as chain and indie bookstores. Where else can you buy them? If you can come up with reasonable options—as she's done here—list them. Alternative sales venues can be quite lucrative for a publisher. A book being sold at Ann Taylor, for instance, isn't competing with ten thousand other books as would be the case at a brick and mortar Barnes & Noble.

new urbanism communities, active adult communities, college towns, etc.), or a network could do an ongoing series about single women and retirement—investigating the special challenges and opportunities that *The Single Woman's Guide to Retirement* examines. She is open and willing to utilize all media to promote the book.[12]

VII. Chapter Outline

Chapter 1: The 5Ds and Retirement[13]

The demographic of the 25 million single women (never married, divorced, or widowed) over the age of forty-five is huge and growing. Cullinane attributes it to the "5Ds": divorce, death, delayed marriage, dumped (or being dumped), and just "don't want to do it" (be married). She summarizes fascinating research about single women regarding the supposed "marriage advantage," their feelings about investing and social support, independence, home buying, psychology, and behavioral economics, and how to use this information to help plan a satisfying and successful retirement. Humor, anecdotes, examples from real single women, and a reference section are included in every chapter.

- The 5Ds
- What makes single women special
- Research on single women
- Application of these studies
- Sidebars (humor/fascinating tidbits)
- *My Life* (examples/anecdotes from real single women)
- Just for Fun (a lighter view)
- 411 (reference)

Chapter 2: Do You Want to/Plan to Work in Retirement?

---

12. Okay, this is pie-in-the-sky stuff, but it shows the author is thinking outside the box and, perhaps more important, thinking big. And you never know. Maybe the publisher has connections in the TV world and has been itching to try something new out. You never know if you don't bring it up.

13. A good, informative title here. These are also very strong, clear, and useful chapter descriptions. The bulleted lists (which you can tell the author likes and uses to good advantage) help convey information quickly. I particularly like the parenthetical comments she uses near the end of the bulleted list to clarify her intentions. I'm not sure what *My Life* or 411 might be otherwise.

Cullinane invites readers to answer these three questions to help them decide if they are ready to retire: Do You Have Enough? Have You Had Enough? Do You Have Enough to Do? This chapter is for those who may want/need to continue to work; the reasons why single women are more likely to *need* to work longer (longer life span, no financial backup, less likely to have a pension, more likely to be in and out of the work force, make less than men, etc.), or why they might *want* to work (social support, intellectual stimulation, provides structure); and includes information on part-time jobs with health benefits; networking, résumé writing for the mature worker, interviewing tips, how to address gaps in employment; working from home, starting your own business, and hot career fields.

- Should you retire?
- Where the jobs are, and how to get one
- Cover letters, résumé writing, and interviewing
- Home shoring
- Sidebars
- *My Life* (examples/anecdotes from real single women)
- Just for fun (a lighter view)
- 411 (reference)

[**Note to the Reader**: This structure continues through the rest of the Chapter Outline section]

Appendix: Checklists, Surveys, and Worksheets[14]

Index

SAMPLE NONFICTION BOOK PROPOSAL #2

Jennifer Armstrong's *Mary and Lou and Rhoda and Ted: And all the Brilliant Minds Who Made* The Mary Tyler Moore Show *a Classic* (Simon & Schuster, 2013)

---

14. Even without a description of these, it's important to note where they'd appear in the text. Because they're located in an appendix, they're simply bonuses. Add-on value. Appendices are things like the bonus features on DVDs—they're not for everybody, but some people find them quite interesting or useful. If the publisher becomes concerned about production costs, appendices are nearly always the first things to go.

Commentary: Since this proposal is also too large (12,000+ words) to include in full, I'm once again only including a few pertinent sections. The About the Market section is absent here, but it appears in full in chapter four. It does contain the Book Description, About the Author, Competitive Titles, Marketing and Promotion, Production Details, the Table of Contents of the book itself, and a brief excerpt from the chapter summaries.

The author notes: "The biggest challenge with this, and with all of the proposals I write, is knowing how much to promise in the way of access to big names without over-promising. There's only so much I can get for a mere proposal, so a lot of what I do is purely on faith that I'll be able to tell the complete, and great, story with whatever interviews I get. I've been pretty lucky so far! (And I don't do this totally on faith, to be honest—I know enough from years of entertainment reporting to tell what will likely fly, and what won't, in the way of celebrity interviews.)"

She also adds that, "It's always hard to know when a proposal is done, mainly for reasons related to the above. I always want more—all the good interviews, all the exclusive information—and it's so hard to get before the book is the real deal. It gets easier the more of these sorts of books you do, but it's still hard. The bottom line is that you're looking for a proposal that tells a story and genuinely shows what you can do as a writer."

Becoming Mary Richards:

How Mary Tyler Moore *and the First Generation of Female Comedy Writers Built an Icon—and the Modern Woman*[15]

Proposal Contents[16]
About the Book[17]
About the Author
About the Market
About the Competition
About Publicity and Promotion
Production Details
Cast of Characters/Interview Targets
Table of Contents

---

15. As you can clearly see, the title changed somewhere along the way. It went from something that feels a bit textbook-like to something that is geared more for a general audience.

16. Make sure you're clear that this is the *proposal's* table of contents and not the one for the book—that comes later. It might seem like a minor point, but any potential area of confusion should be avoided.

17. I like the repetition of section structure here. It feels clear and orderly.

Chapter Summaries
Sample Material
Introduction: What It Means to Be Mary Richards
Chapter 1: Making an Icon

About the Book

Mary Richards remains *the* iconic modern TV woman. Now forty years since she first hit small screens with her sweet brand of female empowerment on *The Mary Tyler Moore Show*, she's made it after all, and then some:[18] The biggest female names in the most popular of pop culture cite her as their #1 role model, from Oprah Winfrey (who dedicated an entire episode to re-creating *The Mary Tyler Moore Show* set and reminiscing about dressing like Mary for her first TV jobs) to Tina Fey, who conceived her hit *30 Rock* as a postmodern take on the quintessential '70s comedy. Joan Jett remade the indelible theme song, "Love Is All Around," into an apt punk-rock version. Indie rockers Weezer name-checked her in their hit "Buddy Holly." The forces behind culture-shaping shows, from *Friends* to *Ally McBeal* to *Sex and the City* cite Mary as inspiration, and for good reason: She was the first female TV character to feel *real* to the women watching—because the forces who helped to shape her, many of them pioneering women writers, wove their very own lives and souls, the good and the bad, into the Mary we saw onscreen, and in the process made an impact on the future of television, and women's lives, that continues to resonate today. Mary Richards navigated the tricky early years of feminism, stronger and edgier than Marlo Thomas's *That Girl* before her, but softer and more accessible than Bea Arthur's *Maude* after, coming out on top with one unforgettable beret toss.[19]

Despite widespread perception, Mary Richards—the tremulous-but-brave, stylish heroine—was *not* the star who played her.[20] Mary Richards was a thirty-something woman

---

18. For anyone who knows the show and the theme song, this line will put a smile on your face.

19. Way to sandwich Mary between two heavy hitters, which reinforces her place in the history of important women.

20. Great observation. Things are not as they seem ... and this book will reveal it. That's a good tactic to hook a reader (and an editor).

anxious to find herself in the big city after leaving a dead-beat fiancé behind. Moore herself was a businesswoman, the producing force behind her own show as well as hits like *The Bob Newhart Show* and *Hill Street Blues*; divorced, remarried, and a mother; and, as it turned out, a nice but pretty tough broad who battled diabetes and alcoholism during the show's run. Mary Richards was *not* her creators, two veteran sitcom writers—and married fathers—named James L. Brooks and Allan Burns. She was *not*, unlike several of her supporting characters and modern cohorts, based on anyone real. (*The Mary Tyler Moore Show*'s Murray Slaughter and Lou Grant were straight from the newsroom Brooks used to work in; *Maude*'s fiercely feminist title character was based on creator Norman Lear's wife.)

So who was Mary Richards? A few parts predecessors like Marlo Thomas's character in *That Girl* and Moore's own *The Dick Van Dyke Show* character, Laura Petrie; a few parts what the network could swallow (an early plan for her to be divorced was nixed); a few parts pushing the network's boundaries (yes, she was on the pill); and, of course, at least one part beret-tossing independence.[21]

But her stories and quirks rang true only because of the women who wrote her life, week after week—women who, prior to *The Mary Tyler Moore Show*, toiled in male-dominated writers' rooms on shows such as *The Monkees* and Brooks and Burns' *Room 222*, or who were shut out of comedy altogether. Women who finally found a place where they could talk out their problems with other women and call it work, who could turn their struggles with dating and body image into plots that future Oprah Winfreys and Tina Feys tuned into, with rapt recognition, every week. That potent combination of foibles and strengths, setbacks and victories, would make the idea of women's liberation easier to swallow for not only the world, but for the men who helped make her a success; it would make liberation seem more accessible to the women

---

21. This description gives a clear sense as to how the author will contextualize Mary's life in the book. There are three ways to go with any topic: be completely neutral, flame it, or champion it. It's quite clear to me that the third option is the choice for this author.

and girls watching her every move; and it would, in a sense, help to liberate the women who wrote her.[22]

In *Becoming Mary Richards, Entertainment Weekly* senior writer Jennifer Armstrong will explore what made the woman with the famous smile into an enduring icon, leading the way for the biggest female names in entertainment today. As *Fifth Avenue, 5 A.M.* did for Holly Golightly and *Breakfast at Tiffany's*, this narrative account will take readers behind the scenes of TV's first—and most enduring—feminist icon, chronicling the struggles behind her conception and introducing the strong characters who made her what she was. *Becoming Mary Richards* will explore how a character with a penchant for crying, a fear of standing up for herself, and an unbreakable habit of calling her boss "Mr." became a feminist touchstone, thanks to the unlikely combination of forces that made her who she was. It will reveal, for the first time:[23]

- Why *The Mary Tyler Moore Show* had more female writers than any other show at the time (and the first female comedy producer ever to win an Emmy solo) and how their offscreen lives were far racier than even their boundary-pushing heroine could've ever dreamed

- How women both behind-the-scenes and in front of the cameras—including Cloris Leachman, Betty White, and Valerie Harper—had unprecedented influence on the show and went on to careers that continue today (particularly the unstoppable White)

- How Mary's best friend, Rhoda, rose to her own cult-icon status (complete with signature head scarves!)

- How the show made its gruffest cast member, Ed Asner, a proud women's libber

- And how Mary Richards influenced a generation of women, including some of the most influential names in modern pop culture, to make it on their own

---

22. So there's a promise to reveal the interconnected lives of writers and actors. Interesting.

23. Bullet lists are easy ways to make a clear argument. It's a sound tactic here.

Through new, exclusive interviews with the creators, writers, cast, and crew[24]—as well as with those whose Mary Richards–worship inspired them to become some of today's biggest comedians, writers, talk show hosts, and rock stars—*Becoming Mary Richards* will chronicle the making of an enduring icon from inside and out.

The cast of characters includes the complex Mary Tyler Moore herself and her no-nonsense husband/producing partner, Grant Tinker; Mary Richards's unassuming creators, family men Brooks and Burns; good ol' boy theme song writer Sonny Curtis; pianist-turned-pioneering comedy writer Treva Silverman; proudly feminist Valerie Harper; the network suits who objected to everything from divorce to stating Mary's age to moustaches; just-out-of-college playwright Marilyn Suzanne Miller and future best-selling author Gail Parent (*Sheila Levine Is Dead and Living in New York City*), both of whom joined the writing staff; and the script continuity woman who saved the show after a disastrous first taping.

The girls who watched from home and emulated Mary's every move included Sandra Bullock, Tina Fey, Joan Jett, Julia Louis-Dreyfus, Sarah Jessica Parker, Martha Plimpton, Oprah Winfrey, and future female writers for *Saturday Night Live* and *Sex and the City*.[25] Together, their stories paint a nuanced, complicated picture of life in the 1970s for girls and women as they realized they *could* make it on their own, even in a world barely ready to admit it.

Becoming Mary Richards will take readers from the heady offices of network powers to the living rooms where young female fans took notes on Mary Richards and plotted their fantastic futures, from the overheated studio where an audience sat stone-faced through *The Mary Tyler Moore Show*'s first run-through to the glowing parties celebrating its tremendous success. It will present the enduring TV idol as we've never seen her before, through the eyes and lives of those who made her and those who loved her.

---

24. Aha. Here we're promised new material from the key people who are best equipped to tell all. Without that access, this book would suffer.

25. Talk about influencing a generation of celebrities and stars!

About the Author

Jennifer Armstrong co-founded www.sexyFeminist.com and has covered pop culture for nine years as a senior writer at *Entertainment Weekly*.[26] She's written cover stories on *Desperate Housewives* and *Grey's Anatomy*, features about Tina Fey and Julia Louis-Dreyfus (among many others), essays about the fruitless search for the next *Sex and the City*, and analyses of the grand significance of Miley Cyrus. Her recent articles include a cover-story investigation of the state of gay teen characters on television, a behind-the-scenes report on the *Teen Mom* phenomenon, and commentary on abortion, teen sex, and rape plotlines in prime time (see links below). She also writes EW.com's feminist blog ShePop (http://pop watch.ew.com/category/misc/shepop/). On SexyFeminist, she's extolled Megan Fox's and Taylor Swift's surprising feminist qualities, questioned the idea of female writers exploiting their sex lives to get noticed, and chronicled changing her life by canceling her wedding (just one more way Mary Richards was *her* role model).

Her first book, *Why? Because We Still Like You*, a history and analysis of *The Mickey Mouse Club*, was published in hardcover by Grand Central in October 2010. (*Booklist* called it a "captivating cautionary tale" of child stardom; *Library Journal* praised its "light and deft touch" in weaving together the Mouseketeers' history.) Her second book is *The Feminist Bombshell*, co-authored with Heather Wood Rudúlph and forthcoming from Mariner Books/Houghton Mifflin Harcourt in 2013.

Before joining *EW*, she worked as a journalist for six years at various daily newspapers; she has a journalism degree with a sociology minor from Northwestern University. Her work has also appeared in *Glamour*, Details.com, Chicago's *Sun Times*, Salon.com, and The Huffington Post (www.huffington-post.com/jennifer-armstrong), as well as in two anthologies, *Altared: Bridezillas, Bewilderment, Big Love, Breakups, and*

---

26. The author could essentially stop right here and have more than enough clout to write this book. The rest reinforces what we already know—she's capable of writing this book and she's passionate about the subject. Both are great things for an editor to believe.

What Women Really Think About Contemporary Weddings (*Vintage, 2007*) and *Coffee at Luke's: The Ultimate Gilmore Girls Gabfest* (BenBella, 2007). She lives in Park Slope, Brooklyn, and is the lead singer of the all-woman '90s-homage band No Ambition.[27]

Select Bylines[28]

"Gay Teens on TV," *Entertainment Weekly*, January 28, 2011 (pdf): http://www.box.net/shared/1zk232t53c

"Teen Mom: How It Became the Most Addictive (And Important) Reality Show on TV)," *Entertainment Weekly*, October 1, 2010 (pdf): http://www.box.net/shared/fqlabxjhuk

"'Glee' goes provocative for 'GQ' and we ask: Ugh, why?" EW.com, October 19, 2010: http://popwatch.ew.com/2010/10/19/glee-goes-provocative-for-gq-and-we-ask-ugh-why/

"Debbie Gibson Wishes and Rockstar Dreams," SexyFeminist.com, January 23, 2011: http://sexyfeminist.com/2011/01/23/debbie-gibson-wishes-and-rockstar-dreams/

"The Search for the Next Sex and the City," *Entertainment Weekly*, February 15, 2008 (pdf): http://www.box.net/shared/static/ta3as5br8r.pdf

"Entertainer of the Year: Tina Fey," *Entertainment Weekly*, Nov. 21, 2008 (pdf): http://www.box.net/shared/5hf2bdie9z

About the Competition
Recent books similar in nature include:

Fifth Avenue, 5 A.M.: Audrey Hepburn, Breakfast at Tiffany's, and the Dawn of the Modern American Woman by Sam Wasson, HarperStudio, 2010, $19.99hc, 231 pages. Wasson chronicles the making of a major female icon who still has an impact on today's women and culture, Audrey Hepburn, just as *Becoming Mary Richards* will do for Mary Tyler Moore. The narrative structure reads almost like a novel and brings behind-the-scenes characters to light, which

---

27. Great final personal detail. And nice band name, too!

28. It's always a smart play to include a few—not every last one, but a select few—links to work you've done. This is especially smart if the stories are relevant to the book you're pitching.

Becoming Mary Richards will also do, simply tackling a different era, the 1970s, and focusing even more on how women
helped to shape their own generation's feminist icon.[29]

*Easy Riders, Raging Bulls: How the Sex-Drugs-and-Rock 'n'
Roll Generation Saved Hollywood* by Peter Biskind, Simon &
Schuster, 1998, $25hc, 512 pages.
This blockbuster book reveals the riveting behind-the-scenes
antics of the 1970s film industry—when auteurs like Martin
Scorsese, Dennis Hopper, Francis Ford Coppola, and Steven
Spielberg rose to power on a new director-centric system, a
gritty aesthetic, and an ultra-artistic bent. *Becoming Mary
Richards* will pull the curtain back on the TV industry of the
same era, which was going through its own unique metamor-
phosis, with a focus on the women who were getting their shot
at writing for TV for the first time. It will plumb the same
rich time in pop cultural history that fascinated so many in
Easy Riders, Raging Bulls, which also became an acclaimed
documentary of the same name. And it will similarly illuminate some of TV's most influential players at the time, with a
comprehensive list of fresh, revealing interviews.

*Live from New York: An Uncensored History of Saturday Night
Live* by Tom Shales and James Andrew Miller, Back Bay Books,
2002, $40hc, 566 pages.
A look at another child of the '70s—*Saturday Night Live*—
mesmerized readers, becoming a national bestseller as well.
Becoming Mary Richards will also take an uncensored look at
the shifting TV landscape of the Vietnam era but will focus
on the even more pervasive landscape of prime time and specifically this one influential comedy's long-reaching effects
on its audience and the culture at large.

*Pictures at a Revolution: Five Movies and the Birth of the New
Hollywood* by Mark Harris, Penguin Press, 2008, $27.95hc,
496 pages.
Harris guides readers through the late-'60s films that were
the precursors to those documented by *Easy Riders, Raging
Bulls*. Through the stories behind such landmark movies as

---

29. Notice how she provides an A/B conversation. The A part is pointing out what the other
book is up to, and the B part is what she'll do and why the B part is needed/better/necessary.

The Graduate and *Bonnie and Clyde,* he describes the seeds of bigger changes to come. This bestseller offers further proof of the public's endless fascination with that tumultuous time in our history and backstage stories of the era.[30]

About Publicity and Promotion
The author can help to promote *Becoming Mary Richards* in several ways, with two major demographics as focal targets: pop culture fanatics[31] eager to see how an icon is made from the very beginning, and women of all ages who idolize Mary Richards or her many pop cultural descendants, from Oprah to the ladies of *Sex and the City.*

Print/Online Media
Hundreds of websites and publications cover pop culture. *Becoming Mary Richards* can target two subsets: those dedicated to women's issues and those that cover mass entertainment. The major players include: Slate's XX blog and podcast, which analyze all things feminist; Feminist. com, a grassroots, user-generated community for feminists; Feministe.us, a longtime, traditional feminist blog; Feministing.com, the brainchild of *Full Frontal Feminism* author Jessica Valenti; Bitch.com and pop culture mag *Bitch*; BlogHer, the largest online collective of women's blogs; Bust.com, *Bust* magazine, and its Girl Wide Web network; MsMagazine.com and the original feminist magazine itself, *Ms.*; Jezebel.com, the irreverent female offshoot of Gawker; iVillage, the Web's largest women's site; EW.com; People.com; *USA Today*'s Pop Candy; PopCrunch; TVGuide.com; Fancast; and TVLine; among many others.

Hundreds more websites and magazines address general women's interests, including major players such as *Glamour, Marie Claire, Cosmopolitan, Allure,* and *Elle.* They're also prime targets. The author's own SexyFeminist.com has cultivated a loyal base of 11,000 users per month[32] and has been cited by prominent outlets such as The Huffington Post, AlterNet,

---

30. It's great when there are bestsellers in your topic area. Point those out!
31. This one seems less clear and smaller in size than the next demographic.
32. The specificity of numbers here is convincing.

Arts & Letters Daily, Bookforum, and Bust. (Armstrong and SexyFeminist partner Heather Wood Rudúlph were named "women in media to watch in 2011" by media blogger Scott Bryant, and the site was named one of the five best feminist blogs by Loosefemme.) In addition to promoting the book on her own site, the author can also pitch and write articles and/or guest blogs for other sites (such as those cited above).

Armstrong has personal connections at several websites and magazines that would be a great fit for *Becoming Mary Richards*, including:[33]

- Josh Wolk, entertainment editor at *New York Magazine*
- Bill McCleary, producer at Premiere Radio
- Margaret Aro, producer at *Good Morning, America*
- Erin Carlson, editor of Yahoo's The Famous blog
- David Blaustein, entertainment reporter on ABC Radio
- Kim Potts, blogger at TVSquad
- Heather Wood Rudúlph, L.A. editor at AOL
- Michael Slezak, senior editor at *TVLine*
- Alynda Wheat, critic at *People*
- Anna Davies, editor at *Cosmopolitan*
- Brian Gianelli, senior editor at *Fancast*

Broadcast Media

Media appearances on shows that focus on similar topics would reach even more potential readers. Daytime talk shows would help speak directly to female audiences, including *The View*, *Ellen*, and shows on the Oprah Winfrey Network. Morning news and cable shows would also provide the perfect forum for discussing *The Mary Tyler Moore Show*'s continuing resonance and perhaps interviewing some of the cast and crew who appear in the book; other key outlets are the TVLand network and Hulu, which could provide partnership opportunities for marathon viewing and discussions. Armstrong has contacts at *The Today Show, Good Morning, America, The View*, ABC Radio, and Headline News. She has also provided

---

33. Note that she's not promising to land blurbs from all of these connections, but if she has a relationship with each of them, she'll get a half-dozen for sure.

expert on-air commentary about pop culture to the likes of *The Today Show*, NPR, CNN, VH1, Headline News, MSNBC, and ABC. Recent appearances have included:[34]

Fox Good Day NY, 8/27/09: discussing Emmy predictions.

WNYC Radio, "The Takeaway," 2/11/10: talking about the Super Bowl being the most watched of all time.

HLN Prime News, 2/17/10: discussing the controversy surrounding *Family Guy*'s mocking of Sarah Palin's son for having Downs Syndrome.

HLN Showbiz Tonight, 4/7/10: discussing Tina Fey's return to SNL and the ratings battle between *Dancing with the Stars* and *American Idol*.

EXTRA, 4/13/10: discussing Conan O'Brien's new show on TBS.

CNN Showbiz Tonight, 5/27/10: discussing *American Idol*.

CBS Early Show, 7/13/10: analyzing Miley Cyrus and what her leaving *Hannah Montana* means for her career.

Showbiz Tonight, 8/3/10: talking about the latest *American Idol* news. (http://edition.cnn.com/TRANSCRIPTS/1004/07/sbt.01.html)

The Insider, 9/8/10: talking about reality TV.

Extra, 9/9/10: talking about the new season of *Grey's Anatomy*.

And many others

Social Media
As noted, the author runs a blog, www.SexyFeminist.com, as well as her own site, www.JenniferMArmstrong.com, and will use both to promote *Becoming Mary Richards*. She will also use her Twitter stream, and SexyFeminist's, to promote the

---

34. Way to give evidence of the author's media connections and presence.

book along with the website. Together, those streams' account for approximately 1,200 followers, including:[35]

- Feminist blogger for the SF Gate Margot Magowan
- Best-selling author Karen Quinn
- RoleReboot, a blog about changing gender roles
- International Women's Day
- The Women's Museum
- Dozens of TV bloggers and pop culture geeks
- Author and blogger Jami Attenberg
- PrettyYoungProfessional.com
- Wayne Hurlbert, host of BlogTalkRadio
- Matt Mitovich, editor-at-large, *TVLine*
- Women's Power Hub

Speaking Engagements/Personal Appearances
Author Jennifer Armstrong can organize her own readings, seminars, and panel discussions about Mary Richards' continuing influence on modern women, pop culture, and television.

Production Details
Length: 80,000 words
Delivery date: Late Summer 2012
Photos: Eight- or sixteen-page color photo insert with archival and behind-the-scenes photos of cast and crew (budget: $5,000 for photo rights)[36]

Table of Contents[37]
Introduction: What It Means to Be Mary Richards **[Included]**

---

35. While the number of followers isn't that impressive, the names of who do follow are quite impressive. Great way to turn a negative (or maybe something neutral) into a positive!

36. With a book like this, photos are critical. People who want behind-the-scenes stuff want to see behind-the-scenes stuff. Always do a little legwork to make sure you're asking for the right amount of money for things like this. Whatever number you ultimately settle on, add 25 percent just to be safe. Odds are, the editor will not give you the full amount asked for, so ask higher than you need.

37. This is a very short table of contents, but since the chapter summaries are so thorough, this can afford to be. It's also broken into four parts that feel organic and structured. Too many nonfiction books feel like the chapters could go in any order. I sense purpose here, which is a very good thing.

PART ONE: THE BEGINNING
Chapter One: Making an Icon [**Included**]
Chapter Two: That Girl Before Mary

PART TWO: THE INFLUENCE AND THE INFLUENCED
Chapter Three: "It Was Wonderful to Have Company, to Be Able to Talk About Women Things"
Chapter Four: Unmarried and Unworried
Chapter Five: The Workplace Family
Chapter Six: People Were Screwing Around
Chapter Seven: The Beret Was Just the Beginning

PART THREE: TV'S OTHER WOMEN
Chapter Eight: Who Could Turn the World on with Her Controversy?
Chapter Nine: The Other Ladies Make It, Part 1
Chapter Ten: New York, This Is Your Last Chance
Chapter Eleven: The Other Ladies Make It, Part 2

PART FOUR: THE LEGACY
Chapter Twelve: The Group Hug
Chapter Thirteen: Love Is All Around

Chapter Summaries

INTRODUCTION: WHAT IT MEANS TO BE MARY RICHARDS
Any modern woman who's made it after all owes a debt to Mary Richards. We can date around without settling down, realize our professional dreams, show our vulnerabilities, and toss our hats in the air to celebrate it all—while still being considered "good" girls—because of this reluctant feminist icon. A brief overview of Mary's key traits and lasting effects on modern women.

PART ONE: THE BEGINNING[38]

CHAPTER ONE: MAKING AN ICON
Here, we look at the major ingredients that went into the future Mary Richards. Mary Tyler Moore herself, known best then as the ingénue wife Laura Petrie on *The Dick*

---

38. Even if you don't put anything else down here, always mark the section breaks.

Van Dyke Show, had been struggling to find her place in Hollywood since that hit ended; she'd just divorced her first husband and married TV executive Grant Tinker, who was determined to get his wife a hit show of her own. Writer-producers James L. Brooks and Allan Burns were working on the acclaimed but low-rated high school drama *Room 222* when Tinker came to them with a hush-hush plan to develop a vehicle for Moore. Dedicated to maintaining their artistic integrity, they came up with the idea for her to play a thirty-something divorcée. CBS network suits, however, wanted more of a Doris Day or Lucille Ball vibe. Thus Mary became a woman who'd left a noncommittal boyfriend to start over. Southern singer-songwriter Sonny Curtis came along with a pitch-perfect theme that asked, "How will you make it on your own?"—and the Mary Richards we'd come to know was captured in song. All she needed was a beret.

CHAPTER TWO: THAT GIRL BEFORE MARY
A flashback to *That Girl*, the single-girl show before *The Mary Tyler Moore Show*, starring the similarly sweet, dark-haired, petite, well-dressed Marlo Thomas. This chapter explores a brief history of that 1966–1971 show, which followed a similar path: It was developed by writers from *The Dick Van Dyke Show*, though Thomas herself created the character through her Daisy Productions, and she insisted on ending the series with her character engaged, but not married—her attempt to draw the line and express some feminist principles. (Yes, this was considered progress then.) So why didn't poor Ann Marie become a lasting feminist icon?[39]

PART TWO: THE INFLUENCE AND THE INFLUENCED

CHAPTER THREE: "IT WAS WONDERFUL TO HAVE COMPANY, TO BE ABLE TO TALK ABOUT WOMEN THINGS"
What happens when a group of mostly male producers decides to create a show about a single lady? They have to hire female writers. Or at least Brooks and Burns, sticklers

---

39. Ending a chapter and a section with a question mark is clever. It's a challenge to deliver nonfiction data in a way that keeps people hooked. Finding ways to use the techniques of good storytelling can help you combat data dump.

for authenticity, did. "In fact, it was quite a major thing that *The Mary Tyler Moore Show* would hire so many women writers," Treva Silverman says. "Jim and Allan were not only open to it, but really looking to see if they could break the stupid prejudice that, 'Oh, women aren't funny.'" The result? The most female comedy writing staff of its time, stocked full of fearless, fabulous single women. We meet them, the female CBS executive who put her job on the line to save the show, and even a female director or two. We also hear from the future pop cultural forces who were watching at the time as girls and young women: Tina Fey, Julia Louis-Dreyfus, and female writers from *Saturday Night Live* and *Sex and the City* reflect on their girlhoods in the 1970s, how the show fit into their lives, and why watching a show about a woman written by funny women helped them become who they are today.

[**Note to the Reader**: This structure will continue through the next four chapters about fashion, singlehood, sex, and the workplace.]

Chapter Thirteen

THE NOVEL PROPOSAL:
TWO ANNOTATED EXAMPLES

One reminder: We covered query letters, the standard initial step when presenting novels to agents and editors, in chapter ten, with numerous examples that illustrate how to create a strong one. The following examples expand those queries into a full book proposal for a novel using many of the same techniques you would for a nonfiction book.

Now, with a nonfiction book proposal, editors feel that if they see a well-written chapter or two of your book, you can probably knock out every chapter with roughly that same level of quality. But for novels, it's easy to start strong and then peter out thanks to plot issues, weak handling of narrative elements, and just an overall lack of control with the story. This is why your novel must be finished before you send your proposal. In fact, agents aren't likely to take you on if it isn't, much less the editors they contact. Editors are far less comfortable buying an unfinished novel after seeing a proposal despite a very strong sample, a great synopsis, and a clear, thoughtful chapter-by-chapter outline. Once you impress them with your query and/or proposal, they'll want to see the whole book right away to make sure you can deliver on your intriguing promises.

However, if you get successful enough or have an especially unique and wide-reaching platform, publishers and agents will learn to trust you to the point that you can do a shortened pitch for your next book or a series, or even less. Brad Meltzer pitches his new book ideas verbally. Julianna Baggott writes her agent a very personal note/letter about a new project. In 1940, renowned actor W.C. Fields sold a scribbled plot idea on a cocktail napkin to a movie studio for $25,000 (the movie was *Never Give a Sucker an Even Break*). But these are best-selling, top-tier authors.

Get yourself a strong track record, and you can play by your own rules, too.

Novel book proposals really shine when you're trying to land a multibook contract for a series. If you're writing *The Hobbit* and you know there's *The Fellowship of the Ring*, *The Two Towers*, and *The Return of the King* all coming, then it makes sense to pitch the trilogy plus prequel novel all at once. Many young adult series are sold this way (think *The 39 Clues*, the Halo books, or The Mortal Instruments series). So, too, are lots of genre book series.

Gina Holmes's *Crossing Oceans*
(Tyndale House, 2010)

Commentary: Here's a proposal for a novel sent *before* it was written—a rare bird, but they're out there, and it's much easier to pull off if you already have an agent. From the author: "It's always an issue that my synopsis deviates from my proposal. I'm a seat-of-the-pantser, so rarely do my books bear much of a resemblance to what I've proposed. The beauty of selling *Crossing Oceans* before it was written was that my editor and I could talk about where I wanted it to go. If I would have written it entirely before selling, I might have given it a happy Hollywood ending thinking that's what the publisher would want. Thankfully, I was wrong. There was some rewriting in the editorial stage, but not much on this book.

"In other books, I've had to go back and do major rewrites because the book barely resembled what I'd promised at all and had gotten off course along the way. That's no fun.

"The biggest challenge in putting together the proposal was getting the numbers right in the marketing section. I had a large platform with Novel Rocket, but with so many ways and avenues people could subscribe or read us, getting accurate numbers for the marketing department was a challenge. We finally had to go to a website/SEO expert. Another challenge is always comparing your book to someone else's. I was told to choose books that were successful, but not overly successful, but still bore similarities to my own writing. I think that took more time than any other piece of the proposal."

Title: *Crossing Oceans*[1]

Byline: Gina Holmes

Copy line: Sometimes love demands the impossible.[2]

Content: After a five-year absence, Genevieve Lucas is coming home to face the ghosts of her past. She intended to keep her five-year-old daughter a secret from the child's father, but being given a prognosis of less than a year to live has a way of changing a person's plans.

---

1. I left the book title and the author name in the original font. Making something larger and using a different typeface makes things stand out. These are two important things to draw attention to.

2. Here's something you don't see in most proposals, but it's a nice touch. It's like that tag-line phrase you see on a movie poster.

Audience: Women, eighteen to eighty. This book will appeal to fans of Nicholas Sparks, Karen Kingsbury, and Charles Martin.[3]

CATEGORY: Contemporary Women's Fiction[4]

SPIRITUAL TAKEAWAY: Readers will be reminded that sacrifice is always required in the Christian walk and that while we all have our cross to carry, we do not bear it alone.[5]

COMPARATIVE TITLES: One comparison for *Crossing Oceans* is Nicholas Sparks's *Rescue*. Like *Rescue* and Sparks's other novels, *Crossing Oceans* is a fateful love story featuring unforgettable characters battling insurmountable odds for a love that won't be denied.

Another comparison is Karen Kingsbury's *Even Now*. Both novels address difficult social issues in a hopeful way, while maintaining a strong thread of romance. In contrast, *Crossing Oceans'* most important love story is between mother and daughter. This novel is written from a Biblical worldview.[6]

Author Bio: GINA HOLMES is founder of the popular fiction site Novel Rocket, featuring interviews with the gamut of best-selling authors such as Dean Koontz, Geraldine Brooks, and Nicholas Sparks.[7] Novel Rocket is regularly named one of *Writer's Digest* Best Websites for Writers and is featured daily on MySpace News. Gina is a registered nurse, mother, novelist, and freelance writer who has contributed to publications such as *Epiphany* and *The Roanoker* magazines. Originally from New Jersey, Gina now makes her home in Southern Virginia where she's learned to forego bagels for biscuits and "yo's" for "y'alls."[8]

---

3. It's a bit bold to compare a first novel to these authors. However, this book and the author's subsequent next two all did quite well (check out the impressive Amazon reviews).

4. A very nice thing to include for novel proposals.

5. Since this book is being presented to Christian publishing houses like Tyndale, mentioning this overarching spiritual theme is a very savvy idea.

6. The author does a very nice job justifying the comparisons to successful authors.

7. This is huge. It means she has access to top-tier authors who might well offer blurbs or other types of support. This is a big asset to her platform.

8. She's funny. It's a nice touch to deliver a small sense of the author's personality like this.

Represented by: Chip MacGregor, MacGregor Literary[9]

Manuscript: 80,000 words to be completed four months after contract signing.[10]

Here's what others are saying about Ms. Holmes's writing ...[11]

"Gina Holmes brings a fresh voice to fiction. In the end, her work shows that faith cannot be extinguished. Ms. Holmes has done us a great favor by sharing her imagination." — Alton Gansky, author of *Angel* and *Zero G.*

"Gina Holmes has an amazing ability to pick the perfect word, the exact turn of phrase, to rise above mundane storytelling and instead pique the interest of fiction fans. This isn't just another novelist, this is the novelist that readers will latch on to and yearn for each new book." — Rebeca Seitz, President of Glass Road PR and author of The Sisters Ink series.

"Gina Holmes has a great story sense, a writing-voice that zings, and a real dedication to the craft." — Kathryn Mackel, author of *The Hidden* and *The Departed.*

"Gina's characters are likable and believable, interacting in tension-filled scenes. Her writing is economic and effective. She has obvious talent!" — Eric Wilson, author of *A Shred of Truth* and *Facing the Giants.*

"Like a skilled musician, Gina Holmes tunes her stories, polishing and refining until each word pulsates with exquisite harmony. Interspersed are moments of heart-pounding drama that leave the reader gasping for breath and ripping back the page, desperate for more. She's one to watch." — Elizabeth Ludwig, freelance editor and author of *Where the Truth Lies.*

---

9. A must-include if you have agency representation. Realistically, the agent is sending this proposal on via e-mail or snail mail, so the recipient has a way to respond. But including contact info here, too, wouldn't be the worst idea.

10. The word count is spot-on for contemporary women's fiction, and the time line is clear enough.

11. General endorsements about one's writing like this could be for short stories, previous books, or any other type of writing that impresses someone. Note, too, how most of these authors work in a similar vein as this proposed Christian book.

MARKETING CHANNELS & SPECIAL MARKETS CONSIDERATIONS: Gina Holmes has a ready-made readership/platform due to the success and notoriety of her site, Novel Rocket, which averages twenty thousand visitors monthly of those interested in Christian worldview fiction. In addition, Novel Rocket's posts are published daily on MySpace News. MySpace is frequented by tens of millions regularly. Novel Rocket was recently named one of *Writer's Digest's* best websites for writers. She will promote her work through Novel Rocket, as well as her review site, Novel Reviews.

Ms. Holmes has helped promote the work of hundreds of CBA and ABA novelists and will solicit promotional assistance by the same authors through their newsletters, blogs, and websites. She is part of an ever-growing Internet network, including the Christian Fiction Blog Alliance, Title Trakk, and others who will be open to promoting a friend.

Ms. Holmes has a relationship with many in the industry and is able to approach the most well-known authors for possible endorsement, including some who frequent *The New York Times* bestseller's list.

As a Registered Nurse, Ms. Holmes is part of an enormous community of health care providers, many of whom are avid readers. As one of their own, Ms. Holmes has a unique opportunity to appeal to book buyers in this market. She will aggressively publicize herself in their many trade magazines through articles and interviews she solicits and/or writes.

Gina Holmes is a recognized book reviewer for Novel Reviews and Amazon. Her endorsements appear on book jackets and publisher websites. Being a reviewer herself, she has a relationship with many critics and their given outlets (including *The Romantic Times, Christian Fiction Review*, and many others) and will use her connections to procure reviews for her own work.

Gina Holmes is a gifted speaker and teacher. She will solicit speaking/teaching engagements on the subjects of running a successful writer's blog, the ins and outs of interviewing, and the journey to publication, with the English departments at the following colleges surrounding her home: Liberty University, Roanoke College, Virginia Tech, Virginia Western, and Hollins University, as well as writing groups both in her area and online. She has already been invited back to teach at the Blue Ridge Mountain Christian Writers Conference and to local writers groups.

Author will write articles that promote her work in the publications of the many organizations she is a member of, whose readers reach into the tens of thousands, including her college alumni magazine, *The Roanoker*, VA Association of Nurses newsletter, Christian Missionary Alliance, and others.

Ms. Holmes will actively seek booksigning engagements regularly.

Shoe Studios has agreed to donate professional film scoring for a movie trailer for her website, www.ginaholmes.com. Gina also maintains personal blogs on ShoutLife and Blogger, which get significant traffic.

Author is an active member of ACFW and will promote her work through the organization and through their popular book club.

Author will solicit online writers and fiction readers groups, providing a link through her website offering speakerphone author chats to libraries and book clubs.

Author will send out monthly newsletters and have promotional contests to gain new subscribers. She has already had numerous requests for her books through her blog and an extensive mailing and e-mail list of potential readers.

Sometimes love demands the impossible.[12]

After a five-year absence, GENEVIEVE LUCAS is coming home to face the ghosts of her past. She intended to keep her five-year-old daughter, ISABELLA, a secret from the child's

---

12. Here's that "copy line" she used at the top. It's a reminder about the overarching theme of this story.

father, but being given a prognosis of less than a year to live has a way of changing a person's plans.[13]

She returns to the sleepy Carolina town she ran from, hoping to find forgiveness and settle her daughter's future.[14]

When Genevieve returns to her childhood home, she learns that her dad and Isabella's father aren't the only two men she must face. Her oxygen-tank toting grandmother informs her that an old high school crush is now renting the apartment over the family saddle-barn. CRAIG'S admiration of her is strong as ever. But knowing how short her time is, Genevieve refuses to water the seed of a love she won't live long enough to see bloom.

Genevieve's father is enraged when he learns that he shares a grandchild with the man who not only misdiagnosed his late wife's cancer but arrogantly continues to deny the mistake. He goes to the doctor's house to once again confront him about his wrongdoing, this time also dropping the bomb of Isabella's existence. When Genevieve learns what her father has done, she's furious. Doctor Preston's son, DAVID, didn't know he was a father. She never told him.

She promptly tracks David down and is met with a combination of anger and indifference. Though she is sad for her daughter, she's relieved that her choice has been made for her. Isabella will be raised by Genevieve's father and grandmother.

Just when she thinks she's got it all figured out, Genevieve gets a visit from David's wife, LINDSEY, who reveals her desire to have children and the painful four miscarriages she's undergone. Though Genevieve doesn't want to like her, she finds her defenses melting, until the woman questions David's paternity. David shows up and chastises Genevieve for not telling him about the pregnancy, then hints he too is not convinced he's the father. Genevieve is angry and hurt beyond words. It was one thing for Lindsey to imply she slept

---

13. Interesting. She's using the movie script technique of putting a character's name in CAPS the first time it's used. If it's good enough for Hollywood, it's good enough for me.

14. Note how the language is clear and simple. It's also written in present tense to give it immediacy. The actual book, though, is first person and written in past tense.

around, quite another for David to do it. He knew the kind of girl she was. She tries to close the door on them when Isabella blocks her path. Two gasps follow, and she knows David's paternity will never be questioned again. The little girl is her father's spitting image.

The next day David calls begging to see his daughter. Genevieve wants to hurt him the way he hurt her. Instead, she looks into the eyes of her daughter and remembers how much this little girl has longed for a father. She asks her if she'd like to spend the afternoon at David's house, and Isabella squeals in delight.

Genevieve receives a frantic call several hours into their visit. Isabella is hysterical. Genevieve discovers that David tried to help the little girl conquer her fear of water by throwing her in the pool. His defense was that was the way he'd learned. Genevieve is furious. Isabella had almost drowned the week before and was now terrified even to take a bath. Fearing for her daughter's future with David, she decides he can have visitation but is not the right man to raise her.

Genevieve meets with David and Lindsey to tell them about her diagnosis and decision. She leaves with Lindsey in tears and David consoling his wife, seemingly unconcerned Genevieve is dying.

Soon afterwards, Genevieve is met with custody papers. David and Lindsey are suing for full custody of Isabella. Genevieve intends to fight them until they gather in the courthouse vestibule and Isabella runs from her to David and Lindsey. Genevieve's heart aches as she watches her daughter laugh at David's jokes as Lindsey lovingly pats her hair.

She realizes then that the child deserves a family and just because David didn't love her, doesn't mean he won't love their daughter. He seems to adore her. She meets with the Prestons and tells them of her decision to give them full custody. They're willing to wait until she passes, but she tells them now would be better. She doesn't want Isabella to have to watch her suffer like she had to watch her own mother.

Genevieve takes Isabella to the ocean to explain her imminent death and their parting. She points across the water and asks if she can see the other side. Isabella says no. Genevieve tells her that she is going to cross the ocean soon but not to cry because someday they'll be together forever when it's Isabella's time to cross. For now she must live with her father and Lindsey.

The night before the custody transfer, Craig's scream wakes the house. Genevieve runs outside to find him cradling a lifeless, sopping Isabella. He explains he heard her yelling for help and pulled her from the lake moments after he saw her go under.

Isabella is hospitalized in the ICU with a ventilator breathing for her and tubes everywhere. While the family gathers around the child keeping constant vigil, Genevieve's father watches Doctor Preston risk his career to get their grandchild the best doctors and care. An olive branch is extended and accepted between the two men.

Doctor Preston convinces Isabella's medical team that taking her off the coma-inducing medication and removing her from the ventilator is her best chance for a full recovery. Unsure of the right thing to do, Genevieve's father convinces her to trust Doctor Preston.

Once she is taken off life support, Isabella's breaths are sporadic and few. Just when the doctors begin a frantic attempt to re-intubate her, she takes several strong breaths.

When the child comes to, Genevieve asks why she went swimming in the middle of the night. Isabella replies in a quiet raspy voice, "I wanted to cross the ocean so we could be together forever."

Genevieve realizes then what she must do. She spends the last months of her life dedicated to transitioning Isabella to her new family. She and Isabella move in with David and Lindsey and when Isabella scrapes her knee, she sends her to Lindsey for kisses and Band-Aids. When Isabella starts referring to Lindsey as "Mommy" too, it eats at Genevieve, but she swallows her pride and pain and encourages their relationship. Craig remains by Genevieve's side, reminding her constantly to make hay while the sun's still shining.

At peace with God and her daughter's future, Genevieve passes, and the story continues with Isabella rewriting the first few paragraphs of *Crossing Oceans*. We find the book was written not by Genevieve, but by Isabella. "I didn't know what compelled me to write my mother's story. I suppose it was to understand her sacrifice. But more than anything, while I was writing it, I could talk with her, be loved by her … while I was writing her, she lived."[15]

SAMPLE NOVEL PROPOSAL #2

S.J. Harper's *Cursed: A Fallen Siren Novel* (Roc, 2013)

Commentary: This proposal has two established authors joining forces for a new paranormal missing persons series. Since this proposal is extensive (thirty-plus pages), I've excluded most of the 8,400-word synopsis as well as the character list. What's interesting is that all the marketing information appeared in a separate query letter.

FALLEN

AN EMMA MONROE/ZACK ARMSTRONG MISSION

JEANNE C. STEIN AND SAMANTHA SOMMERSBY[16]

Real Name/Pen Name: Jeanne C. Stein[17]
Address:
Contact Phone:
E-mail address:

Real Name/Pen Name: Lori James/Samantha Sommersby

---

15. While every author feels the inclination to not "spoil the story," that's the wrong approach for a synopsis or any agent/editor correspondence. Do spoil the story for them. Give the clear, decisive ending. Spill the secrets. They absolutely need to know how you'll wrap things up in the end.

16. While I usually cut the header or title page off of the sample proposals, I left this here to show how the authors are trying to create clarity for this new branded series.

17. The authors front-loaded this information again for clarity. This proposed series is written under a pseudonym, and one of the two authors also writes under a different name. Lots of names to keep track of. This is a fine way to get everyone on the same page from the start. Also, the full contact info was filled in, of course.

Address:
Contact Phone:
E-mail address:

Working Title (include series name if applicable): *Fallen*
(An Emma Monroe/Zack Armstrong Mission: Book 1)

Word Count: 70,000

Genre/s: Urban Fantasy, Paranormal, Romance[18]

Pitch: *Without a Trace* meets *Angel*, only this Angel is an
age-old Siren turned FBI Agent who is cursed by mortality
and partnered with a hunky alpha werewolf. In search of
redemption for past sins, they use the powers of seduction
and strength, along with their knowledge of the supernatural, to rescue damsels, bring big bads to justice, and capture
one another's hearts.[19]

Possible Log Lines: Meet FBI Agents Emma Monroe
and Zack Armstrong. She's a cursed Siren. He's a damned
Werewolf. They're on a mission of redemption. Today it could
be one rescue away.[20]

SYNOPSIS

Special Agent Emma Monroe is a no-nonsense woman who
is all about the mission, and her mission is redemption. Once
a Siren, Emma failed to prevent Hades from kidnapping
Persephone. Cursed by Demeter and ejected from Mount
Olympus, she's now bound to this world. A nomad of sorts,
she's had many names and many lives. For thousands of years,
she's been searching for and rescuing missing women, hoping
that each save will be the one that will tip the scales of justice
and be her salvation.

In addition to being banished to the mortal world, Demeter's
curse ensures that Emma will never find lasting love. Seduction

---

18. You don't pitch a genre series without knowing exactly which genre(s) it fits in.

19. This is a strong Hollywood-style pitch that explains a new story by referring to similarities
with older stories, like how *Passenger 57* is *Die Hard* on a plane.

20. While log lines are typically one or two sentences, these five short sentences do a fine job
of communicating a short summary that still has the power to hook a reader quickly. And
since they wisely say "possible log lines," they show that they're open to feedback and revision.

may be second nature, and superficial sex may momentarily fill a need, but there can never be anything real, anything meaningful. Having lost other lovers, she's learned the hard way the ultimate price is simply too high to pay. Emma relies on her best friend, Liz Greyson, a witch with mad magical skills, to keep her "Plain Jane" reverse glamour in place and periodically cast a dampening spell that allows her to dial down her innate powers of seduction.

Working missing person cases for the FBI is the perfect cover. She has a steady stream of women to save. Because Emma's most recent partner was promoted, she's been assigned a new partner. Zachary Armstrong transferred into the San Diego office from South Carolina. Zack is six foot three, dark, rugged … and a werewolf.

Although Emma recognizes Zack for what he is, his supernatural nature, as well as Emma's, is otherwise unknown at the Bureau. Zack intends to keep it that way. A former Special Forces sniper, he's been exploited by the government before and faults himself for being too loyal and too trusting. The long string of faceless kills he'd once been proud of now haunts him. He beats back the demons by doing penance. Instead of taking men and women from their families, he finds them and brings them back.

Case One: Amy Patterson[21]

Tuesday, April 10

If the stack of newspapers and mail is any indication, Amy Patterson has been gone for approximately two weeks. Her landlady reported her missing. She also reported that Amy was an author who rarely left her apartment, had few friends, and has *never* left town without telling her. She pushed the San Diego District Attorney, a personal friend, to ask local FBI to review the detective's work on the case since the police department is making no progress. The case has been referred to Emma … and her new partner. During their search of Amy's apartment, Emma and Zack find precious little in the

---

21. Instead of a chapter-by-chapter breakdown, they go with a date-by-date structure.

way of clues. Among other things, mention is made of tinted windows overlooking the San Diego bay and the fact that both the cupboards and refrigerator are bare.

[**Note to the Reader:** The synopsis continues with the same date-by-date structure for the entire arc of the story.]

Chapter Fourteen

THE ANTHOLOGY PROPOSAL:
TWO ANNOTATED EXAMPLES

Whether you're pitching a thematic poetry anthology to a university press or an essay collection by best-selling authors to a major publisher, the proposals look the same—you're the editor, and you're hawking wares that you didn't create. Not that you didn't choose, order, and edit the material, of course, but these types of books are far different than a business how-to or memoir where every word is written by you.

One of the dangers with this kind of book (and I've seen this happen time and time again) is the editor putting out a call for submissions online and in magazines to see if they can get enough good material to produce the book. Once the submissions come in, the editor wants to get the rights to them or else she might lose out, right? What does she promise the potential contributors for permission to use their work? Money from a contract she doesn't have? Contributor copies for a book that doesn't exist? What if the material has already been published and the rights are owned by a publisher?

Even if she somehow secures the right to use all the material she wants, she's done exactly the thing we've said *not* to do many times throughout this book. Don't create a full manuscript until *after* the contract is in hand— novels excluded, usually. Sending in an already finished anthology feels like a "take it or leave it" situation, whereas a proposal feels like a collaboration that has plenty of room to adjust. It's not uncommon for a publisher to want to swap out a few of the contributors with some of their own authors, and that feels more doable when promises and rights arrangements haven't already been put in place.

So how does an editor get sample material if a call for submissions isn't an option? Typically, it's by finding representative samples of the type you intend to include (which is along the lines of saying, "It's going to be something like this …"). Another option is to hit up a few authors you know and have a good relationship with and see if they can provide you with sample material completely on speculation. If you're asking for already written and/ or already published material, then so much the better.

Just be clear about who's on board and who isn't, which samples are part of the future book and which ones are just approximations, and you should be fine. Putting together anthologies is a time-intensive job that requires meticulous record keeping, so don't get involved with one of these projects unless you're confident you can keep it all under control (or you have a partner who can).

SAMPLE ANTHOLOGY PROPOSAL #1

Gary L. McDowell and F. Daniel Rzicznek's
The Rose Metal Press Field Guide to Prose Poetry:
Contemporary Poets in Discussion and Practice
(Rose Metal Press, 2010)

Commentary: This book was pitched as *Wonders of the Field: Contemporary Poets on the Prose Poem.* As you can see, the final title changed a good deal. No problem. If a publisher wants to buy your book and requests a few changes, say "No worries!" unless it's something you absolutely can't live with. I like the new title better—it's provocative and inviting. While there's nothing wrong with random titles like *Wonders of the Field,* if you use such a title you absolutely need a subtitle to go with it.

Purposes:

Over the last two decades, the prose poem has become an increasingly vital, flexible, and exciting literary creature, but no lively discussion among its practitioners and readers has yet to appear in book form.[1] Therefore, one of our main purposes is to illuminate the craft and process of this otherwise critically neglected form (quickly becoming a subgenre) of poetry—the prose poem. The essays in the book will speak to teachers, students, readers, and writers of poetry. The goal, instead of how to instruct a writer to write a prose poem, is to illuminate how and why prose poems generate so much excitement in the literary world.[2]

Another purpose is to offer insights to readers and writers alike from a variety of poets at different stages in their careers. Whether the author of the essay has made his or her career writing prose poems or just begun experimenting in the form, their essays offer insights to both the novice and the

---

1. If you have a choice, you want to be the first or the best of something. Here they're pitching to be the first book that does this.
2. Good distinction here. I might've assumed this was a creative writing how-to.

veteran. We have also tried to include writers of great cultural and aesthetic diversities in order to better accentuate the many approaches that each generation has taken toward the prose poem.[3]

Outstanding Features:

Essays: The accessibility of the personal narrative over the traditional critical approach to the essay is advantageous because it allows the reader to connect with the author's views and opinions without closing the door on the reader's reactions. While we hope that teachers and students alike will find great value in the book, the personal aspect of these essays will hopefully appeal to larger audiences outside of academia.[4]

Prose Poems: Unlike a traditional collection of essays, we've asked our authors to include one of their own prose poems alongside each essay to give the reader a concrete example of concepts discussed in the accompanying essays. We feel this combination (essays with prose poems) offers a unique opportunity for readers to see the prose poem from both sides: in theory and as a finished work on the printed page.[5]

Introduction: Upon completion, our introduction will outline the purpose of the book, explain our motivations for creating the book, discuss the importance and vitality of the prose poem in contemporary American literature, and discuss why we have chosen to invite personal essays over reviews or similarly critical works.[6]

---

3. This is that range of voices that textbooks and anthologies make a point to have. It's good to note that this is already part of the plan.

4. Essays can be very inviting and fun (like those of Dave Barry or David Sedaris) or stuffy and academic in the worst connotations of the word. It's useful to point out that the goal is to have a strong personal aspect here, which suggests a less stodgy feel to the text.

5. It's interesting to note that the final book has thirty-four essays but sixty-six poems.

6. This introduction is simply going to be a shortened version of this proposal, which is quite appropriate for this kind of project.

Significance:

This book will provide readers with a firsthand opportunity to get inside the minds of contemporary poets[7] and see how the prose poem has influenced their lives as artists. By inviting our contributors to write personal essays detailing their relationship with the prose poem, we have tried to bridge the gap between poet and poem, writer and reader. One disadvantage of the critical essay is the possibility of a disconnect between the text and the audience. This is the exact reason we have asked our poets to speak about the impact of the prose poem on their personal lives and aesthetics. We have used the personal essay as a launching pad to get at the critical aspects of the prose poem through personal anecdotes and histories. While we both enjoy and respect the power of the critical essay, we feel that the lack of personal essays about poetry, and especially prose poetry, is a gap that must be filled. Our anthology merges the personal with the critical, and the result is a unique and dynamic look into the life of prose poetry.

Market Considerations:

Primary Audience: Our primary audience is all poets and readers of poetry, whether they are longtime admirers of prose poems or newcomers to the form. Also, readers interested in the lives and artistic processes of writers will appreciate the personal approach each essay takes. The prose poem has been steadily gaining popularity over the last three decades, but no attempt at collecting the personal narratives and reflections of poets working in the form has existed until now.

Secondary Audience: Creative writing instructors and students of writing and literature will also have use for this anthology. A surge in popularity of prose poems has given way to a large literary market with many major publications featuring prose poems in every issue, as well as journals dedicated solely to prose poems and the study of prose poetry. Coupled

---

7. This is the same kind of rare access I championed in my textbook *Contemporary American Poetry: Behind the Scenes* (see chapter sixteen). Many scholars, teachers of creative writing, and poets are quite interested in getting the inside scoop, the behind-the-scenes stuff of writing. That's essentially what they say as well in the market considerations section.

with the continued growth of creative writing programs, we feel there is a developing academic market for resources dedicated to the prose poem.

Structure:

Since our essays display a wide variety of voices and styles, we will order the anthology (as we have with our proposal) so that there is a range of aesthetic approaches and personal views. One overall goal of the book is to create a dialogue between different perspectives on the prose poem. The poems provided by each essayist/poet will follow each essay and act as bridges between the poets' thoughts and practices.[8]

Competition:

While there are plenty of prose poem anthologies from major poetry presses (such as Oberlin College Press, Scribner, Tupelo Press, and others),[9] there are no anthologies that have collected personal essays by prominent, contemporary poets on the prose poem. While Michel Delville's *The American Prose Poem: Poetic Form and the Boundaries of Genre* is the first, and as of yet only, book-length critical study of the form, it is not a personal approach and contains only Delville's point of view. *The American Prose Poem* is a fine study of the form, but our anthology will present a side of the prose poem that has yet to appear in print. What makes our anthology most unique, besides the inclusion of both essays and prose poems, is how it reveals the very personal role the form has played in each of our contributor's artistic lives.

Status of the Work:

The anthology will be an exhaustive look into the contemporary prose poet's methods and influences; therefore, we are

---

8. Anthologies have a lot of material to deliver from a lot of different writers. How that's delivered is just one of the critical decisions an editor has to make. Some of my anthologies were ordered alphabetically by authors' last names, while some were organized thematically. Here they explain the strategy is to create a dialogue between pieces—an interesting approach that's not at all unlike putting together a single author book of poems.

9. Because the publishers they're approaching are specialists in this field, the editors didn't feel the need to give titles for these competing books. Note, too, how they immediately point out the common lack those prominent titles share.

aiming for a book of between 250–400 pages with a total of forty to fifty essays accompanied by prose poems. To fulfill this goal, upon acceptance we plan to further solicit established contemporary prose poets and, if needed, to make an open call for submissions.[10]

A list of poets we intend to approach might include:

Kim Addonizio, Nin Andrews, Eric Baus, Claire Bateman, Stephen Berg, Joel Brouwer, Killarney Clary, Sean Thomas Dougherty, Mike Dockins, Russell Edson, Carolyn Forché, Amy Gerstler, Noah Eli Gordon, Arielle Greenberg, Gabriel Gudding, Matthea Harvey, Lyn Hejinian, Bob Hicok, Tyehimba Jess, Peter Johnson, David Keplinger, Mary Koncel, Sabrina Orah Mark, Harryette Mullen, William Olsen, Michael Palmer, Mary Ruefle, Maureen Seaton, Reginald Shepherd, Charles Simic, Larissa Szporluk, James Tate, Rosmarie Waldrop, Bruce Weigl, Joe Wenderoth, Franz Wright, and David Young.[11]

Authors:

Gary L. McDowell's poems have appeared recently or are forthcoming in *Colorado Review, The Pinch, Ninth Letter, The Southeast Review, DIAGRAM, Bat City Review, RHINO, Copper Nickel, Pebble Lake Review*, and many others. His chapbook, *The Blueprint*, appeared in 2005 from Pudding House. He has been twice nominated for a Pushcart Prize and is pursuing his Ph.D. in Literature and Creative Writing at Western Michigan University, where he is the Poetry Editor of *Third Coast* and an assistant editor at New Issues Poetry & Prose.[12]

F. Daniel Rzicznek's first book of poems is *Neck of the World*, winner of the 2007 May Swenson Poetry Award, published by Utah State University Press. He is also the author of

---

10. Here and elsewhere, the editors are reinforcing their goal of comprehensiveness on their coverage of the prose poem. The page range—250 to 400—is a huge difference in terms of production costs, though. It's typically better to pick one number and say "about 350 pages."

11. No promises as to who they'll get since they admit these are poets they "might approach," but it gives a sense to the editors' sensibilities. One look at this list and it's clear they really mean "contemporary," despite the prose poem having been around for decades.

12. Gary is a graduate student. How cool is it that he's part of this and got a book out of it? It helped that he had a number of literary journal credits. It also helped that his co-editor has authored a few books of poetry and won prizes. Together, they make a formidable team.

the chapbook *Cloud Tablets* (Kent State University Press, 2006). His poems have appeared in *Boston Review, The New Republic, The Iowa Review, Gulf Coast, AGNI,* and *Mississippi Review,* and have been nominated for the Pushcart Prize. He currently teaches English composition at Bowling Green State University.

SAMPLE ANTHOLOGY PROPOSAL #2

Ryan G. Van Cleave's *City of the Big Shoulders:*
An Anthology of Poems About Chicago
(University of Iowa Press, 2012)

Commentary: My earnest hope for this book was to have the 2016 Summer Olympics come to Chicago. This place-based poetry anthology seemed like a great pocket-sized gift that thousands of tourists could take back with them, along with any Olympic souvenirs they picked up. Alas, they lost the bid to Rio De Janeiro. Still, books centered around geographical places tend to have a long shelf life. And more important, I love Chicago and was happy to do a book about it regardless of the book's sales record.

Unlike all of my other book proposals, I had only a single publisher in mind for this book, and I sent it to that one place. Too few publishers are interested in publishing poetry anthologies, but the University of Iowa Press is one of those. Since they have an interest in all things Midwest, plus I've published four other poetry anthologies with them by this point, they were the perfect fit.

And don't assume the pitch was a formality. I've sent the same publisher other proposals before and came up short. This one struck a chord with them. It did with me, too. I knew it was a winner as I was writing it.

> **Project Description:** My intention is to edit an anthology that represents a generous gathering of the best poems about Chicago (and Chicago-related subjects) from natives, visitors, and fans of this great city.[13] One of the largest cities in North America, Chicago's metropolitan area boasts 10 million residents, making it one of the world's twenty-five largest urban areas by population. A leader in transportation, telecommunications, and finance, Chicago is a city of

---

13. Talk about leading with a log line! This is it. Clear and direct.

great architectural significance, ethnic diversity, and cultural wealth—rich sources for poetry, indeed.[14]

Contributors: The anthology's title comes from Carl Sandburg's famous poem "Chicago," from his book *Chicago Poems* (1916). Other memorable Chicago poems come readily to mind: Marge Piercy's "Visiting a Dead Man on a Summer Day," Ezra Pound's "Epilogue," Maxwell Bodenhelm's "South State Street: Chicago."[15] Collecting new and existing work on Chicago will be relatively simple, considering the sizable list of poets/wordsmiths who were either born in Chicago or have a strong Chicago connection. To name just a few:[16] Sherwood Anderson, Gwendolyn Brooks, Hayden Carruth, Ana Castillo, Reginald Gibbons, David Hernandez, Edward Hirsch, Paul Hoover, Tyehimba Jess, Li-Young Lee, Haki Madhubuti, Edgar Lee Masters, Lisel Mueller, Simone Muench, Elise Paschen, Keith Preston, Bin Ramke, Luis Rodriguez, Carl Sandburg, Lew Sarett, Shel Silverstein, Charles Simic, Patricia Smith, Mark Strand, John Tipton, Mark Turcotte, Kanye West, Yvor Winters

Marketing: Beyond the obvious strategy of marketing this text to Chicagoans (and all high schools, colleges, and universities throughout Illinois and the Midwest), tourists (Chicago welcomed 44 million visitors in 2006),[17] and those interested in urban poetry, this book is quite timely. How so?

---

14. Thank you, Wikipedia. While it's not the only place to go for information, it's a fine place to start.

15. While I knew the fine folks at the University of Iowa knew their poetry, I still gave both full name and title of these noteworthy poems about Chicago in case they wanted to look them up.

16. This list is very strong, indeed. I knew it was more of a wish list than a realistic list since some of those authors were dead and their literary estates would charge me a fortune to use their poems (Carl Sandburg and Gwendolyn Brooks, ahem ahem). But I felt good that I could get some of them, and I managed to do so. I also promised new and emerging voices, so that's where some of the lineup came from as well.

17. Again, here's that tourist angle. Even without the Summer Olympics rolling into town, 44 million visitors is nothing to sneeze at.

Since President-elect Barack Obama is from Chicago, the anthology has the opportunity to be both topically current and politically relevant.[18]

Chicago is one of four final cities on the short list for hosting the 2016 Summer Olympics, with the potential site being Washington Park (connected to Jackson Park by the Midway Plaisance). Recent Olympics in Europe and Asia should give Chicago an edge. A former colleague of mine who wrote a novel set in Australia saw his book's sales quadruple during 2000, when Sydney hosted the Summer Olympics.[19]

With the 2009 AWP Conference being in Chicago, it'll be quite easy to put out a Call for Submission to the thousands of writers there to obtain new, exciting work for this anthology to go with poems I solicit from the above list of well-known and established Chicago poets.[20]

Poems: What might this anthology look like? Of course, a number of poems will reflect Chicago's architecture, famous locales, and general history. Other poem topics, though, might readily include:[21]

- The Great Chicago Fire of 1871
- O'Hare International Airport, the second busiest in the world
- Al Capone
- Chicago's Native American background (Potawatomis, Miami, and Sauk)
- Lake Michigan
- Grant Park, Lincoln Park, and Jackson Park

---

18. This seemed like a rich topic. Sure enough, a few of the best poems deal with Obama in one manner or another.

19. I mentioned this goal in the commentary. It would've been a huge marketing opportunity to capitalize on, as my friend Todd James Pierce did with his book about Australia (see the synopsis for that novel on www.theweekendbookproposal.com).

20. The University of Iowa folks regularly attend this conference, and they know full well that I could easily do what I promised: pass out fliers for this anthology and be bombarded with submissions.

21. Here's where I guess at the range of topics that might appear in the poems. Remember that at this point in the process, I didn't have a single poem for the book yet. These were just educated guesses on the many poem-worthy things about Chicago that I could think of.

- The Chicago Bulls/Bears/Blackhawks/Cubs/White Sox
- The TV show *ER* was set in Chicago
- Lake Effect snow
- The El
- The "Magnificent Mile"
- Soldier Field
- Navy Pier
- Chicago pizza
- The Chicago Loop
- The Sears Tower
- Mayor Richard J. Daley and his son, Mayor Richard M. Daley
- McCormick Place
- Chicago is the birthplace of house music
- Chicago is home to the original Poetry Slam

Manuscript Details: The book will be approximately 175 pages in length. The full manuscript delivery date will be six months from the upcoming AWP Conference (February 11–14, 2009). All submissions from potential contributors will be handled via e-mail to expedite manuscript preparation and ensure a timely final manuscript.[22]

Contents: (page counts refer to final book pages, not manuscript pages)[23]

- Editor's Note by Ryan G. Van Cleave (2 pages)
- Introduction by Edward Hirsch (he wrote the introduction to my *Behind the Scenes* textbook), Lisel Mueller (winner of both a Pulitzer Prize and the National Book Award—I've worked with her before, too), or a similarly high-profile Chicago writer (4 pages)
- 100 poems (approximately 150 pages)—all of the accepted poems will either be new work written specifically for

---

22. As I like to, I offer a specific page length count as well as a firm delivery date for the manuscript.

23. In my earlier proposals, I didn't go into such clear section-by-section page counts, but I find editors like this. It also makes it seem like I'm really, really sure about what I'm doing.

this anthology or older work that writers donate without reprint fees

- Contributors' Notes (approximately 14 pages)
- Title and First Line Indexes (4 pages)
- For reasons of timeliness and economy, the entire book will be compiled in a MS-Word 2000 file prior to turning in the final manuscript

Samples: Available upon request.

About the Editor

- **Career Background:** Raised and educated in Chicago, Ryan G. Van Cleave was the 2007–2008 Jenny McKean Moore Writer-in-Washington at The George Washington University. He has taught creative writing and literature at Clemson University, the Florida State University, the University of Wisconsin-Madison, the University of Wisconsin-Green Bay, as well as at prisons, community centers, and urban at-risk youth facilities. He lives in Sarasota, FL, where he creates educational books and films with New Realm Productions; he also works as a freelance writer, editor, and consultant. He serves as director of C&R Press, a nonprofit literary organization based in Chattanooga, TN.

- **Publishing Background:** The author (or co-author) of twelve books, Van Cleave's poetry, fiction, and nonfiction have appeared in such publications as *The Boston Review, The Christian Science Monitor, The Iowa Review, The Missouri Review, Ploughshares, The Progressive, TriQuarterly*, and *Writer's Digest*. His work has also been featured in *Mooring Against the Tide: Writing Fiction and Poetry* (Prentice Hall, 2000), *The 15th Annual Year's Best Fantasy & Horror* (St. Martin's 2002), *Never Before: Poems About First Experiences* (Four Way Books, 2005), and *In a Fine Frenzy: Poetry Inspired by Shakespeare* (University of Iowa Press, 2005).

- **Editorial Background:** Van Cleave has worked in an editorial capacity with *Black Box Recorder, International Quarterly, The South Carolina Review, Sundog: The*

Southeast Review, and *The Dictionary of American Regional English*, as well as on dozens of books, movies, and poetry books as a freelance editor.

Anthology-Specific Editorial Background: Previous poetry anthologies edited by Van Cleave include:

- *American Diaspora: Poetry of Displacement* (University of Iowa Press, 2001)
- *Like Thunder: Poets Respond to Violence in America* (University of Iowa Press, 2002)
- *Vespers: Contemporary American Poems of Religion and Spirituality* (University of Iowa Press, 2003)
- *Red, White, and Blues: Poets on the Promise of America* (University of Iowa Press, 2004)
- *Breathe: 101 Contemporary Odes* (C&R Press, 2009)

Potential Reviewers:[24]

---

24. As Delia Poey did with her proposal (see chapter sixteen), I listed four poetry experts who would be ideal candidates to review the proposal and report on its merits (Names and contact info not shown).

Chapter Fifteen

THE MEMOIR PROPOSAL:
AN ANNOTATED EXAMPLE

While memoir is much like fiction in that publishers care as much about the writing as the facts/happenings of the story, it is also much like nonfiction in that a solid proposal and dynamite sample chapter or two can be enough to seal the deal. I sold my memoir, *Unplugged: My Journey Into the Dark World of Video Game Addiction* (HCI, 2010), that way. Psychiatrist Doreen Orion sold *Queen of the Road: The True Tale of 47 States, 22,000 Miles, 200 Shoes, 2 Cats, 1 Poodle, a Husband, and a Bus with a Will of Its Own* (Broadway Books, 2008) that way, too. Michelle Au, Rachel Resnick, and plenty of other memoir writers also found publication through the memoir book proposal.

INSIDER TIP

Don't make a rookie mistake and confuse memoir with autobiography. Here's a way to decipher the difference.

Memoir: a true narrative story that focuses on a special period of a life that will be of interest to a larger audience.

Autobiography: the true narrative story of a famous person's life (like Abraham Lincoln, Leonard Cohen, or Michael Jordan) written by that person. If someone else writes it, it's a biography.

William Zinsser explains the difference by saying, "Unlike autobiography, which moves in a dutiful line from birth to fame, memoir narrows the lens, focusing on a time in the writer's life that was unusually vivid, such as childhood or adolescence, or that was framed by war or travel or public service or some other special circumstance." So unless you're superfamous, you should write a memoir. If you *are* superfamous, call me—I want to split a piña colada with you in a ritzy New York bar and bask in your greatness.

People will tell you that memoir is *totally* different than other nonfiction books. You *have* to write the whole thing first. Like I said, I didn't. Doreen Orion—who queried "a lot" of agents, reported that less than 1 percent wanted to see the whole book. And none of the editors the book went to (after she secured an agent) asked for more than the proposal and two sample chapters. My experience with memoir jibes with hers. My meaty proposal and sample chapter were enough for them to make an informed decision.

The same people telling you that you must write the entire memoir first are infected with the same unhelpful ideas as people who say you must write your business how-to, your history textbook, your biography of Nelson Mandela, and your illustrated cookbook before sending it out. It's simply not a hard fact. It's just one way of doing things.

Yes, some editors or agents will insist on seeing a full manuscript for your memoir. Yes, some will not. Try the ones who won't first. Why? Save yourself time and heartache. I know too many memoirists who had to throw out or redo hundreds of pages because the editor (or the head of marketing or the VP or …) "strongly preferred" the writer to do things differently. It's much easier to throw or redo an outline and chapter descriptions, isn't it?

Here's just one example: Dinty Moore wrote his entire memoir, *Between Panic & Desire*, before sending it to the University of Nebraska Press. After peer review, they asked for major revisions, so he tossed out six chapters, wrote six new ones, and revised the rest of the book. All of that effort earned him a contract. But that's a lot of extra writing, no?

Dinty Moore, though, confesses, "The one thing I've learned about publishing is that there are always exceptions, and every book finds its path differently." If you'd prefer to go the route of selling a completed memoir off a proposal, fine. I just find life too short to write that much on speculation.

Regardless of whether you subscribe to the "write the entire blasted thing first" philosophy of memoir or not, the following proposal demonstrates plenty of ways memoir book proposals differ from other types of books.

SAMPLE MEMOIR PROPOSAL

Carol Ross Joynt's *Innocent Spouse: A Memoir*
(Crown, 2012)

Commentary: This is a big proposal, clocking in at nearly 18,000 words. Joynt's agent admits, "It's a little longer than what I usually like to send out, but I think the individual components are quite strong." I agree. The project sold at auction to Crown.

For space considerations, I've excluded the marketing and publicity section, the comparable and competitive titles (although this appears in chapter five), Appendix B, the sample chapter, and most of the chapter summaries (which are so detailed that they run thirty-three pages in total). I'll leave one chapter summary in to show you how impressively she handled this part of the proposal.

"You will cheer for Carol as she fought back and won!" — Walter Cronkite

"A searing personal journey … [Carol] is unafraid to turn an unerring spotlight on herself, examining the flaws and mistakes from every angle. Yet what emerges from this fascinating story is a courageous woman who is a survivor and above all else a mother who would do anything for her child." — David Baldacci[1]

INNOCENT SPOUSE

a memoir

by

Carol Ross Joynt

Represented by:

Laney Katz Becker

You hear the term "Innocent Spouse" and you think, *Ah, poor dear, she caught him cheating with the summer intern.* In my case, you'd only be partially correct. My husband was cheating, yes, but on an entirely different playing field: his infidelity was *financial.*[2]

Innocent Spouse is a code of the Internal Revenue Service that is used in criminal tax fraud cases. It's awarded in situations where a spouse dies and the surviving spouse, usually a widow, is hit with a surprise IRS debt. The code says that the surviving spouse cannot be charged with the crime, is not personally liable for the debt, and may keep any money and property that is in his or her own name. But first, (ah, isn't there always a *but*?) the surviving spouse must be able to prove—beyond a reasonable doubt—that he or she knew nothing about, nor participated in, the shenanigans that caused the fraud. It sounds simple, but it's not: Innocent Spouse is very rarely granted in criminal tax fraud cases. It

---

1. Agent Laney Katz Becker said that these blurbs came *after* she took on this client. What a great way to start things off, no? And even more amazing, the agent approached her after hearing Carol on NPR. Together, they created this proposal.

2. This is an interesting twist. I'm intrigued and will keep reading for sure.

is the IRS, after all, and they are not known to blithely let people off the hook.[3]

ENDORSEMENTS

"This is an inspiring story by an accomplished journalist who found that nothing in her challenging career prepared her for the complexities of her very daunting life. You will cheer for Carol as she fought back and won!"[4] — Walter Cronkite

"A searing personal journey where the pages fall away from one's hand like meat from a bone. Ms. Joynt takes on her life with both a hatchet and a scalpel and is unafraid to turn an unerring spotlight on herself, examining the flaws and mistakes from every angle. Yet what emerges from this fascinating story is a courageous woman who is a survivor and above all else a mother who would do anything for her child." — David Baldacci

"For those who read *The Pilot's Wife* by Anita Shreve and wondered how a loving husband could possibly keep a secret life hidden from his family, wonder no more: Carol Joynt reveals in sad and searing detail how it can happen and the price she, as a wife, had to pay to save herself and her young son." — Kitty Kelley, investigative journalist and *New York Times* best-selling author of biographies about Jacqueline Kennedy Onassis, Elizabeth Taylor, Frank Sinatra, Nancy Reagan, etc.

"Anyone who's ever ended a long marriage or love affair and looked back at the ex-partner with one question in mind— who was THAT?—will be instantly hammered by Carol Joynt's story of her journey from storybook marriage to an unending dunk in the pool of dark reality. Carol tells her tale with equal measures of equanimity and disbelief, as the onion of her relationship gets peeled after her husband's sudden death, revealing a loving but mysterious man who planted a poison pill in the rest of her life ... so far. Never stooping to

---

3. Love it. It's Woman vs. the Government. It's a story that promises secrets, conflict, financial gain/loss, and sleuthing. Who wouldn't want to know more?

4. Note that this is the longer version of the quotation. The one that led into the proposal was the pithier teaser version. It's the same way that a phrase from a longer quote appears on the front cover of a book, like when Stephen King says "A real heart-racer ..." about a new thriller.

self-pity, and never forgetting why she loved this man, Joynt shares the stunning bumps in the road of a single woman with child—a road my own mom took—with warmth, humor, and intelligence. What's not to love?" —Harry Shearer, star of *The Simpsons* (Mr. Burns, Smithers, Ned Flanders), comedian, and radio host

"Think you know your husband? Read this book. Carol Joynt takes us on a harrowing roller-coaster ride through a system that viewed her as guilty until she proved her innocence. A riveting, inspirational account of one woman's dreamy life turned nightmare and her ultimate triumph. I couldn't put it down." — Jane Stanton Hitchcock, *New York Times* bestselling author; Edgar and Hammet Prize nominee (*Social Crimes, One Dangerous Lady, Trick of the Eye*, etc.)

SECURING MORE ENDORSEMENTS:
I have personal and professional relationships with hundreds of accomplished and well-known journalists, newsmakers, and celebrities, which I will use to seek endorsements for *Innocent Spouse* when the time comes. Many of these contacts and connections are with people I've interviewed for my cable television show *The Q&A Café*—the only talk show that takes place in a saloon. A partial list of these newsmakers appears in Appendix B (pg. 67) of this proposal.[5]

PROPOSAL TABLE OF CONTENTS

---

5. As if the list of celebrity endorsements we've already seen isn't enough, she's got two pages of people she's interviewed for her cable TV show or knows through her years of broadcast work. What are the odds that a few of them will help her out? I'll bet the odds are quite good, and good odds excite editors.

OVERVIEW

I moved out of my parents' middle class suburban home at age eighteen to begin life as a journalist. I had no college education, but that didn't deter my ambition to have it all—assignments in big cities and war zones, scoops, front-page bylines—and by age twenty-two, I was well on my way to achieving my dream. I had an exciting job in New York City, where I was the first full-time woman writer for Walter Cronkite,[6] the nation's top anchorman. I was working hard at something meaningful and building the foundation of a serious career during one of the most climactic times in our nation's history—Watergate and Vietnam.

But my dreams extended well beyond my career. I also wanted a Knight in Shining Armor, romance, and a sense of security. Several years later, that dream also came true when I met my future husband, J. Howard Joynt III. He embodied all things glamorous and romantically dangerous. He was part James Bond, part Jack Nicholson. He had style, family money, an Ivy League education, and he owned Nathans, a sizzling Georgetown bar. Howard was both prince and pirate; stability and risk—but I didn't focus on the contradictions—in fact, they were part of his charismatic charm.[7]

We lived a fantastical life, and shortly after our marriage I quit my job as the network assignment editor in the NBC News Washington bureau. For the next ten years it was a wild ride: You name it, we did it—or bought it.[8] But then the tempo settled down to something calmer. I missed my work, and Howard needed to focus more on Nathans. I returned to television as a producer for Charlie Rose. I won an Emmy. Later, I was selected as the Washington bureau chief for a syndicated start-up, and shortly thereafter, I sailed to ever bigger producing roles with icons like David Brinkley, Ted Koppel, and Larry King.

---

6. Aha. The mystery of where his quotation came from is now solved.

7. What a description! He sounds too good to be true . . . but that's the point, isn't it?

8. We love rags to riches stories, but we also love riches to rags, and that's where this is headed. The tension mounts as we wait for the financial KABOOM.

On the home front, Howard and I found our dream house on the Chesapeake Bay, and we had a son, Spencer. Life was satisfying, secure, and stable. Twenty years after we met, we were still in love, our marriage was comfortable, and we were both ecstatic about being parents. When I looked at my husband I noticed some gray hair and a slight paunch, but I still saw my beguiling prince and pirate.

Then Howard died, and just like that, my world collapsed. I learned I wasn't living in a dream, but in a house of cards—with a man I did not know. Howard, it turned out, had secrets. He was involved in a federal criminal tax fraud case; he owed millions of dollars to the IRS. And with his passing, I, as his surviving spouse, was responsible for repaying the debt.

While I thought Howard's death was the worst thing that could happen, I soon learned it was only the catalyst for worse things to come: I had a lifestyle I couldn't afford, a business that was a mystery to me and a bankrupt money pit, and a lease that was a noose around my neck.[9] The future for Spencer and me was a battle for survival on every front because, even if I sold everything, I couldn't come up with the millions of dollars necessary to settle our debt. But it wasn't my fault. I didn't know. I was innocent.

Innocent Spouse is a story about my attempt to hold onto my thirty-year journalism career along with our home, all while raising a son, trying to understand the restaurant business, and learning to deal with a daunting new world of lawyers, debt, and the IRS. It is a story of a fairy-tale life gone awry, and my struggle to pick up the pieces and become something I'd never been before: self-sufficient. But my story is also a cautionary tale for any woman who has ever decided it was easier not to know, too difficult to learn, or "not my thing"—and allowed "the other half" in her life to handle the finances.[10] Finally, *Innocent Spouse* is a tale that will have book groups everywhere asking: How well does anyone ever know

---

9. What a great way to explain the tension in her life! And she didn't deserve this. Now we'll root for her like we're watching *Rocky* for the first time.

10. So it's not just a tell-all, there's a self-help element to this, too. The message is "Women! Educate yourselves about the things that truly matter." It's also an important warning call.

his/her spouse? And what, if anything, can we do—should we do—to protect ourselves?

SPECS: A full manuscript could be delivered to the publisher six to nine months after signing a contract. It will contain approximately 85,000–95,000 words. Photos are available upon the publisher's request.[11]

ABOUT THE AUTHOR

Carol Ross Joynt was a military and academic brat who was born in Denver and raised in Europe, Ohio, and on the East Coast. She skipped college and jumped right into national news, joining the staff of the Washington bureau of United Press International the same week that Richard Nixon was inaugurated President for the first time. She started at the bottom, taking dictation on breaking stories from Helen Thomas and Merriman Smith. Her first "beat" was reporting on the antiwar movement; she also covered politics and the Apollo space program. Later, Carol was hired by *TIME* magazine and moved to New York. Among her many diverse assignments, she traveled on the McGovern campaign bus, reported from the presidential conventions in Miami, and even covered the premiere of *The Godfather*.

In 1972, Walter Cronkite asked Carol to be one of his three writers on *The CBS Evening News*. She accepted immediately. For four years she worked alongside the influential icon as Cronkite informed viewers about the death of LBJ, the Watergate scandal, the resignation of Richard Nixon, the kidnapping of Patricia Hearst, and the end of the Vietnam War. Each year, Carol and her colleagues received the Writer's Guild Award for best news script, and *The CBS Evening News* was commended on many fronts for its outstanding coverage of Watergate and Vietnam, including Emmys and Peabody Awards, among other accolades.

After a year off to crew on a racing boat in the West Indies, and to live in France, Carol returned to Washington and network news in a succession of positions, which included

---

11. Nice, tidy description of all the pertinent publication details. Not all memoirs need photos, but why not offer them and let the publisher decide?

producer roles at NBC News, CBS News *Nightwatch, USA Today the TV Show, This Week with David Brinkley, Nightline, Larry King Live,* and *Hardball with Chris Matthews.* For these broadcasts Carol focused on subjects ranging from global politics and the world's leaders to the latest successes or scandals involving the talented, the royal, or the merely celebrated. At *Nightwatch,* Carol and Charlie Rose won the national news' "Best Interview" Emmy Award for an hour CBS News broadcast interview with Charles Manson at San Quentin Prison.

Outside the world of journalism, Carol also directed documentary films and oversaw several film projects for clients such as the National Gallery of Art (NGA). She directed a video retrospective of the NGA's 50th Anniversary and a film tribute to the Kress family and their contribution to the Gallery's collections. She also directed a film for the American Academy in Rome, celebrating its 100th anniversary.

In 1997, when she was a producer for *Larry King Live,* her husband of twenty years, J. Howard Joynt III, died suddenly from pneumonia. Joynt inherited his landmark Georgetown restaurant, Nathans,[12] where she created *The Q&A Cafe,* the only known talk show that takes place in a saloon. In 2008, *Forbes Magazine* listed Nathans as one of Washington's top "power restaurants," due to *The Q&A Café.* Today, in addition to running Nathans and booking and producing her talk show, Carol also writes a weekly column about Washington for NewYorkSocialDiary.com, a social and cultural website that attracts more than 600,000 unique visitors each month.

On the domestic front, Carol's priority is making a home for her teenage son, Spencer, and their animals: Leo the dog and Ozzy the parrot.

---

12. In the proposal itself, the author includes this footnote: "ZAGAT 2009 described Nathans: On Georgetown's busiest corner, this 'great local joint' with a 'very Washington,' 'old-school club' look attracts loyal locals who 'always feel comfortable' either at its 'great people-watching bar' or in its 'cozy' back dining room; 'reasonably priced' American fare and a 'fabulous brunch' keep regulars returning, and even foodies who insist it's 'not for serious diners' find it 'fun'; N.B. owner Carol Joynt interviews a 'who's who' of news-making personalities at her popular 'Q&A Cafe' lunches."

CHAPTER OUTLINE AND SUMMARIES

PART I

Chapter One
Howard is in the intensive care ward; he's unconscious and on life support. Faceless people in helmets and jumpsuits prepare to airlift him to another hospital that's better equipped to handle his pneumonia. When they strap his seemingly lifeless body onto a gurney, I can barely see his face through the oxygen mask, or his body under the tubes and equipment.[13]

A few weeks ago we were in the Caribbean on a family vacation. Ten days ago we were in New York, celebrating the New Year. Now the gurney rolls past me—urgently.

I sit in a tiny room outside the ICU of the trauma hospital. One week stretches into two, then three. I leave the hospital only to hug our five-year old son, Spencer, change clothes, and occasionally to sleep. Howard remains on life support; he is never conscious. When the doctors tell me Howard won't make it, I return home. "I need to talk to you about Daddy," I say to Spencer. "I know," he says. "He's going to die, isn't he?"

I take my son to the hospital to say good-bye to his daddy. I leave them alone, but from outside the drawn curtain I hear Spencer sing, "You Are My Sunshine."

With his hand in mine, Howard dies on Saturday, February 1, at 10:16 a.m.

TARGET AUDIENCES
INNOCENT SPOUSE covers many different themes which makes it ideal for a wide range of readers. Those most likely to gravitate toward this story include:

---

13. Doesn't the first-person, present tense work powerfully here? And if every chapter summary is as detailed as this, do you see why an editor doesn't need to see a completed manuscript to know this story is a winner?

- Women—Especially married women. Especially women who have turned over financial matters to their spouse. This memoir will keep those women up at night. Promise.[14]
- Reading groups—This memoir is ripe with questions that married people will likely find thought-provoking, if not controversial: How well do you know your spouse? All marriages have secrets, don't they? How much (financial) control should you yield to a spouse?[15]
- On a lighter note—This memoir will also appeal to anyone with an interest in pop culture and/or journalism, as the behind-the-scenes stories in the world of entertainment are both fun and fascinating.[16]
- Single moms who struggle to balance work with raising their child(ren)[17]
  a. www.singlemom.com
  b. www.singlerose.com
  c. www.singlemothers.org
- Widows/Widowers[18]
  a. www.CaringInfo.org
  b. http://widow-speak.org
  c. http://www.widownet.org
  d. www.ywow.org
- Anyone who has ever worried about their finances and/or been audited by the IRS
- Readers with an interest in the restaurant business
- Anyone who enjoys a fresh story and learning something new

---

14. This kind of informality wouldn't fly with a regular nonfiction book. But with this extremely personal memoir? It's a nice touch.

15. Great point. Reading groups are primarily made up of women, and this topic will readily appeal to that audience.

16. Who wouldn't enjoy hearing how the author hobnobbed with the rich and famous?

17. Yes, yes, yes. The Pew Research Center shows that 40 percent of households with kids under eighteen include mothers who provide the sole or primary source of income for the family. Those parents are going to be interested in this book for sure.

18. This story starts with the death of a spouse. That's powerful stuff and will find an eager audience with widows and widowers. (The URLs here and for the bullet before it are another nice touch. Make things easy for an editor to confirm or learn more about.)

- In an economy where many "haves" have suddenly become "have nots" this story about surviving financial ruin will resonate more than ever before.

Appendix: Hyperlinks[19]

---

19. This is a single page (not included here) many authors couldn't provide, but why not give more social proof for editors to see firsthand? It's in an appendix, after all, so it can be easily ignored if an editor doesn't care much. But I think it's a very nice and not overly long list of URLs that gives context for this story. The links included were for videos, print, and Internet articles relevant to the memoir.

Chapter Sixteen

THE TEXTBOOK PROPOSAL:
AN ANNOTATED EXAMPLE

I have to be honest—I know a few dozen people who've written textbooks, and none of them wrote the book first in the hope of getting a contract later. Textbooks can take an insanely long time to build, and since they often use published material as samples, you have to pay for permission rights to reprint the material. No writer is going to fork over big bucks on such a speculative venture. To give you a sense of how much such a book can cost, I've included in this chapter a textbook proposal of mine that rang up more than $15,000 in permissions, and that's with me literally begging some authors to beg their publishers to reduce the reprint costs.

So as you can imagine, it's the norm to sell a textbook via book proposal due to the financial realities mentioned above, but also because so many textbook companies and editors are very hands-on. They expect you to make many changes in response to their concerns. Plus the proposals are regularly sent out to academic peers for review, and those responses, too, help shape the final product. After all, the publishers want teachers to want to teach from the book, so that feedback is taken very seriously.

Ryan G. Van Cleave's *Contemporary American Poetry: Behind the Scenes* (Longman, 2002)

A little context: I was finishing up grad school in 2001, and I attended the late December conference of the MLA (Modern Languages Association) because that's where nearly all of the hiring is done for professor jobs. I was wandering through the book fair between interviews, and I met a bored-looking person at the Longman booth. On a whim, I said, "I have a great idea for a book that'll fill a niche in your publishing line." The guy gave me his card and said to follow up with him. As you can see from the date of the cover letter, it took me a few weeks to pull something together since I had absolutely no idea for a book. I just said that to see what would happen.

What happened was a book! (Warning: Don't try this tactic unless you're prepared to work fast!)

January 30, 2001

XXXXX, Acquisitions Editor
Mailing Address 1
City, State, Zip

Dear XXXXX:

It was a pleasure meeting with the Longman reps at the MLA conference this past December. After speaking with them for awhile, they suggested I send something your way,[1] so enclosed please find a proposal for *Best of the Best: A Poetic Chrestomathy*.[2] It's a very different type of anthology,[3] but one I feel would complement books such as the Friebert and Young anthology among others.[4]

Who am I to be editing this book? Formerly a Kingsbury Fellow at Florida State University where I received my Ph.D. in poetry and American Literature, I am now the Anastasia C. Hoffman Poetry Fellow at the University of Wisconsin-Madison's Institute for Creative Writing. My poetry (nominated for seven Pushcart Prizes this year) has appeared in recent issues of *Arts & Letters*, *Quarterly West*, and *Ploughshares*; new poems are forthcoming in *TriQuarterly*, *The Journal*, and *The Christian Science Monitor*. I am author of four books, including most recently the poetry collection *Say Hello* (Pecan Grove Press, 2001) and the anthology *American Diaspora: Poetry of Displacement* (University of Iowa Press, 2001). I am including a flier for *American Diaspora* so you can get a sense of the quality of writers that you can expect to appear in this anthology.

---

1. Notice how I lead with my "in" for this person I never met. She wasn't at the conference—her colleagues were.

2. While I like the word *chrestomathy*, which means selection of literary passages on one topic, it's a bad title. About it, one reviewer wrote: "What the !@#($!*@ is a chrestomathy"? He was right. We changed the title.

3. See how I called it an "anthology"? When the editors at Longman asked for more teaching apparatus to make it more like a textbook, I gave them a fast "You bet!" (Tip: Say "you bet!" as often as possible when editors ask you to do something.)

4. I mention other popular titles of theirs to show that I do know their catalog and am not being ignorant by sending them an idea that's the same as what they've already done.

I include an SASE for your response. Thanks in advance for your time and attention.

Best Wishes,

Ryan G. Van Cleave, Ph.D.
Mailing Address
Email Address
Website
Phone
encl./ *Best of the Best: A Poetic Chrestomathy*, a proposal.

PROPOSAL

Best of the Best: A Poetic Chrestomathy

Sure, every American poetry anthology includes Simic's "Fork" and "Knife," as well as Mark Strand's "Keeping Things Whole" and "Courtship" but what poems would these poets pick as their own favorites? And why? This anthology intends to answer those questions through the two meanings of chrestomathy, (1) a collection of one's best work and (2) a selection of passages used especially to help in learning a language; in this case, it's the language of poetry from the viewpoint of the poets themselves. This book lets contemporary American poets pick a selection of their own best work, then provide a brief original commentary (specifically for this anthology) on their choices. It's a different type of anthology for a different type of reader—those poets and teachers of poetry who want the "inside scoop" on a poet's views, concerns, and personal aesthetic choices.

Working List of Contributors:
(poetry and commentary samples available upon request)
Sherman Alexie, Agha Shahid Ali, Margaret Atwood, Jimmy Santiago Baca, Ray Young Bear, Mei-mei Berssenbrugge, Marilyn Chin, Andrei Codrescu, Billy Collins, Victor Hernández Cruz, Jacqueline Dash, Martín Espada, Diane Glancy, Joy Harjo, Linda Hogan, Garret Hongo, Carolina Hospital, Jesse Lee Kercheval, James Kimbrell, Timothy Liu, Adrian C. Louis, Pablo Medina, Czeslaw Milosz, David Mura, Josip Novakovich, Ed Ochester, Sharon Olds, Alberto Ríos,

Pattiann Rogers, Charles Simic, Gary Soto, Mark Strand, Edwina Trentham, Derek Walcott, Ron Wallace, Li Young-Lee.

Best of the Best: A Poetic Chrestomathy will be a reader-friendly anthology of no more than three hundred pages, following an introduction by the editor and a preface by a high-profile American poet. Most of the poetry included in this anthology will be reprinted, but some will be very new work by some of America's best poets.

Best of the Best: A Poetic Chrestomathy can be ready for publication in Spring of 2002. Course adoption possibilities for this anthology are extremely high as it appeals to a wide variety of curricular needs, from Contemporary American Literature to Creative Writing classes to current issues in History, Psychology, and Sociology.

Feel free to share your comments, observations, and concerns regarding this project. I look forward to hearing from you at your earliest convenience.

Sincerely,

Ryan G. Van Cleave, Ph.D.

Part Three

INSIDER ADVICE

Chapter Seventeen

INTERVIEWS WITH TWO EDITORS

Since editors are the ones who offer book contracts to authors, let's see what we can learn from speaking with two experienced ones. No two are alike, but they all share the same passion for acquiring good books and supporting quality authors.

CAROL TRAVER, SENIOR ACQUISITIONS EDITOR AT TYNDALE HOUSE

Carol Traver has acquired *The New York Times* bestsellers *Coming Back Stronger* by Drew Brees, *Growing Up Amish* by Ira Wagler, *The Winners Manual* by Jim Tressel, *Don't Bet Against Me!* by Deanna Favre, *The 4:8 Principle* by Tommy Newberry, *First Things First* by Kurt and Brenda Warner, and *Game Plan for Life* by Joe Gibbs. Specializing in inspirational memoirs, Carol has worked with a wide range of authors in both the American Booksellers Association and Christian Booksellers Association markets, including former presidential candidates Rick Santorum and Tim Pawlenty, *American Idol* Season 5 Finalist Mandisa Hundley, and *New York Times* bestsellers Jerry Jenkins, David Jeremiah, and Randy Alcorn.

How many book proposals have you run across in the last year alone?

Between agented and unsolicited submissions, I see several hundred proposals every year, out of which I typically pursue a dozen or so. About five or six actually make it all the way through to final publication.

How many of those hundreds of proposals annually are knockouts?

Very few (typically between 1 and 5 percent) of the proposals that come across my desk actually merit a serious look. In some cases, the topic, content, or author simply isn't a good fit for our Christian publishing house, which is basically a sign that the agent or author didn't do their research before sending the proposal out. The majority of these come through attached to a generic form letter (always a dead giveaway) that gives no indication as to why they think our house (or I personally) would be a good fit for their project.

What stood out about the few you decided to pursue?

The few that do make it past the slush pile typically come from agents we have a long-standing relationship with who know the types of books, genres, and markets we excel in (and those we don't) and what interests us personally as acquisitions editors.

These book proposals are professionally done, personalized, present a clearly articulated hook, show evidence of thoughtful market research, provide accurate and realistic competing book information, strong writing samples, and a full profile of the author's platform, past sales history, marketability, and professional network.

Yes, the concept has to be great and the writing strong, but at the end of the day, the book also needs to be highly marketable. A good proposal will provide solid evidence of all of these things.

What is the most important thing you'd like would-be authors to remember when creating their book proposal?

Wow, there are a lot of things, but I'd probably say know your competition. Very few first-time authors take the time to do their research and see what else is already out there on their topic. In today's overcrowded marketplace, both retailers and consumers are extremely hesitant to take a chance on an unknown—especially when there are other more established, successful authors out there writing on the same topic. That's not to say if you have a passion for a certain topic that's already been covered that you *can't* write about it. But familiarizing yourself with what's already out there can help you tweak your concept so that it is unique enough to occupy its own space in the marketplace. Know what else is out there, what's worked, what hasn't, and find a way to make *your* book stand out from the crowd.

Acquisitions editors look at proposals through the eyes of the end user. If they feel your proposal doesn't offer any new insight, they're going to pass. We're looking for what's new and exciting, not what's already been done—even if it has been done successfully.

Likewise, to gauge consumer interest most publishers will check the sales histories on comparable titles when considering a new proposal. If the topic you're pitching doesn't seem to have much life in the marketplace, they're going to be extremely hesitant to take a chance on another one—especially from a first-time author.

And finally, be realistic with your comparables. Don't just grab the biggest runaway bestseller out there and say, "My book is just like X." First off, it's not. And if it *is*, you haven't created anything new, unique, or noteworthy. Bestsellers are bestsellers *because* they are unique. Knockoffs never work, and publishers know that. I would take a proposal for a book that is unlike anything I have ever seen before over a proposal I feel as though I've already read a dozen times any day of the week.

Publishing is hard, and the competition is fierce—you need to know what you have, know what you don't have, and be willing to do whatever you can to make your concept stand out. Go stand in the middle of a bookstore and ask yourself, "Why would anyone buy my book over everything else that's already out here?" Good acquisitions people do that often themselves. It's a sobering but extremely helpful exercise.

Who's a tougher audience for a book proposal, literary agents or editors?

I would say an editor is a tougher audience, because they are the ones who are going to be asking their companies to invest a significant amount of money in your book. If an agent can't sell your proposal, they're just out time (not to minimize the importance of time, of course. Editors also spend a significant amount of time working on manuscripts before they are published). However, if a publisher can't sell your book, not only are they out a significant amount of time and energy, but between the advance, marketing, cost of goods, overhead, etc., they can also be out hundreds of thousands of dollars. Publishing is a creative partnership, yes, but it is also a business. Not only are editors evaluating the quality of the writing, the distinctiveness of the idea, and the marketability of the finished product, they are also running every proposal through a fiscal feasibility lens as well. There is a great deal of financial risk involved in publishing a book, and at the end of the day, there is no guarantee that we are going to be able to sell a single copy. That's why writer's platforms, sales histories, ministries, and corporate affiliations are so important.

You've been fortunate enough to acquire celebrity books like Drew Brees's *Coming Back Stronger*, Kurt and Brenda Warner's *First Things First*, and Joe Gibbs's *Game Plan for Life*. Are the "rules" for book proposals different for high-profile people like them?

Yes and no. Because of their name recognition, visibility, media appeal, and built-in fan bases, personality-driven books like these do have a natural edge over no-name authors, simply because we don't have to overcome the hurdle of "introducing" them to the market. The audience is already there. However, because the cost of publishing high-profile authors is significantly higher, so is the financial risk. In that sense, yes, the same rules do apply. Regardless of who the author is, the book still has to serve a purpose. The story and/or message have to be compelling enough to justify a consumer plunking down $25 to read it. And yes, even high-profile authors (typically their agents) are expected to put together a formal proposal that outlines what the book is going to be about, what makes it unique, and how they (the author) are going to help promote it.

Granted, when it comes to high-profile names, the roles are sometimes reversed. In other words, *we* approach the celebrity with a book idea. When we do, however, the same rules apply to us that apply to them. We still put together a formal proposal complete with concept, expected time commitment on behalf of the author, etc.

TODD STOCKE, VICE PRESIDENT AND EDITORIAL DIRECTOR OF SOURCEBOOKS

A bookseller at heart, Todd Stocke now works for Sourcebooks, one of the world's leading independent book publishers. He oversees all imprints and acquisitions in every category, including adult nonfiction, fiction, romance, mixed media, calendars, young adult, and children's books.

During his time at Sourcebooks, he has guided the growth of its list from just ten new titles a year to its current annual output of three hundred–plus, with regular appearances on *New York Times* bestsellers lists.

How many book proposals come to Sourcebooks a week? How many eventually move on to become books in your catalog?

We publish more than three hundred books a year across a wide array of genres such as adult fiction and nonfiction, including a thriving line of romance novels, children's books of all stripes and ages, and young adult.

We receive several thousand unsolicited proposals every year. We open every one of them, and although 99.8 percent of them don't or won't work for us, we have found things in the slush pile. We just bought a great memoir for 2014 called *Seven Letters from Paris* that our assistant editor plucked out of the slush. Such a find is hugely exciting, though somewhat rare. The vast majority of our books are bought from literary agents, plus some from packagers and some from foreign publishers.

What was it about the *Seven Letters from Paris* proposal that not only caught an assistant editor's eye but carried it all the way through to the finish line?
The easiest answer here is that this project was in our wheelhouse because we'd recently been highly successful with a Paris-based memoir called *Paris My Sweet* by Amy Thomas. So internally we had identified that kind of book as a tiny subgenre, and our editors had tracked upon a spreadsheet the sales history on a whole pile of memoirs, from all publishers, that we identified as Paris themed. So this was a space we'd had a strong track record in already—and what that means is that our sales, marketing, and publicity folks had already been through the experimentation phase of who's interested in that sort of thing and who's not. That means prior knowledge for us on what might work in marketing and publicity and what might not. That's tough to find, with memoir especially, so it was a leg up.

From there it was a matter of the story, the voice, the author. First and fundamentally, is it good? Secondarily, can I pitch it? Beyond that are author-related questions, starting with whether the author is amenable to work on the creative end— i.e., the developing and positioning of the work. For us, the answers in all cases were yes.

On a scale of one to ten, how important is it for a would-be author's book proposal to have a strong PR/publicity component? Why? And is this different than it used to be?
Three. This is actually a real hot-button topic for me. Yes, it's wonderful when an author has a platform. There's a lot we can do with a built-in audience. But that's sort of the rub—the job of the publisher is to work *with* the platform. To augment it. To build it. To capitalize on it. In other words, the book doesn't sell just because of the author's platform. Otherwise, why the heck do they need us? In so many ways, our job as the publisher actually is to *be* the platform.

I was on a panel for a writers group recently, and in Q&A someone asked how important an author's social media platform was. Now, the unspoken part of that question is "Um, hey, I don't have *any* social media platform—no real Twitter, Facebook, or Pinterest followers—so how on earth do I build that?!?" My response was that if you have it, great, but if you don't, don't worry about it. That's actually our job as the publisher—to help guide you through what you should and should not be doing with social media. If anything at all, by the way.

Would it be fair to say that if an author doesn't have a strong platform that they need to clearly communicate that they're willing to work with a publisher to develop and maintain one? How might that be shown at the proposal stage?

I think it's useful for an author to somehow express that they're familiar with and at least conversant in platform-related subjects. There's a wide chasm between "I don't have a Pinterest platform" and "I've never used Pinterest, what is it again?" That's applicable to pretty much every platform-related thing—TV, radio, magazines (especially specialty ones), and the various social and online things. It helps us if authors are at least familiar with them and open to discovery in areas that may have impact. That initial familiarity, in fact, can help the author begin to identify what may and may not have impact for them, and the "may not" is just as important as the "may."

What is the most common misconception authors have about book proposals?

In many ways I think authors sometimes need two pitches—one short, one long. Most initial proposals are probably too long. Tell me the heart of what I'm looking at and why it's cool, then let me read some of the work. If I want to see more, with that give me the longer pitch and a more blown-out proposal with marketing/media/competitive/comparative elements. Perhaps most important, give me some suggestion that you've set foot in a bookstore lately and thought about where your book would sit. That thinking should educate how you pitch your work.

Chapter Eighteen

INTERVIEWS WITH TWO LITERARY AGENTS

Throughout this book, I've talked about how you basically have two audiences for a book proposal. One is a literary agent, who (if they accept you as a client) can help polish and shape your proposal so it has a better chance of success with audience #2, the publishing house editor. At an agency, you typically have to sell your proposal only to one person. As you learned in chapter two, you have to sell to an entire room full of people at a publishing house (called the pub board). Anything you can do to prepare yourself and your proposal for that gauntlet is worth doing.

Even if you choose to skip the agent route and directly approach publishers who accept unsolicited manuscripts and queries, you can still share in the wisdom these in-the-publishing-trenches folks have to offer. Read on, and see what these industry veterans have learned about the book proposal.

LANEY KATZ BECKER OF LIPPINCOTT MASSIE MCQUILKIN

Laney Katz Becker is an agent at Lippincott Massie McQuilkin (www.lmqlit. com). Prior to becoming an agent, she was an advertising copywriter and freelance journalist, as well as an award-winning author of fiction (*Dear Stranger, Dearest Friend*) and nonfiction (*Three Times Chai*). Laney uses her extensive writing background to help her authors shape and revise their projects. She specializes in debut authors, and her "newbies" have made the *New York Times*, national, and international bestsellers' lists. She is a graduate of Northwestern University, is married, and has two kids.

What's one of your favorite book proposal success stories?

I got a memoir query (slush pile) from someone who was living in L.A., and though I didn't know it at the time, his big dream included breaking into the scriptwriting/sitcom world in Hollywood. His proposal needed work, and I called him to discuss it. He was open to my ideas for revisions, and I signed him. Months went by as he and I worked on getting his proposal ready for submission. Finally, I sold the proposal, he wrote the full manuscript, and around publication time the author developed a book trailer—which was hilarious and immediately went viral. It quickly garnered more than a million YouTube views. (It's now around 4 million.) Anyway, the trailer created such a splash that the author was interviewed about it in newspapers, radio shows, and some comedy icons posted links to the video on *their* web pages. Yes, my author sold some books, but the real success here is that the book trailer and its huge appeal opened all kinds of opportunities for the author with managers, film agents, and so many of the Hollywood elite he'd previously tried to connect with and failed. But now, the stars had aligned in the least expected way, and he was able to take those sitcom ideas and scripts from his desk and parlay his notoriety into something that went well beyond the book. If you want to check out the book trailer you can search for "50 State Stereotypes (in 2 minutes)" at YouTube.

What do you see most authors getting wrong with their proposals?

The things most writers get wrong in their proposals varies, depending on the proposal category.

Prescriptive/self-help proposals: I often get proposals from writers who say something along the lines of "There are plenty of books about [insert subject matter they want to write about], but they're all from the point of view of experts or celebrities. Mine is different. It's from the perspective of a real person." This is not a selling point! It's a competitive market, and publishers are always concerned about how they'll make readers aware that a book exists. That means that from the get-go, agents, editors, and publishers are all eager to work with a recognized expert or celeb who already has an established national platform. Why? Because it dramatically increases the chances of landing those coveted media interviews, which are so necessary in getting word out about the book. Now, if you're "a normal person" who wants to write about parenting a child with special needs, or rebounding after a divorce, or how to care for a chronically ill loved one, etc., you can still share your tips, but a book is probably not the best forum. There are other avenues open to writers whose credentials for writing about something are nothing more than "I've walked the walk." But when it comes to self-help books, publishers are looking for experts, or celebrities who have expertise and some name recognition.

Memoir Proposals: Most lives are not worthy of a memoir that anyone other than friends and/or family members care to read about. Sorry. But it's true. (And the same goes when you find your grandparents' love letters.

Nice for you and the rest of your clan, but to me, it's like being invited to look at your family photos. I'd rather pass.)

But, even if you have a wonderful, fresh, and inspiring story to tell, how do you break through the clutter? Sometimes being a great writer with a unique voice who has an amazing story to tell is enough. But often it's not. Publishers are platform obsessed, which means that as an agent, I have to be, too. So, unless a proposal contains some concrete ways/connections that can convince me (and that I, in turn, can use to help convince publishers) that your story can break out and garner some review/publicity attention, it's a tough, tough sell.

I also see too many writers who are jumping on a trend too late. For a while those "year-long experiment" memoirs were hot. But now? Not so much. Yet I still get queries from people wanting to write about what happened when they decided to sell everything and live on a boat for a year. Or sleep in a different bed every day for a year, or bake a different cupcake … whatever wacky thing they want to try. A subscription to something like *Publishers Marketplace* is such an easy way for writers to stay on top of what's being bought and sold *today*, which can help them stay on top of what's in and what's out. (Remember, it typically takes more than a year from the time a proposal is sold to when it's published; something to keep in mind when trying to determine if you're jumping on an already downward-spiraling trend.)

Memoir proposals that don't really have a story arc but are more about "this happened, then this happened, then this other thing," are also problematic for me. The chapter summary/outline for a memoir proposal needs to have more than a laundry list of events. It needs a story arc—similar to that found in a novel.

Others may disagree, but I don't want a "memoir" written by someone other than the writer. So "I've written a memoir about my grandmother, who came over from Europe during the war" is not going to fly for me.

Narrative proposals: I don't see enough of these (and wish I saw more) especially from great journalists. But when I do see them the biggest problem is lack of focus. The writer is trying to cover too much, and he or she's all over the place. Also, the rambling nature of these types of proposals leaves me yearning for better storytelling, which is what makes a narrative work really come to life, for me.

How many proposals do you see a month (or year, if you'd prefer)? And how many merit serious consideration?

I get over one hundred queries a week. About a quarter of those are for nonfiction projects. (I handle more fiction than nonfiction, so that's about the right ratio.) Unless the topic is one I know I'm not interested in, I always take a quick look at the proposal. Sometimes I don't read more than the opening lines or paragraph before I decide that the writing isn't strong enough or the voice isn't compelling. But, basically, I'll keep reading a proposal until I know it's not for me/not something I'm excited to take on. (If I think it's a good or better fit for one of my colleagues, I pass it along to them.) So the generous answer is that I give every proposal serious consideration. But I probably read an entire proposal and am interested enough to want to talk to the author about it only 2 to 5 percent of the time. I know, not a great percentage. But I spend a lot of time working closely with my authors to help revise their proposals and get them sparkling for submission to editors, so I have to love the topic, believe we can make it salable, and make sure that the writer is up for doing the necessary revisions until it's good to go!

What does it mean to have "a great hook"? How do you know when you've got one?

To me, the words *great hook* are synonymous with *great idea.* It's the thing that intrigues people so much they're dying to read your book/know what comes next. How do you know if you've got one? There's a terrific barometer that I learned from another agent that I think works like a dream; it's called "the wow test." First, develop an elevator pitch for your book—you know, that one-sentence description that you can rattle off when asked, "What's your book about?" Now, once you share that pitch with someone, what's the person's reaction? If it's "wow," you've got that great hook, that big idea, that thing that can get agents' and editors' attention.

For regular nonfiction books, what's a good researching/ writing ratio? How can you tell when that's off?

I think different topics require different amounts of research, so that ratio is fluid depending on the topic—and the writer. Some writers feel they need massive amounts of research so they, themselves, understand a topic inside and out. *But, just because a writer knows something or has learned something during the research phase doesn't mean it belongs on the page.* (Can I repeat that because it's soooo important!) When I'm editing a manuscript or proposal I'm big on putting notes in the margins, and my authors can tell you that the words *info dump* are not foreign to them. That's my way of letting them know that they either need to better integrate their research into the text or think about getting rid of it all together. Because just dumping it onto the page is boring, heavy-handed, and even a bit lazy. I also complain about "info dump" to some of my novelists; the temptation to dump is especially great in historical fiction. (In fact, I'm reading a novel now—not one of my authors—and I'm not going to finish it, simply because the info dump is so frequent that I've lost track of the story!)

LISA HAGAN OF LISA HAGAN LITERARY

Lisa Hagan Literary has a history of anticipating future book trends and creating appropriate projects with its clients—scientists, writers, and innovators from around the world. Lisa began her literary career with Paraview Literary Agency in 1993 and purchased it in 1999. Her areas of interest are in nonfiction properties only: self-help, metaphysical, spiritual, health, travel, science, and business. Lisa is always on the lookout for a good story that will inspire others to become who they are truly meant to be.

How close to being "done" does a book proposal need to be for you to take that project on?

Of course, I prefer to receive a completely polished proposal according to publishing standards. Every agent does. However, if the content is so exciting or current, I will assist the writer in crafting what I deem to be the best possible proposal. In my twenty-two years, I have written many proposals with experts in their fields. It's usually because I am excited about the idea and want to sell it right now. Everything sells faster when I am super hot for an idea. I can be impatient, which is not necessarily a bad thing. Sometimes writers need a little push out of their comfort zones.

What are some of the biggest misconceptions authors seem to have about book proposals?

That there are no existing comparative titles. If you are the first ever with your idea, then good for you, but I have yet to see that happen.

Can you give an example of a book proposal a client of yours used that was so well done that the project sold far easier than it would've had you sent in the finished book alone?

Many years ago, when I was first starting out, I pitched a well-written and engaging proposal on the secrets of the ancient Incas, which I found fascinating. I sold it right away. I was excited to sell it and couldn't wait to read the final draft of the manuscript. When the author turned it in, it was so poorly written that the contract was canceled. Fortunately, that has only happened one time. I never did learn who wrote the proposal, but I'm sure it wasn't the author.

How often does a publisher cancel a contract after receiving the full manuscript?

I've only had the one book canceled, but I've certainly seen it happen, though I'm not sure how often. One of my co-workers had this experience when the head of the imprint was let go and the new person didn't care for the subject matter, as it didn't gel with her belief system. But more often than not, it's usually because the author either can't write or is plagiarizing. A freelance editor can always be brought in to fix any problems if the subject matter is worth pursuing.

The worst is when an editor that has acquired the proposal leaves the publishing house and you are turned over to an editor that (a) doesn't get the material or (b) doesn't care. You are left in limbo land. This is rare, but it has happened to me and it stinks!

Do you have a story about how a great idea hooked you despite the proposal not being up to par?

A friend of a friend sent me a proposal for *Babylon's Ark: The Incredible Wartime Rescue of the Baghdad Zoo*. Even though it was poorly written, I requested the manuscript, which was not in any better shape. I passed. But I could not stop thinking about the story and what the author had accomplished. After some deliberation, I contacted him, took him on as a client, wrote the proposal myself, and we reworked the two chapters to add to it. I sold it to a terrific editor who did a sensational job editing. I am very proud of how it turned out.

Chapter Nineteen

TEN INSIDER TIPS THAT MIGHT MEAN THE DIFFERENCE BETWEEN SUCCESS AND DISASTER

Here are some final thoughts and ideas about what I wish I'd known when starting out in the writing business, as well as at various times in my career where I struggled. We all struggle at times, and let's be frank—struggling sucks. My intention is that sharing this information might help you avoid some of that suckiness.

I could've called this chapter "Ten Insider *Secrets* That Might Mean the Difference Between Success and Disaster," but the truth is that they're not all that secret. Some are plain common sense. Some are just the lessons writers often learn via the School of Hard Knocks. Some are things that I've seen writers do wrong thanks to my years as a writing coach, book doctor, and editor of a nonprofit literary press. Writers run afoul of these all the time, so trusting that people easily overcome these challenges on their own isn't a good bet.

So here they are in no particular order beyond how they came to me. No one is more or less important than any other. I truly hope these help keep you on the path to success.

And P.S. Use the contact form on www.theweekendbookproposal.com to tell me about any successes this book helped bring about.

TIP #1: IF YOU'RE NOT ENJOYING THE PROCESS OF WRITING YOUR BOOK, STOP AND ASK YOURSELF WHY.

Ask yourself this question: Why do people read? There are many answers to this because reading offers a lot. Mind-blowing ideas. Sensuality. Excitement. Adventure. Fun. Triumphs. Wonder. Insight. Catharsis. At the root of all of those things is enjoyment, satisfaction, gratification. In short, the common denominator of every reading experience is some form of pleasure.

If you're not experiencing any type of pleasure while writing your book (the sample chapters, the outline, any of it), how on earth do you expect a reader to derive pleasure from reading it?

WORDS OF WISDOM

"No tears in the writer, no tears in the reader. No surprise in the writer, no surprise in the reader." — Four-time Pulitzer Prize winner Robert Frost

If you find yourself dreading the obligation of writing more on your project, don't plow ahead and hate every minute of it. Instead, stop and take a moment to figure out what it is that you're dreading. A lot of times, that dread is an indication that you've got something wrong. Maybe you know that your main premise isn't fully developed. Maybe the book you're talking about writing isn't a book you're actually that interested in writing. (That happened to me once. I was twenty pages into a book proposal, and I dreaded the idea of getting a contract and actually having to write the thing! It was a really fine idea for a book, only it wasn't a book I needed or even really wanted to write. Life's too short to spend doing things you loathe.) Or maybe you fear success.

Take the time to uncover the root cause of your resistance. Deal with it however you need to. Then return to writing, renewed and refreshed. That's how you'll rediscover that pleasure that called you to writing to begin with.

TIP #2: READ, READ, READ.

When I was an undergraduate at Northern Illinois University, I took an introductory poetry writing class because I fell in love with Wallace Stevens's poetry in high school. I'd carried around a slender volume of his verse for so long that the only things holding it together were two thick rubber bands.

When asked about our favorite poets on the first day of that poetry class, many fellow students didn't name one. It quickly became clear that most of my peers didn't know many poets, let alone have favorites. Our professor then asked how many of us had bought a book of poetry in the past year. The only hand that went up was mine. Nineteen other kids were in that class, all hoping to write good poetry one day. The class was an elective, so it's not like they had to be there. They chose that class over a host of other options. Maybe they didn't want to be professional poets (that might well be an oxymoron, I realize), but they clearly wanted a better handle on how to write quality poetry.

How in the world is that going to happen if they don't read to know what good, publishable-quality poetry looks like?

I am blessed to have found reading at a very young age, thanks to a good school librarian who passed me a copy of *The Hobbit* when I was in third grade. I was hooked. From then on, I've read at least three books a week, and from that constant exposure, I have developed a keen awareness of what makes good writing. I'm able to appreciate striking turns of phrase and word choices, too, which helps me do more of that in my own writing, I'm certain.

If you didn't grow up with a love of reading, no worries. It's never too late to cultivate this fine habit. Read books, magazines, newspapers, blogs, anything you can find. All writing offers lessons in what does (and doesn't) work. And don't feel limited to print material, either. Listen to audio books or quality documentaries like those by Ken Burns or Errol Morris. If your local bookstores have live author events, go hear those, too. Experience the craft of wordsmithery in all of its forms. It's like a vitamin you need to keep your own writing healthy.

TIP #3: THE #1 KILLER OF WRITING CAREERS IS PROCRASTINATION.

Part of the idea of a title like *The Weekend Book Proposal* is that there's no time for procrastination. *No* writer has time for procrastination. This probably sounds a little Yoda-like, but writing is *doing* and procrastination is *not doing*. See the problem?

A few ways to combat procrastination:

- **Give yourself public accountability:** Announce to all eleven thousand of your Facebook friends that your novel will be done by Christmas, and you'll get so tired of fielding questions and comments about it that you'll get writing. A spouse or family member can similarly provide the ongoing presence that doesn't let you off the hook.

- **Break your project into small, easily manageable steps:** Don't get overwhelmed by the idea of writing an entire book proposal. Start with one thing that's easy—your author bio. Or the elevator pitch, which is what, twenty words? Who can't write twenty words? Then take on one other small task. Then another. And so on.

- **Change up your environment:** Write at home versus the coffee shop. Write at the library. Write in a park. Write on a long train ride. Write in a bus station. Write at a church. Write in your garage. Write in a hotel room. Go somewhere different than you normally do for writing and see if a change in place fires up your creativity.

- **Reward yourself:** Give yourself a reward/treat for completing the project. The idea of getting a slice of raspberry pie or watching a rerun of *Dr. Who* does wonders for my motivation regarding an onerous freelance writing assignment. Don't go overboard with this, but the occasional carrot dangled before you can be a good incentive. (If you need to call it a bribe, fine.)

- **Hang out with go-getters:** I'm convinced that we pick up (by osmosis, perhaps) the habits of those we associate with. Spend enough time with successful people who get stuff done, and you'll start to be one of those people, too. Model your behavior after them, and you'll be knocking down writing tasks in no time. Reading books like Steven Covey's *The Seven Habits of Highly Effective People*, too, can't hurt if you don't have easy access to successful people.

TIP #4: FIRST DRAFTS ARE *NOT* FINAL DRAFTS.

You can do everything right but still end up without getting a publishing contract if you skip the revision and editing stages. First drafts are great for figuring out what you want to say and how you want to say it. Now say it more clearly, more efficiently. That's what a good revision can do for you. It tightens your writing. It makes it stronger. It puts the pizzazz into your piece.

Yes, it's hard work to revise. Sometimes it's very hard. It's certainly much harder for most writers to do than sitting back and dreaming up new stuff in the first place. But here's where the big payoff happens. Here's where you go from being a would-be writer to a professional (meaning paid) writer. If you sincerely want that book contract, then don't skimp on the revision stage.

TIP #5: JEALOUSY IS OKAY IF YOU USE IT TO FUEL YOU VERSUS LETTING IT DISCOURAGE.

A lot of famous people are the same age as me right now: Eminem, The Rock, Shaquille O'Neal, Ben Affleck, Jennifer Garner, Jenny McCarthy, Jude Law, and Gwyneth Paltrow, to name just a few. As we were all growing up together, it was easy to dismiss their successes because they were in different fields than mine. She's an actress, I'm a writer, right? He's just scoring baskets. What's that got to do with manuscripts and query letters? Rap music? Pshaw.

But before long, sure enough, some same-aged writer friends started killing it in the literary world. Starred reviews in *Publishers Weekly*, advances huge enough to buy mansions, and major publishing awards—these guys and girls were raking it in.

I'm human. I had moments where I thought, "Jeez. I took classes with that guy. He wrote one story that was bad enough to peel the enamel off my teeth. Why do such good things happen to *him*?" Moments like this are fine as long as they're brief. What they need to quickly lead to is: *If so-and-so can do that, then so can I.* And then you work like heck to prove it to yourself and the rest of the world.

Jealousy is something most writers won't talk about. It's often ugly. And it sometimes reveals our worst faults. Plus we all put ourselves into everything we write, so when the world responds better to someone else's work, it's like the world likes them better. That sucks. But let it fuel your own efforts, and jealousy suddenly has a positive outcome.

TIP #6: THERE'S ALWAYS MORE TO LEARN.

There's a reason why Writer's Digest keeps putting out new writing how-to books. The act of writing hasn't changed all that much in the last few hundred years, admittedly, but the insights and ideas we have regarding it are always evolving. In short, there's always something more to learn.

WORDS OF WISDOM

"You'll never know everything about anything, especially something you love." — Julia Child

"Education is the kindling of a flame, not the filling of a vessel." — Socrates

NBA great Michael Jordan always practiced and evolved his game despite being the best basketball player on the planet. He was Michael freaking Jordan! If he can keep working and learning, why should we feel that we can kick back and say, "No more! I've got it licked!"?

Don't spend overmuch time studying your craft because to be a writer you need to write, right? But do humbly add to your existing body of knowledge about writing from time to time. Take a class. Read another Writer's Digest book. Listen to writer interviews on YouTube. Spend some time being introspective about your own writing. It'll all pay off.

TIP #7: KNOW THAT WRITING A SUCCESSFUL BOOK IS HALF COMMERCE, HALF ART.

The world has changed. No longer do writers live as recluses in cabins and knock out bestseller after bestseller, leaving all the marketing, publicity, and selling to the publisher. Back in the 1920s, that might've been the case. This isn't the 1920s anymore. PR guru Steve Harrison claims the best investment a writer can make is to learn more about marketing. In his teleseminars and workshops, he cites numerous examples of how the most successful books aren't often the best, but they're the best marketed books. Just think about Dr. Phil. There's no way he's the best shrink on the planet, but if he's not one of the most famous and successful ones, then I'm an orangutan. He's a media marketing creation.

Editors know this reality. They're aware of the critical importance marketing and publicity have with every book they acquire. Make sure that you take off your "Grand Artiste" hat at some point and put on your Don Draper *Mad Men* fedora before zipping off your proposal to New York. You don't have to be happy with the realization that having a strong business IQ will help your writing career, but don't be in denial about that, either. Make sure your book proposal shows a bit of your business IQ and savviness, too.

TIP #8: JOIN A WRITERS' GROUP.

Writing can be a painfully solitary business. It's not unreasonable to desire a little practical or emotional support from time to time, and a good writers' group can offer those things. Who better to understand the challenges a writer faces than other writers? If the group you choose has deadlines for delivering material to be discussed, you might satisfy Tip #3 as well. Other members might well have information about agents, editors, and contests that you could find useful. Talk about a good bonus! And speaking of bonuses ...

Super bonus tip: When I wrote *Memoir Writing for Dummies* in 2013, I had too much material, so we put an entire chapter up on the Web for free. That chapter, "Making the Most of a Writing Critique Group," is something you can check out, too. Learn all about writing groups, including how to find the right one for you. (www.ryangvancleave.com/bonuschapter.pdf)

TIP #9: DON'T UNDERESTIMATE THE VALUE OF ATTENDING A WRITERS CONFERENCE.

I'm a fan of writers conferences. The panel discussions are a great way to discover what editors and agents want firsthand. Plus you can often pay a little extra to have some of your own work evaluated and responded to by a publishing professional. Not a bad way to get your writing sample up to snuff, which makes your entire book proposal stronger. It's also a fine opportunity to widen your circle of literary friends. You never know who will be your next co-author or have the perfect contact for your proposal.

Writers conferences can be big, busy things and can intimidate first-timers. Check out the full schedule far in advance, and don't try to do every last thing (especially for multiday conferences). Select those events that hold the most appeal, and make the most of those. Remember, too, that the purpose of going is to help with your writing. Don't get too caught up in the socializing, drinking, and gossiping—all very popular things to do at conferences!

TIP #10: THERE ARE OODLES OF DIFFERENT GOOD ROUTES TO SUCCESS AS A WRITER.

Read enough stories on how debut authors got published and you'll quickly see that there's no single path to publication. Just because a published author went about it differently than you're doing isn't a problem. Every writer is different. Every book is different. Every situation is different. Don't spend a lot of time trying to unearth the secret blueprint for publishing success. A good idea, some hard work, and sincere effort in the ways described in this book are all you need. You can't do much about dumb luck or Mercury being in retrograde.

I often get approached by would-be writers at conferences or workshops who tell me, "Well, so and so did it this way." I don't care. Sorry, but it's true. Anecdotally, I suppose I might find the story interesting, but in terms of being nuts-and-bolts useful? Not at all. Just trust your own process and give 100 percent to it plus a little patience. It'll pay off. Trust me.

SUPER BONUS TIP #11: DON'T FALL PREY TO ROOKIE MISTAKES.

Note: Yes, I realize that I promised ten tips, but just as you should do with your entire book proposal (and every aspect of your writing career, in fact), I have underpromised and overdelivered. That's why you get #11! Boom!

Don't tell me you're not excited about Super Bonus Tip #11. Heck, I'm excited about it, and I know these tips well.

Here's a laundry list of what rookies—and even experienced writers—must not do. I call these "boomerang boo-boos," because most editors will instantly reject your proposal and send it back to you if you commit them.

Don't include a copyright symbol on your work: So much good work already exists, why would someone bother to steal yours (even after being vaguely inspired by the Ira Levin play/film *Deathtrap*)? And your work is technically copyrighted the moment it's written, anyway, whether you officially register it with the U.S. Copyright Office or not (the online filing fee is currently $35 per piece copyrighted). Never use the © symbol nor the word *copyright* on your documents. Never.

Don't misspell an editor's name: I get this a lot. One day I'm Van Cleave. The next I'm G. Van Cleave. Or Ryan Cleave. Ryan Van. Etc. It's annoying. It's rude. It also shows that you didn't take the time to find the correct spelling. Or you're a sloppy typist who doesn't revise. In any event, this is a silly no-no.

Don't use clip art in your presentation: If you're using professional-level art that's appropriate to your presentation (as I said I did in my proposal for *You Know You're a Video Game Addict If*, which is an illustrated humor book), then fine. If you're worried that an editor won't know that you're a writer so you include something like a clip-art pencil, resist that temptation. Clip art is fine for Christmas letters to the family and scrapbooks—nowhere else.

Don't trust spell-checker without fail: Spell-checker is only as smart as the people who programmed it, which is to say it isn't perfect. It also can lead you astray because you meant *from* and typed *form*, which is a perfectly valid word, so spell-checker ignores it. Trust spell-checker at your own peril. I'm sure that its a misteak to due sow. (See what I mean?)

Don't get chatty in e-mails, queries, and cover letters: You might think that being casual is a refreshing change of pace from the stuffy "Dear Mr. High-Falutin' Editor" things they usually get. It's not. From time to time, I have a problem with students at my college who send me e-mails like this.

Prof
U want me 2 bring Story 1 2 class? Its not done yet. lol.
A-Dawg
W o o F!

If A-Dawg and I are pals, this sort of abbreviated, loosey-goosey communication is fine. For any correspondence between you and an editor you're trying to impress, err on the side of formality and respect.

Don't talk your rejection into a yes: If you get a rejection, move on. Don't blog about that editor's poor judgment and million-dollar mistake. Don't whine to every writer you know about "that stupid publishing house." And don't call that editor and try to convince her that she made a gross error. Just hike up your shorts and move on.

Don't send more than one version of your work to an editor: So you're committed to revision? Great. It's not unheard of for writers to be tweaking a manuscript or proposal long after it's been sent out. But don't fire off version 1.1 to replace version 1.0, especially before version 1.0 has been responded to. And certainly avoid sending versions 1.2 and 1.3 to replace the earlier ones. The one you originally submitted is the one you'll live or die with for that editor. Feel free to send later (hopefully better) versions to the next editor. But let me ask you—did you submit too quickly in the first place? Why not wait until you have version 1.4 versus 1.0 before sending out at all? (See Tips #4 and #6.)

Don't follow up too soon or too often: While the single proposal you're circulating might be the most important thing in *your* world, it's not the most important thing in the editor's world. She has many clients under contract, and she needs to deal with them first. She might well have a family and other obligations, too, which take precedence over your submission. In short, it might take an unbearably long time for her to respond to you. Resist the impulse for one of those "Didja get it? Didja like it? Didja didja didja?" e-mails.

If it's been an inappropriately long time and you've not heard back (such as a few weeks past stated reply times, or three months in general), a short, polite follow-up that includes all the pertinent information for your original submission is appropriate. What's pertinent? The date of submission, your name, your contact info, the title of what you sent, and a brief (seriously—one sentence is enough for this part) explanation of what you sent. That's it. Offer to resend if they need you to. Other than that, it's a "get in and get out" kind of thing.

Note: 99 percent of the time, nudging an editor like this isn't going to result in a "Yes, good Lord, yes!" Just think about the situation. You're superbusy, overworked, and underpaid, and someone's asking you to do something for them. The easiest way to get past that request? Say no. So don't expect much with your request here. What you're really trying to do is get the 100 percent confirmation that this is a No so you can cross that name off the list and move on to the next one. (I have had a Yes after nine months, so it's not entirely hopeless if it takes a long time.)

Additional note: A few agents consider not responding to be a "no." You can find out who these are by checking their agency websites for this stated policy, or by checking your agent out through online resources such as www.QueryTracker.net or www.AbsoluteWrite.com.

Don't miss deadlines: The writing community is smaller than you'd think, so a reputation for being a deadline misser (i.e., pain in the butt to work with) is easily earned. But you can screw up with deadlines even before you've signed a publishing contract. If an editor is truly interested in your book, he might say something like, "I've got an acquisitions meeting next Thursday. Have two sample chapters and the revisions we suggested ready by then, and I'll pitch it."

WORDS OF WISDOM

"I love deadlines. I like the whooshing sound they make as they fly by."
— Douglas Adams

If you agree to that arrangement and then send an "Oops, I forgot I was participating in a Dungeons & Dragons marathon this week. I didn't get to it. Sorry!" e-mail, you're well on your way to being officially labeled "untrustworthy" and "difficult."

Don't use extra spaces at the ends of sentences: Back in the good old days of typewriters, it was appropriate to put two spaces after a period. Like this. See the difference from these and the sentences above? The reasons why this was done are complex, but the main thrust is that typewriters used monospaced type, meaning every character used an equal amount of space on the page. This inserted lots of extra space around skinny letters like *i* or the number *1*. To distinguish between ends of sentences and that extra spacing between letters, people typed two spaces at the end of a sentence. Modern fonts (which all computers use) correct this spacing issue, so the double space is no longer necessary as a visual cue.

But c'mon, you might be saying. Why is avoiding the double space such a big deal? Because it's annoying for someone at the publishing house to have to manually fix every one of those. Even if they use a "find and replace" option, they still have to check to make sure it worked correctly. So just be nice. One space after end punctuation is enough. Really. And for those who argue that two spaces after a period make something more readable, I say: Show me the research. I can't find any. And just giving the page the old eye test, I don't notice an increased level of reading difficulty with the single space versus the double space.

SUGGESTED READING

BOOKS WHOSE PROPOSALS ARE INCLUDED AS EXAMPLES

Armstrong, Jennifer. *Mary and Lou and Rhoda and Ted: And all the Brilliant Minds Who Made The* Mary Tyler Moore Show *a Classic*. New York, NY: Simon & Schuster (2013).

Cullinane, Jan. *The Single Woman's Guide to Retirement: Everything You Need to Know*. Hoboken, NJ: Wiley (2012).

Harper, S.J. *Cursed: A Fallen Siren Novel*. New York, NY: Roc (2013).

Holmes, Gina. *Crossing Oceans*. Carol Stream, IL: Tyndale House (2010).

Joynt, Carol Ross. *Innocent Spouse: A Memoir*. New York, NY: Broadway Books (2012).

McDowell, Gary L. and F. Daniel Rzicznek. *The Rose Metal Press Field Guide to Prose Poetry: Contemporary Poets in Discussion and Practice*. Brookline, MA: Rose Metal Press (2010).

Van Cleave, Ryan G. *City of the Big Shoulders: An Anthology of Chicago Poetry*. Iowa City, IA: University of Iowa Press (2012).

Van Cleave, Ryan G. *Contemporary American Poetry: Behind the Scenes*. New York, NY: Longman (2002).

ON RESEARCH

Berkman, Robert. *Find It Fast: How to Uncover Expert Information on any Subject Online or in Print*, 5th edition. New York, NY: HarperResource (2000). No writer's bookshelf is complete without this handy reference book. This book goes beyond just listing experts and information "supersources"—it also explains how to identify experts and offers tips on dealing with them.

Booth, Wayne C., Gregory G. Colomb, and Joseph M. Williams. *The Craft of Research*, 3rd edition. Chicago, IL: University of Chicago Press (2008). Though this book is primarily for classroom use (writing research papers), much of the book is dedicated to understanding good reasoning in the writing process—a good skill for any writer. The sections on evaluating and using primary, secondary, and tertiary sources is useful, as is the chapter on visual communication (using charts, tables, and graphs effectively).

Fogg, Christine, and Bruce Grundy. *Release the Hounds: A Guide to Research for Journalists and Writers.* Sydney, Australia: Allen & Unwin (2006). This easy-to-follow Australian-published guide explains how to find, identify, and use quality Internet resources. It also talks about developing research skills, using special libraries and collections, and government documents. The book plays with the title metaphor throughout, using such chapter headings as "Marking the Territory" and "Picking Up the Scent."

THE WORLD OF PUBLISHING

Curtis, Richard. *Mastering the Business of Writing: A Leading Literary Agent Reveals the Secrets of Success.* Amazon Kindle Editions (2004). This updated version of his 1995 paperback is a comprehensive look at nearly every aspect of the publishing world through the eyes of a leading literary agent. For those who want to know about copyright, contracts, advances, subsidiary rights, and publishing protocols, this book will help.

Gallagher, Helen. *Release Your Writing: Book Publishing, Your Way.* Virtualbookworm.com Publishing (2007). Suitable for beginners and intermediate writers, this book examines the changing publishing industry and advocates self-publishing and/or print on demand for those whose work is unlikely to attract the attention of agents and publishers. It also includes marketing strategies, promotion tips, and even advice on how to write more effectively with your computer.

Sambuchino, Chuck. *Formatting & Submitting Your Manuscript*, 3rd Edition. Cincinnati, OH: Writer's Digest Books (2009). If you want to see more examples of query letters, novel synopses, and book proposals, then Sambuchino's book is a fine complement to this one. If you like lots of dos and don'ts, Sambuchino's book delivers. Many people find this a must-have for the reference shelf. Make sure you get the most recent edition, though, or you might be missing out on the information about online submissions.

Shaw, Lisa. *How to Make Money Publishing from Home: Everything You Need to Know to Successfully Publish: Books, Newsletters, Greeting Cards, Zines, and Software.* Rocklin, CA: Prima (2000). This revised edition is still decidedly behind the times on the Internet and electronic publishing, but for a beginner, this book covers a lot of topics in a short space. Use it to get a handle on what's possible and supplement with other books as needed.

Walsh, Pat. *78 Reasons Why Your Book May Never Be Published and 14 Reasons Why It Just Might*. New York, NY: Penguin (2005). The founding editor of MacAdam/Cage and a former reporter for the *San Francisco Chronicle*, Walsh is generous with his insider information. His ninety-two short chapters are informative and eminently useful. Punctuated with anecdotes from a long career as a writer and editor, this book is an entertaining wake-up call to writers.

ON NONFICTION WRITING

Poynter, Dan. *Writing Nonfiction: Turning Thoughts Into a Book*. Santa Barbara, CA: Para Publishing (2005). This updated edition by writing coach Dan Poynter brings marketing savvy, publishing know-how, and plain common sense together in an approachable 156-page package. Well-organized, this book has loads of tips and examples from people who have used his techniques to find publication. Readers of his *The Self-Publishing Manual* will find much of the advice and information redundant, however.

Van Cleave, Ryan G. *Writing Memoir for Dummies*. Wiley (2013). What can I say? It's yet another book I sold off a proposal and a single chapter. If you're interested in the world of writing memoir, give it a shot. You'll learn to mine the past for great stories, choose the best structure to highlight your story, get your memoir published, and market your finished memoir.

Zinsser, William. *On Writing Well (30th Anniversary Edition): The Classic Guide to Writing Nonfiction*. New York, NY: HarperCollins (2006). Zinsser's guide "has been praised for its sound advice, its clarity, and its warmth of style." The techniques he clearly explains will vastly improve one's writing, even in such areas as humor, technical writing, science writing, and sports writing. This small book is a must-have for all nonfiction writers.

ON FICTION WRITING

Camenson, Blythe, and Marshall J. Cook. *Novel Proposal: From Creation to Contract*. Cincinnati, OH: Writer's Digest Books (1999). This all-inclusive guide to novel proposals collects advice from more than nineteen agents and editors. Accessible and informatively organized, this book is perfect for first-time novelists with a finished manuscript. Even experienced writers might find some of the information surprising and helpful.

Gardner, John. *The Art of Fiction: Notes on Craft for Young Writers.* New York, NY: Vintage (1991). This classic text is *the* book on the craft of fiction. Gardner's examples are a little dated, though his advice is sound and understandable even for those who have not read the classics he regularly refers to. There's a reason this book is regularly adopted by creative writing programs as a textbook—it works.

Van Cleave, Ryan G. and Todd James Pierce. *Behind the Short Story: From First to Final Draft.* New York, NY: Allyn & Bacon/Longman (2007). Here's another book I sold off a minimal proposal—eleven pages, which included only two pages of sample text! With specific craft advice from twenty-seven of America's best fiction writers, this book compiles critical analysis, writing exercises, representative contemporary stories, and useful insights into the writing process for short story and novel writers. The collaborative, multiperspective approach mirrors the strengths of a good writing workshop while also covering the elements of fiction.

WRITING, CREATIVITY, AND INSPIRATION

Goldberg, Natalie. *Writing Down the Bones: Freeing the Writer Within.* Boston: Shambhala (1986). A classic text on creativity, writing, and inspiration, this book can get writers (or would-be writers) writing. Couched in personal anecdotes, the writing advice is simple but profoundly effective. Beginners especially will get a lot out of this book.

Heffron, Jack. *The Writer's Idea Book 10th Anniversary Edition: How to Develop Great Ideas for Fiction, Nonfiction, Poetry, and Screenplays.* Cincinnati, OH: Writer's Digest Books (2012). This idea-generating book has stood the test of time and helped countless writers on the path to publication. This book will be a hit with beginners who need help getting started.

Lamott, Anne. *Bird by Bird: Some Instructions on Writing and Life.* New York, NY: Anchor (1995). This classic book of advice and inspiration is perfect for beginners and useful for seasoned writers. Its humor and easygoing style is entertaining—you can't miss with this book. It's full of pithy quotes that you'll want to share with your friends and tape to your wall.

Rico, Gabriele Lusser. *Writing the Natural Way.* New York, NY: Tarcher (2000). For some (especially those who are visually oriented), this book brings them to a complete breakthrough in their relationship with writing. For the rest of us, the well-considered prompts and exercises will have to be enough. Her ideas on brainstorming, left brain/right brain, and the "inner writer" are intriguing and worthwhile.

Ueland, Brenda. *If You Want to Write: A Book About Art, Independence, and Spirit.* bnpublishing.com (2008). Out of print for a long while, this book from 1938 is now available again. Her discussions of authenticity, the divine expression in each individual, and the power of nature are especially interesting. This book has inspired thousands—with good reason. I particularly recommend it for younger readers and beginning writers.

White, Fred. *Where Do You Get Your Ideas?: A Writer's Guide to Transforming Notions Into Narratives.* Writer's Digest Books (2012). This fairly new book has advice, exercises, and techniques on finding the kernels of stories right in front of you. White also breaks down the creative process into six clear steps: idea recognition, idea incubation, outlining, research, drafting, and revision. If you're unsure what you want to write a book on, you can't go wrong by using his techniques.

REVISION

Bell, James Scott. *Revision and Self-Editing.* Cincinnati, OH: Writer's Digest Books (2008). Geared primarily for the relatively new writer of fiction, some of the tips and ideas will translate into other genres. End-of-chapter exercises, a witty tone, and contemporary examples make this an easy-to-read book. This book does not, however, review grammar.

Bishop, Wendy. *Elements of Alternate Style: Essays on Writing and Revision.* Portsmouth, NH: Boynton/Cook (1997). Bishop was a former professor of mine, and her common-sense style helped my writing immensely. Though many of these essays are about the teaching of writing and improving student work, the lessons and ideas are quite valuable. Individual essays discuss revision in different genres: poetry, research writing, creative nonfiction, alternate styles, and hypertext.

Browne, Renni and Dave King. *Self-Editing for Fiction Writers: How to Edit Yourself Into Print.* New York, NY: Quill/HarperResource (2001). Two senior editors share their proven techniques and expertise for turning manuscripts into polished works of fiction. While targeted specifically to fiction writing, their advice is useful for all genres.

Cook, Claire Kehrwald. *Line by Line: How to Edit Your Own Writing.* New York, NY: Houghton Mifflin/Harcourt (1985). Don't let the year of publication fool you—good writing is good writing no matter how old the advice.

This book is comprehensive in guiding you through decisions on sentence structure, choosing the best words, and utilizing punctuation. It's also quite good at troubleshooting stylistic faults and other things that doom a writer's prose.

Lukeman, Noah. *A Dash of Style: The Art and Mastery of Punctuation.* New York, NY: W.W. Norton (2007). While not exactly a book on revision, the high-powered advice and examples on how to manipulate punctuation like a master are best utilized in the later draft stages (revision). Full-length chapters on the comma, period, dash, and other punctuation marks are extremely helpful for writers of any genre. Lukeman knows his stuff.

Truss, Lynne. *Eats, Shoots & Leaves: The Zero Tolerance Approach to Punctuation.* New York, NY: Gotham (2006). Who would've thought a grammar book could be a bestseller, but that's what you have here! This thing is funny, funny, funny, but the lessons are as serious as anything Strunk & White believed. This impassioned manifesto is a great read.

BOOK PUBLICITY

Bodian, Nat G. *How to Choose a Winning Title: A Guide for Writers, Editors, and Publishers.* Oryx Press (1989). This out-of-print title compiles Bodian's thirty years of experience in one readable, quick-reference volume. Through examples and understandable rules, he shows you how to create memorable titles regardless of topic, genre, or style. It's worth trying to find a used copy of this book if you have any question about your own book's title.

Cole, David. *The Complete Guide to Book Marketing.* New York, NY: Allworth Press (2004). Cole's book is full of straight talk and insider insight on publicity, promotion, and marketing. His focus on marketing strategy is something few other books match. This book is very realistic about the publishing world and discusses self-publishing and selling outside traditional channels.

Howard-Johnson, Carolyn. *The Frugal Book Promoter: How to Do What Your Publisher Won't.* Loretto, PA: Star Publish (2004). For the few dozen free ideas on how to promote a book for free (or nearly so), this text is worth the $17.95 price alone. Of particular use are her sections on media kits, media interviews, book signings, and book fairs. The production quality of this book is a little weak, but the contents are not.

Katz, Christina. *Get Known Before the Book Deal: Use Your Personal Strengths to Grow an Author Platform.* Cincinnati, OH: Writer's Digest Books (2008). This easy-to-use book explains how to create an author platform from scratch.

Whether you're truly starting with nothing or you've got a few things in place, the ideas here will be useful.

Kremer, John. *1001 Ways to Market Your Books—For Authors and Publishers*, sixth edition. Fairfield, IA: Open Horizons Publishing Co. (2006). With so many time-tested ways to promote a book, writers could never do them all. Still, the advice and examples are both creative and useful. The only downside is that Kremer regularly references his other books, urging people to buy those for more information. Then again, cross promotion is one of his tips!

Levinson, Jay Conrad, Rick Frishman, Michael Larsen, David L. Hancock. *Guerilla Marketing for Writers: 100 Weapons for Selling Your Work*. Cincinnati, OH: Writer's Digest Books (2001). Levinson is an expert on fusion marketing, free media coverage, direct-response campaigns, and online marketing. He's one of the top marketing experts in the world—you can't go wrong applying any of his ideas to your own PR campaign, though many of his books are targeted at small business owners, inventors, and salesmen. With some imagination, his tips can translate into massive PR success in the publishing world.

Mcauley, Jordan. *Celebrity Leverage: Insider Secrets to Getting Celebrity Endorsements, Instant Credibility, and Star-Powered Publicity*. Los Angeles, CA: Mega Niche Media (2010). If you've ever wanted to get your book (or book proposal, hint, hint, hint!) endorsed by someone a lot more famous than you are, this book can help. Use this in conjunction with McAuley's website www.contactanycelebrity.com for the one-two publicity punch your book needs.

LITERARY AGENTS

Larsen, Michael. *How to Get a Literary Agent*. Naperville, IL: Sourcebooks (2006). This highly recommended book by a veteran literary agent promises "everything you need to know about using an agent to launch and sustain your literary career." Larsen does a good job explaining the whole story of the industry and shows how newcomers can realistically break in.

Lukeman, Noah. *How to Write a Great Query Letter*. Amazon short (eBook). A bite-size look at the query letter from a veteran agent, this e-book is very informative and grounded in expert advice. He even details how fiction and nonfiction queries should differ. Considering that this e-book is available at Amazon.com for free, this is another must-have for any aspiring writer.

Reiss, Fern. *The Publishing Game: Find an Agent in 30 days!* Boston, MA: Peanut Butter and Jelly Press (2003). Best-selling author Fern Reiss shares tips on finding top agents, wooing them, and helping them sell your proposals. A very clear, readable book, you can't go wrong with this title if you don't know where to start. For those who already have a strong background, this might seem like a basic book.

MARKET GUIDES

Guide to Literary Agents. Annual publication. Cincinnati, OH: Writer's Digest Books. The 2012 edition of this yearly publication features contact and submission information for eight hundred–plus individual agents worldwide. Included is a bonus eighty-five pages of original articles and interviews that help would-be authors better understand how to succeed.

Herman, Jeff. *Writer's Guide to Book Editors, Publishers, and Literary Agents.* Annual publication. Rocklin, CA: Prima Publishing. At one thousand–plus pages, the 2012 edition has specifics for hundreds of US and Canadian publishers, including contact information for book acquisition editors, subject interests, and a list of recent sales. The literary agent directory section has almost two hundred listings that detail likes, dislikes, and other insider information. This is a powerful resource for writers to keep handy.

Literary Market Place. Annual publication. New York, NY: R.R. Bowker. With a hefty list price ($300+), this book is not for the private collection—use it at libraries. Its value is the comprehensive listing of forty thousand–plus individuals and companies that work in the publishing field. In fifty-four sections, everything and everyone in the business (publishers, ad agencies, associations, events, agents, and distributors) is organized and at your fingertips.

Writer's Market. Annual publication. Cincinnati, OH: Writer's Digest Books. With over 3,500 listings for book publishers, consumer magazines, contests, and literary agents, this book is an inexpensive way to get "in the know." Each book also contains articles and interviews with industry professionals to help writers transform their hobby into a career and to help make seasoned pros even more effective.

OTHER BOOKS THAT YOU MIGHT FIND USEFUL

Beckwith, Harry and Christine K. Clifford. *You, Inc.: The Art of Selling Yourself.* Warner (2011). Lots of practical knowledge is offered here about salesmanship, the business world, and becoming successful. It's quite readable and has some very good ideas on communicating, listening, and writing.

Burt-Thomas, Wendy. *The Writer's Digest Guide to Query Letters*. Writer's Digest Books (2009). From hooks to using research to communicating your platform, this book has it all. Since queries are often the make-or-break point for new writers in search of their break, this book is a valuable resource to have handy.

WEB RESOURCES

While you can certainly Google on your own to find writing websites, the following are places to start when you want more quality information to help you succeed. Use the links pages at these websites to guide you to other worthwhile online resources.

A GREAT PLACE FOR ALL THINGS BOOK PROPOSAL–RELATED

My website for this book: www.theweekendbookproposal.com

GOOD WRITING ORGANIZATIONS AND ASSOCIATIONS

Academy of American Poets: www.poets.org
American Christian Fiction Writers: www.acfw.com
The Authors Guild: www.authorsguild.org
Military Writers Society of America: www.mwsadispatches.com
National Association of Memoir Writers: www.namw.org
National Society of Science Writers: www.nasw.org
National Writers Union: www.nwu.org
PEN American Center: www.pen.org
Science Fiction & Fantasy Writers of America: www.sfwa.org
Writers Guild of America, West: www.wga.org

INDUSTRY MAGAZINES FOR WRITERS

Midwest Book Review: www.midwestbookreview.com
Poets & Writers Magazine: www.pw.org
The Writer Magazine: www.writermag.com
Writer's Digest: www.writersdigest.com
Writers' Forum: www.writers-forum.com

PUBLISHING INDUSTRY RESOURCES

AgentQuery: www.agentquery.com
Association of Authors' Agents: www.agentsassoc.co.uk
Association of Authors' Representatives, Inc.: www.aaronline.org
Authorlink: www.authorlink.com

Book Marketing Tips for Book Authors: www.bookmarket.com
Bookwire: www.bookwire.com
Literary Marketplace: www.literarymarketplace.com
Preditors & Editors: www.pred-ed.com
Publishers Lunch: www.publisherslunch.com
Publishers Marketplace: www.publishersmarketplace.com
Publishers Weekly: www.publishersweekly.com
R.R. Bowker: www.bowker.com
Writer's Market: www.writersmarket.com

CONFERENCES, WORKSHOPS, AND RESIDENCIES FOR WRITERS

Absolute Write University: www.absoluteclasses.com
Association of Writers and Writing Programs: www.awpwriter.org
Corporation of Yaddo: www.yaddo.org
Gotham Writers' Workshop: www.writingclasses.com
Internet Writing Workshop: www.internetwritingworkshop.org
MacDowell Colony: www.macdowellcolony.org
NewPages: Writers' Conferences: www.newpages.com/writing-conferences/
ShawGuides: Writers' Conferences: www.shawguides.com/writing
Vermont Studio Center: www.vermontstudiocenter.org
Write 101: www.write101.com

WRITERS' GROUPS

Coffeehouse for Writers: www.coffeehouseforwriters.com
Scribophile: www.scribophile.com
Writers Meetup Groups: www.writers.meetup.com
Writers on the Net: www.writers.meetup.com
Writers Write: www.writerswrite.com

INDEX